THE
PATH OF
EMOTIONS

THE
PATH OF
EMOTIONS

Transform Emotions Into Energy
to Achieve Your Greatest Potential

DR. SYNTHIA ANDREWS, ND

 New Page Books
A division of The Career Press, Inc.
Pompton Plains, N.J.

THE PATH OF EMOTIONS
EDITED AND TYPESET BY KARA KUMPEL
Cover design by Lucia Rossman/Digi Dog Design
Printed in the U.S.A.

To order this title, please call toll-free 1-800-CAREER-1 (NJ and Canada: 201-848-0310) to order using VISA or MasterCard, or for further information on books from Career Press.

The Career Press, Inc.
220 West Parkway, Unit 12
Pompton Plains, NJ 07444
www.careerpress.com
www.newpagebooks.com

Library of Congress Cataloging-in-Publication Data
Andrews, Synthia.
    The path of emotions : transform emotions into energy to achieve your greatest potential / by Synthia Andrews ;
    foreword by Iona Marsaa Teeguarden.
        p. cm.
    Includes bibliographical references and index.
    ISBN 978-1-60163-238-8 -- ISBN 978-1-60163-560-0 (ebook) 1. Mind and body. 2. Emotions. 3. Vitality. I. Title.

    BF161.A62 2013
    152.4--dc23

                                                    2012039160

The primary tenet in every spiritual tradition is to love one another.
This makes the path very clear: Remove from
within every resistance to love.

In memory of Suzanne Smith Ramsby
October 24, 1934 to October 7, 2012

This book is dedicated to my husband,
Colin Andrews,
who shines the light of true North.

Acknowledgments

First and foremost, I must always thank Johanna Sayre for her endless help in developing and proofreading my manuscripts. Her guidance is never restricted to phrasing and grammar. She has an innate ability to feel the heart of what I am trying to say and help me say it. My thanks to her come with deep gratitude.

Next, the two intrepid artists:

Mark Johnson (1957–2011), who originally prepared the art in this book for my earlier Career Press publication, *The Path of Energy*. The art in this book is among the last he offered the world, and was done with a shaking hand as he entered his last months. There were mornings when neither of us thought he would finish, yet his dedication never wavered. I like to hope the meditations that he illustrated helped in the days before his passing.

Wayne Mason, who has repeatedly come to the rescue with artwork for illustrations, and Website and cover design, has never disappointed with design or deadline. My gratitude and thanks abound! You can view his art on my Website, *www.thepathofenergy.com*.

Thanks to my Jin Sin Do® Bodymind Acupressure® teachers: JSD creator Iona Marsaa Teeguarden, Deborah Valentine Smith, and Jasmine Ellen Wolfe. A special thank you to Iona for helping fashion the description of her emotional kaleidoscope, which redefined an aspect of my approach. Opinions in this book are mine and should not be taken as a reflection of JSD. Also, a thank-you to mentor Louisa Poole, who introduced to me to myself.

Thank you to all those at Career Press who have supported this project and made the work go easier: Kirsten Dalley, Michael Pye, and Laurie Kelly-Pye, as well as line editors, formatters, and all the others whose work adds to the final product.

And finally, but not least, many thanks to my agent John White and the Career Press acquisitions editor, Adam Schwartz, who were willing to take a chance.

Contents

Part III: Engaging Emotional Awareness

Introduction

The Path of Emotions celebrates the creative enjoyment of life through embracing the power of emotions. Emotions command our life-force and direct our choices. They provide information and guide our exploration of subtle energy. My personal journey into this realm began after reading a book on auras, the radiant energy fields that surround us, by medical intuitive Edgar Cayce. Within a few years I found Carlos Castaneda's book *The Teachings of Don Juan: A Yaqui Way of Knowledge (1968)*, and my life was permanently altered.

Castaneda wrote a series of books that detailed his experiences with his mentor, Yaqui Shaman Don Juan Mateus. Reading his books created an internal shift of perception that expanded my awareness into the energy level of reality. Especially liberating was Don Juan's treatment of emotions, highlighted in this quote from *The Teachings of Don Juan*: "No person is important enough to make me angry." The implication to me is that we can, to some extent, choose our emotions.

This countered everything I previously understood. I believed myself trapped in cause and effect, whereby people, events, and circumstances caused me to react with anger, happiness, fear, and so forth. I behaved as though expression or suppression of what I felt were my only choices. However, Don Juan indicated that events create an emotional response based on our beliefs, on the paradigm in which we live. Some emotions are purely survival, such as the fear that impels us to run from danger, but others are choices based on preconceived ideas. What if we change our preconceived ideas and, by doing so, choose a different set of emotional responses? Can we then consciously engage our emotions and direct their power? The possibility of this was mind-boggling, and entirely changed the manner in which I approached life. For me, it emphasized two important principles.

First, emotions are gateways to our personal power. Today it is commonly understood that nobody can define another's worth, or cause another person to act or behave in a certain way, unless the person being influenced abdicates his or her power. In 1974 this thought was revolutionary and it reoriented my life. In the blink of an eye, I moved from being a victim of my circumstances to being an explorer of enormous vistas of possibility. The question became: Was I going to give away my personal power by allowing events and people to determine my emotions, or did I have a choice?

Accepting one's personal power requires taking responsibility for all the circumstances in one's life. Common wisdom says we cannot choose our emotions; they are instinctive. I suggest that by moving to the formative level of emotions, we can extract the information they carry and consciously transform the powerful force they exert. I am not advocating suppressing emotions—far from it. I am advocating embracing them. It is a shift in paradigm.

Shifting paradigms requires disciplined attention and takes work. The challenge is to respond to every experience not as good or bad, but as an opportunity to grow. In the words of Don Juan, "The trick is in what one emphasizes. We either make ourselves miserable, or we make ourselves happy. The amount of work is the same."[1] Sometimes we meet the challenge well; sometimes we don't. How well we walk the path is not as important as being committed to staying on it, regardless of how long it takes us to become elegant in our effort.

The second, more scintillating principle is that there is a link between emotions and subtle energy. Emotions are more valuable than gold; they carry our intent into the world. What is personal power other than the ability to gather and command our own energy—to use it, build it, or store it with intent? Mastering the use of emotions is one of the keys to personal power, opening a door into the kingdom of subtle energy. Wasting them siphons away our vitality. Consequently, understanding the mysterious and intractable connection between energy and emotion became the central focus of my life. As Don Juan would say, it is my "path with heart."

Once attuned to this level of reality, interpreting world events and personal interactions in terms of gains or losses of energy exposes an undercurrent of meaning. For example, looking at the teachings of Gandhi with an awareness of energy reveals nonviolence to be less of a political strategy than a means to access the deepest levels of personal power. Using nonviolence mobilizes a force beyond what we currently understand in a society governed by competition where greed and self-interest are the guiding principles of action. Gandhi said, "The force generated by nonviolence is infinitely greater than the force generated by all the arms invented by man's ingenuity."[2] Where once I would have read this statement to mean a social force working for social change, now with a view to energy I see it as a spiritual force geared to the highest good of all that is ignited within each person. Nonviolence refuses standard definitions in favor of consciously mobilizing energy.

My training in the use of energy and emotion has been focused on individual healing methods, and I've been gifted with several extraordinary mentors: Louisa Poole from Rockport, Massachusetts, taught me how to use my body to feel subtle energy and how to discern different types of energy. A Native American friend taught me the power of living with intent. As much as I learned from what they taught, I learned more from how they lived, and I hold them both in a high place of honor.

The person who brought my search into brilliant, technicolor focus is psychotherapist Iona Marsaa Teeguarden, LMFT, who created a bodywork method called Jin Shin Do® Bodymind Acupressure®. The Jin Shin Do (JSD) system combines the theories of classic Chinese acupuncture, a traditional Japanese acupressure technique, Taoist philosophy, and Qigong (breathing and exercise techniques) with Western psychological tools such as Reichian segmental theory and principles of Ericksonian psychotherapy. It is a brilliant synthesis of body-centered emotional processing and meridian methodology.

An important part of the philosophy underlying JSD® Bodymind Acupressure® is Iona's inspired treatment of emotions and feelings in her "Emotional Kaleidoscope" diagram. You can see and read about the "Emotional Kaleidoscope" in Iona's book, *The Joy of Feeling* (Japan Publications, 1987; Jin Shin Do® Foundation, 2006; *www.jinshindo.org*).

Through Jin Shin Do®, I understood that the two primary functions of emotions are: to provide information and to generate energy. They are part of the body's exquisite information-gathering system; collecting, synthesizing, and responding to the vast array of stimuli in this extraordinary universe. Learning how to use emotions allows one to marshal the forces of subtle energy, enhancing all aspects of life.

The Path of Emotions is divided into three parts: **Part I: The Elegant Dance of Emotions** describes the world of subtle energy and how emotions decipher energy information. It explains the physiology and embodiment of emotions providing foundational information for the process introduced in the following parts. **Part II: The Language of Our Core** explains how emotions become derailed and seem to control our actions and responses to life. It describes the role emotions play in unprocessed trauma, causing physical pain and dysfunction. It also introduces the keys to understanding the language of energy and the practices necessary to master intent. **Part III: Engaging Emotional Awareness** covers the many ways we can use emotions and intent to clear past trauma and work with subtle energy for creative expression.

It is my sincere hope that this book opens greater access for each reader to his or her own magnificent spiritual center.

PART I
THE ELEGANT DANCE OF EMOTIONS

Emotions are the intersection in an elegant dance between the world of form and the formless world of energy. Learning how to interpret the dance steps is a journey into the heart-of-self and the exploration of interior planes where imagination is the paintbrush that creates our personal reality.

Part I wends a path through definitions of subtle energy, emotions, and feelings. It engages the esoteric realms of the human energy system as well as the science of emotion. It describes the route emotions take into our body where they impact our attitudes, beliefs, and dreams. Part I provides the foundation for a leap into the possibilities presented in Part II. I hope the read is informative and fun for all!

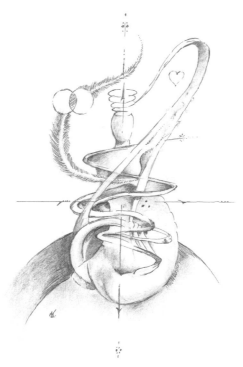

The Dance of Emotions
Illustration by Mark Johnson

Chapter I
The Energy-Emotion Matrix

Happy, sad, angry, joyful. Emotions provide rhythm, context, and meaning to life. Without them we would find little of value in our successes and minimal learning from our failures. Emotions convey the essence of being alive, yet most of us spend a considerable amount of time and energy avoiding and controlling our emotions rather than using them. We don't like to feel anger, fear, sadness, shame, or guilt, and strive to escape or suppress them. We value happiness, excitement, satisfaction, and joy—and who wouldn't? They are comfortable, energizing, and uplifting. We label some emotions good and others bad as we confuse comfortable and uncomfortable with value. But what if there is more to emotions than how they make us feel?

Emotions are a source of information. Comfortable or uncomfortable, they tell us about ourselves: where we need to grow, what traumas haven't healed, what we have to offer the world, and more. They also tell us about our surroundings: what direction to take, whom we can trust, when to make a business move, and so forth. Enjoyable emotions may lead us toward activities and relationships; however, unpleasant emotions have equal function. They provide vital information for survival, alerting us to threats and warning against foolish actions. The value of emotions doesn't end with information; they also energize our life. While informing our perceptions, they liberate energy for action, delivering the power to enable our goals and pursue our dreams.

Research shows that emotional intelligence is more important than IQ in career success and fostering happiness in relationships.[1] Typically, however, we tend to undervalue emotions and view them with distrust, something taught to us as children. Do you remember being a kid and knowing from your own emotional response that a parent was angry with you, but being told you were wrong and that "nothing was the matter"? Denials of this nature send a twofold message. First, they dissuade us from trusting our senses. Coming to terms with contradictions between what we sense and what we are told undermines our ability to trust our perceptions, thus damaging self-confidence. A person who is always second-guessing his or her instincts is unable to act with conviction or access personal power.

Second, it implies that emotions are somehow bad and that we should deny what we feel. We are trained to believe that the mind is good and emotions are bad; that emotions take us away from logic, leading us into the addictions of pleasure over the virtues of hard work. They trap us in limitation through fear, anger, and shame. Many religions teach that emotions are tricksters, seducing aspirants away from faith. Emotions have even been described as parasites, as though one of the attributes in the magnificence of life is non-functional. The message is clear: Emotions should be suppressed and overcome in favor of either logic and rationality or blind faith.

Once emotions are denied, their message and energy are suppressed, and instead of empowering us, they become saboteurs to happiness and success. Distrust of emotions seems vindicated when they cause us to make limiting decisions or influence rash behavior. Many people attribute the worst mistakes they've ever made to decisions induced by wild emotion. However, bad decisions don't mean emotions can't be trusted; they mean we have unlearned how our emotions work; we have become separated from their function. Debased and suppressed, emotions become an unconscious ruling force rather than an attribute of wisdom.

The opposition between mind and emotion is an illusion; the two are meant to work together, each augmenting the other's unique contribution. Accessing emotions is the key that opens the door to higher consciousness, helping us to understand our selves and the world better. Emotions do this by being a direct link to subtle energy, the vital force that flows within and around us, creating the ambiance of life and carrying the information that directs our inner convictions. Emotions are the language of subtle energy— the body's translation of frequency. Through emotions, energy interactions are brought into direct awareness.

Today more than ever before, there is an awakening to the energy level of reality. The prevalence of yoga, Tai Chi, and energy healing in helping people live happier, healthier lives is generating acceptance of this mysterious substance. People are feeling the flows of energy in their bodies and becoming aware of the energy interactions in which they engage. Consequently, there is an upsurge of interest in the ability to consciously participate in energy realms to create meaningful, life-affirming change. Emotions are the language of interpretation.

Paying attention to subtle energy attunes us to deeper layers of reality. It brings unconscious awareness into the realm of conscious choice. Information we receive can indicate:

- ☯ Whether we are in danger.
- ☯ What the best decision may be in a given situation.
- ☯ Whether we can trust someone.
- ☯ Whether a person has ulterior motives or hidden agendas.
- ☯ How to be more intimate with people we love.
- ☯ What our limitations are and what fears we hide.
- ☯ What we value, what has meaning, what carries truth for us.
- ☯ What career path to take.
- ☯ The presence and meaning of underlying connections between people and events.
- ☯ The importance of synchronicity.

Energy awareness is also a deepening of our spirituality. Through it we can access:

- ☯ Heightened states of being and altered states of awareness.
- ☯ Our innate understanding of the spiritual qualities in Nature.
- ☯ Connection to Universal Consciousness, Divine Love, and/or God.
- ☯ Frequency shifts associated with change.
- ☯ The ability to assist healing.

- ☯ Paranormal abilities such as communication with deceased individuals, precognition, and telepathy.
- ☯ The ability to see the forces behind social issues, politics, religious orders, and so forth.
- ☯ Our ability to manifest the life we want.
- ☯ Our spiritual essence.

When we become proficient at using the emotional language of energy, we can receive the information emotions hold, direct the force they entrain, and then release them. We no longer need to harbor feelings that hurt or cause injury, and no longer need to allow them to dictate our actions and behaviors. We can choose to step into our personal power and take command of our emotional terrain so that our actions become conscious, creative, potent, and fulfilling. We become the master creators of our life.

Chapter 2
The Kingdom of Subtle Energy

The first time I met my husband, a flood of perceptions engulfed me that I was ill-equipped to intellectually define. We were in a crowd of people, yet when he glanced in my direction, our eyes locked. I was immediately overcome with an internal quickening, a very fine vibration that felt as though it originated in my cells. The sensation was like bees buzzing in a hive. Waves of energy streamed between us, and the chakra energy centers in my body expanded. My heart physically burned as boundaries disappeared and internal resistance melted.

It was impossible to explain what was taking place. I had never experienced anything like it before. However, my emotions were clear. I felt love, and my feelings informed my understanding. They also provided the motivation to take a risk and connect with this stranger before me as well as the drive to follow through. It was a rare moment of complete coherence of mind, body, and emotion, and a perfect example of how emotions function.

The body is processing energy information all the time. Each of us is in continual exchange with the people around us and with the world at large.

Emotions and sensations inform the importance and meaning of our energy interactions, creating our gut reactions. Rarely, however, do we have the experience of time slowing so that each component of an event can be individually felt and explored. These infrequent moments are unique and life-altering, occurring most often during times of heightened meaning such as accidents and near-death experiences, and when meeting significant people. In those moments of percipience we feel alive; life force streams through our body and nerve endings are on fire.

Most people have had at least one experience of heightened awareness. The questions for many are: *What is being transferred, and can we consciously engage it?* To answer these we need to explore the dynamic world of subtle energy and form a foundation for understanding the role emotions play.

Subtle Energy Overview

Subtle energy has many names in many cultures; it is called *etheric energy* in the spiritual writings of Theosophy, *akasha* or *prana* in Vedic and Hindu traditions, and *chi*, or *qi*, in Chinese philosophy. Subtle energy is said to be the medium through which consciousness acts. It carries life force, that which makes the difference between inert material and life.

Flowing into, through, and beyond matter, subtle energy is both the substance of matter and the creative force that organizes it into form. It is the motivating and animating principle of the universe, forming the matrix of life. This formative level of reality is interactive. Into the energy field matrix we pour our dreams and desires as well as our fears and limitations, and out of it are formed the circumstances of our lives.

Though separate, everything is a part of everything else, connected through the matrix of the energy field. One of the children I work with likened the idea to fish in a fish tank. The fish are suspended in the medium of water that supports them, moving into, through, and around them. The water connects the fish to everything else in the tank. Every move one makes is felt by all as a vibration through the water. Though the metaphor is limited in similarity, imagining it provides a visceral experience of the concept.

As the force that organizes matter into structured form, subtle energy transmits information as frequency. *Frequency* is defined as either the number of traveling waves in a specified period of time, or as the rate at which a particle vibrates. Vibration in the energy matrix forms templates for physical matter. If we consider consciousness to be the creative force of the universe, then subtle energy is the carrier wave for consciousness.

Although the topic seems esoteric, using frequency to code information on energy carrier waves is a foundational concept in the technology revolution. The principle is used every time cell phone signals are transmitted on microwaves, or music and conversation are transmitted on radio waves. The same principle occurs when the body receives information from light and sound. Light frequency is received through the eyes and translated into visible information in the brain; sound frequency is received through the ears and translated into audible signals. Similarly, the body receives subtle energy information and translates it into emotional experiences. How this happens is discussed in Chapter 3.

The flow of subtle energy is life enhancing. It nourishes and vitalizes the body at a cellular level, promoting health and well-being. It promotes body wisdom and forms our innate intelligence. When we learn how to consciously interact with subtle energy, it increases our understanding of the world around us and can be used to transmit thought, healing energy, and personal intent. As such, it is a vehicle for self-empowerment.

In summary, subtle energy has several important attributes:

- ☯ It is an organizational force forming an energy matrix.
- ☯ It transmits information in the form of frequency.
- ☯ It is the medium for transmitting consciousness.
- ☯ It is life force, carrying information that produces health, well-being, and vitality.
- ☯ It is both substance and force.

Furthermore:

- ☯ The energy matrix is an energy field that produces templates that organize matter into discernible form.
- ☯ The body receives subtle energy information and translates it into emotions, physical sensations, and direct knowing that form gut reactions, instinctive responses, and intuition.
- ☯ Subtle energy can be used for healing, thought transmission, remote viewing, and other so-called paranormal abilities.

Historical Perspective

The majority of cultures around the world have a word for subtle energy and a practice to manipulate it. Chart 2.1, Energy Systems From Around the World, provides a few examples. Many indigenous cultures describe it as the web of life, a similar description to that of a matrix or energy field. Complex rituals and mind-expanding drugs along with meditation, breathing, and movement practices have been used for thousands of years to provide access to this realm. The prevailing belief is that humans are not powerless bystanders to mysterious processes; rather, we are participants interacting with a greater whole that guides the evolution of consciousness and the refinement of reality.

Ancient cultures consciously engaged subtle energy for healing, fertility, manifestation, guidance, and so forth. Maps of the body were made that diagrammed energy pathways and collection centers. The best known today are the maps of meridian pathways used in Traditional Chinese Medicine (TCM) and the charts of the chakras from the Hindu tradition of India, both of which date at least to 3000 BCE.

The widespread ancient understanding of energy pathways in the body can be demonstrated with the discovery in 1991 of a naturally mummified man. The 43-year-old, 5-foot 5-inch male corpse, found frozen in the Alps between Italy and Austria, was dated at 5,300 years old. Known as Otzi the Iceman, or the Tyrolian Iceman, he was significant for many things, including charcoal tattoos found in specific locations on his body. The tattoos were made by slashing the skin and filling the cut with charcoal.[1]

Unlike ornamental tattoos found on other mummies from this time period, the tattoos on Otzi the Iceman were clearly not artistic. Instead, they indicated knowledge of the same pathways of energy used by today's TCM practitioners: Placement of the tattoos had a very high correlation to acupuncture points. An article on the Iceman's autopsy in *The Lancet,* a British peer-reviewed medical journal, reported that the tattoos were placed on points along the Bladder Meridian that would be used by TCM practitioners to treat lower back pain and inflammation. Radiographic pictures (X-rays) of the skeletal structure showed lumbar degeneration indicating pain and inflammation in his lower back.[2] These correlations are well beyond chance.

Is it accidental that two ancient cultures from different parts of the world developed similar healing methods? Or is it possible that ancient people were aware of energy pathways in the body? Has the modern human lost touch with innate energy senses that help us survive?

Chart 2.1: Energy Systems From Around the World

Culture/Person	Name for Subtle Energy	Practices
India-Hindu	Prana Akasha	Yoga Pranic Healing Kundalini awakening
China	Chi	Tai Chi, Qi Gong, Acupuncture
Japan	Ki	Acupressure
Hebrew	Ruach	Kabala
Sufi	Baraka	Transmission for enlightenment
Peru	Huaca	Shamanism
Native American Iroquois Tribe	Orenda	Shamanism
Native American Sioux Tribe	Wakan	Shamanism
Maoris (New Zealand)	Atua	Traditional healing practices

Frank Anton Mesmer	Animal Magnetism	Hypnotism
Wilhelm Reich	Orgone	Body-centered psychotherapy Cloud-busting Orgone accumulating chamber
Harold Saxton-Burr	Life-field	Organization of embryo development

Information in the first two columns is from the book Future Science *by John White and Stanley Krippner.*[3]

The Science of Energy

There is little scientific proof that subtle energy exists; however, the exciting frontier of physics offers a foundation for its presence. This subject is fascinating and complex, and only an overview is provided here. Those who are interested will find articles and books for further study in the resource appendix.

The discovery that light can display characteristics of both particles and waves (Young's double-slit experiment) sounds strikingly familiar to the substance-energy duality of subtle energy. Einstein's revolutionary formula $E = MC^2$ (energy=mass x the speed of light squared) also states that energy and matter are the same substance; the difference between them is simply the speed at which they vibrate.

Although Einstein may not have been espousing the existence of a medium for consciousness, his equation implies that vibration underlies reality. Superstring Theory takes this idea further. Superstring Theory proposes that everything in the universe, from galaxies to subatomic particles, is made up of microscopic strands of vibrating energy termed Strings. The deepest, most indivisible level of matter, it suggests, are patterns of vibration that give specific types of matter their specific form and property. Physicist Brian Greene explains that all of the different properties of particles that make up matter are "the manifestation of one and the same physical feature:

the resonant patterns of vibration—the music, so to speak—of fundamental loops of string."[4]

Using music as a metaphor is apt because sound provides an excellent demonstration of the effect of vibration on matter. This phenomenon was first observed by Robert Hooke in 1680 during an experiment at Oxford University. With the use of a violin bow and a plate of flour, he demonstrated that sound vibrated the individual flour particles into geometric patterns. In 1787, physicist Ernst Florens Friedrich Chladni, the father of the science of acoustics, repeated Hooke's technique and published the patterns in a book entitled *Discoveries Concerning the Theory of Music (Sound)*. Drawing his violin bow across the edge of a flat plate covered with sand, Chladni showed that different tones vibrated the sand into different, repeatable patterns. The patterns were named Chaldni figures.[5]

The current study of sound vibration on matter, called Cymatics, was developed by the late Swiss doctor Hans Jenny. In 1967 he published a book titled *The Structure and Dynamics of Waves and Vibrations*, which was followed in the 1980s by a video called *Cymatics* that visually demonstrated the principles. His technique was to mix particles such as sand, spores, and iron filings with a liquid such as water or oil, and place them on a metal plate. Using a sound generator to vibrate the plates, he demonstrated the ability of frequencies and combinations of frequencies to produce complex geometric patterns.[6] This has become the standard for demonstrating the ability of vibration to organize matter.

Einstein's formula also advises that matter and energy are not polar opposites; the separation between them is one of degree. The world is expressed along an electromagnetic spectrum, a gradient from lower frequencies to higher frequencies, and everything we know in the world emits a signature frequency, including bodies, organs, and cells, and even thoughts and emotions.

The ability to determine and understand radiations of the electromagnetic spectrum has grown with technology, and we can be certain there is more to the electromagnetic spectrum than what current instruments can detect. With the advent of more sensitive measuring devices, we will find additional energy waves at higher and lower frequencies, and it's entirely possible that proof of subtle energy will be found in these regions. For example, the Superconducting Quantum Interface Device known as SQUID is a magnetometer that measures extremely low magnetic fields. Invented in 1965 by Robert Jaklevic, its ability to measure the magnetic fields of organs has changed our understanding of neural activity and the function of the heart. The SQUID device may well provide the needed breakthrough into subtle energy detection.

Another possibility is that the vibrational matrix of subtle energy is not a specific frequency, but is a force that underlies the electromagnetic spectrum. Nuclear physicist David Bohm, one of the fathers of quantum physics, postulated a fifth force to explain the behavior of particles at the subatomic level. In what is termed the Aharonov-Bohm Effect, he called this fifth force a "subtle energy field underlying electromagnetism" and theorized that it explained the class of phenomena outside the four known forces of physics. To be clear, Bohm's concept of subtle energy may not be the same substance as the medium of consciousness we are considering, although articles on what he calls the "implicit order of the universe" seem more aligned than not.[7] The unexplained phenomena Bohm refers to are quantum anomalies such as non-locality and entanglement, the ability of related particles to affect each other at a distance.

The concept that subtle energy is also a substance has an interesting correlation to dark energy and dark matter. *Dark energy* is theorized in astrophysics to explain why the expansion of the universe is accelerating. The theoretical existence of *dark matter* explains anomalies seen in gravitational effects on bodies in space. Although dark energy and dark matter are undetectable and of unknown composition, it is proposed that dark energy constitutes 70 percent of the entire universe, and dark matter accounts for 25 percent. So-called normal matter constitutes only 5 percent. As explained on the NASA Website, this 5 percent is "everything on Earth, everything ever observed with all of our instruments."[8]

So, dark matter cannot be directly observed, as it does not emit or absorb light or other electromagnetic radiations,[9] and dark energy cannot be measured.[10] Yet, like subtle energy, their existence is inferred based on the observations of their effect. Dark energy exerts a force and dark matter is substance; the correlation to subtle energy can't be missed.

Most interesting, however, is that dark matter, which we can't see or measure but only infer, is thought to create the structure for normal matter. Because there is more dark matter than normal matter, and it has a stronger gravitational pull, scientists say the "normal matter flows gravitationally into dark matter scaffolding."[11] Physicist Chung Pei-Ma, an associate professor of astronomy at UC Berkeley, said in a UC Berkeley press release, "The ghost universe of dark matter is a template for the visible universe," and later in the press release, "Dark matter in the Milky Way is a dynamic, lively environment in which thousands of smaller satellites of dark matter clumps are swarming around a big parent dark matter halo, constantly interacting and disturbing each other."[12] Compare this to the mystical description of subtle energy and the lines that separate the world of science and mysticism waver.

Now that we have explored the concept of subtle energy, we can return to the real question: Can emotions interact with this realm, and can we use them to expand our lives?

Emotional Interaction

The influence of emotions is beautifully visualized by the work of Japanese author Masaru Emoto. His unorthodox experiment purports to shows that different thoughts and emotions create different crystallization patterns in frozen water. In his work, people projected specific emotions and thoughts toward water as it froze, and Emoto then examined the crystals under a microscope. He found that water subjected to thoughts of love while freezing produced crystalline structures that were more elaborate and symmetrical than those that formed when focused on by people holding negative thoughts.[13]

The effect works in reverse as well: Vibration impacts emotions and thought, as seen in a study of the Mozart Effect (the influence of music on mood and brain function, reported in the *Journal of Social Medicine* in 2001). In this study, music was shown to improve mood, enhance brain function, and improve certain types of mental illnesses.[14] Is it any surprise that science is confirming what every person who listens to music experiences? Perhaps we shouldn't wait for science to validate what we already know and feel through our bodies about subtle energy and emotion. We can start right now. Take a moment and try this exercise:

Exercise to Enhance Your Energy Field

- Take a quick scan of your body: Are your shoulders pulled up to your ears; is your face closed in concentration; is your back tight? Notice every place where you feel tight, hard, or closed.

- Take a deep breath, and on the exhalation release tension. Move your body; let what is tight unwind, what is hard soften, what is closed open. Inhale light, exhale tension. Do this for three slow cycles.

- ◑ Imagine around you a field of energy—your own personal matrix. Breathe into it and develop your sense of it. Let it grow in your imagination. Extend your awareness and explore this personal envelope. If there were geometrical patterns in your field, what would they look like? What would they feel like? Are they sharp and angular? Soft and round? Intricate or simple?

- ◑ When you are ready, pretend this space is another person whom you like, so smile at it. Smile into your energy field until the feeling of acceptance and enjoyment permeates the ambiance. Enjoy the feeling of enjoyment.

- ◑ Visualize again the geometric patterns in your field. Have they changed? In what ways?

- ◑ Carry this feeling with you, transmitting its frequency to all you meet.

If we accept the presence of subtle energy and the idea that emotions are translations of energy information, then embracing our emotions and learning to understand their language will change our lives. As this exercise demonstrates, all we need are attention, feelings, and imagination.

Chapter 3
Body Sounding:
Receiving Energy Information

Everyone wants to walk a path with heart, to find purpose and meaning in life. This, more than anything else, is the reason to understand and employ the power of emotions. Emotions illuminate the path and enliven the journey. They read the ambiance and connect us to the flow of life force. The information they provide is our gateway into the world of subtle energy.

The experience when I met my husband seemed as though time had slowed. I became aware of nuances that are typically under the radar of perceptions; however, they are not indiscernible. Once we start to pay attention, energetic interactions become apparent, exposing the truth in relationships, the significance of events, and the ecstasy of spiritual alignment. In addition to learning essential information about our surroundings, we learn about the quality of our inner and outer lives as well, and in so doing become more connected to our authentic self.

The first step in the journey of exploring our emotional link to energy awareness begins with looking at the structures in our body that receive energy and translate it into emotional and physical information. In my previous book, *The Path of Energy: Awaken Your Personal Power and Expand Your Consciousness* (New Page Books, 2011), I synthesized information from several different models. Here I am sharing my personal and professional experience of the human energy systems in the Body Sounding Model. This is a long chapter, and there is no need to labor over it; how to use the information will be made clear in Part II.

The Body Sounding Model for Energy Integration

Our bodies are equipped with a subtle energy system that receives and transmits energy information. It maintains the physical and spiritual templates that govern our experience as conscious beings in physical bodies. The system is composed of three primary subsystems: the aura, the chakras, and the meridians. The aura is the radiant field around each person, the chakras are energy centers in the body that connect with the aura, and the meridians are channels of energy that provide vital life force to every cell. Current understandings of auras and chakras are based on Hindu tradition made popular by the Theosophists at the turn of the 20th century. Some of the oldest teachings originate in Upanishad texts that date to the early centuries BCE. Details on meridians come from Chinese medicine dating to 2000–3000 BCE. Hindu texts also talk of channels of energy in the body called *nadis*, which have a strong correlation to Chinese meridians. My understanding is based on traditional descriptions with notable departures.

Many different models for working with energy structures exist, and thousands of books are written on the subject. Whereas certain basics are the same, details and approaches vary depending on the focus and perspective of the writer. No two systems are exactly the same because no two people are exactly the same. It is said that there is a face of God for everyone who looks, meaning that the road to the divine is personal, and the perspective is individual. No one can define this territory for another.

Many will debunk information on energy structures because of the differences in some of the descriptions. However, everything we understand depends on focus. Here's an example of how focus impacts medicine: To a cardiologist, the heart is a pump distributing blood and the focus is on the mechanics: the ability of the arteries to expand and contract, the reliance of valves, the functioning of heart chambers, and so on. A neurocardiologist looks at the nervous control of the heart: its rhythms, electrical conductance, and coordination with the sympathetic nervous system. More recently it has been discovered that the heart is also an endocrine organ, producing hormones that help regulate blood pressure and heart rate.[1] In the 1990s, an entirely new model was formulated based on the research of neurocardiologist Dr. J. Andrew Armour. He maintains that the heart is a sensory organ as well as a sophisticated information encoding and processing center sustaining a continuous two-way dialogue with the brain.[2]

Each doctor focuses on the function of the heart he works with, the same way energy practitioners focus on the function of the energy systems that validate their personal experience. With enough information, an overarching pattern is found that brings all perspectives together. Although each model offers a different approach, they all provide life-changing information. People choose to work with the method they resonate with, the one that offers them the most growth, and which one it is can change as the person changes.

As humans evolve, the energy structures that support and serve our development evolve as well. Rudolf Steiner, the founder of Anthroposophy, stated that people's energy structures today are very different from what they were thousands of years ago and very different from what they will be years from now.[3] Many believe we are in a transitional time in history and rapid evolution is taking place, precipitating unprecedented changes in our energy structures. Therefore, systems and models must change as well.

Appendix C provides my favorite books on energy anatomy. The Body Sounding Model may or may not correspond to others, but it's not an either/or situation. This information is another view, an addition to existing truth, and it will grow and evolve and parts will fall away.

Body Sounding and the Aura

The aura is a multi-layered field of energy surrounding the body. It emanates from a core of energy in the center of our being, radiating outward and surrounding us in the shape of an egg. Researcher Joseph Chilton Pearce called it the Cosmic Egg. It represents our personal space, and everything that happens inside of that space is a direct reflection of the compilation of who we are: our thoughts, attitudes, emotions, beliefs, desires, and more. It holds the karmic patterns we are born with and the soul growth we hope to achieve. All of these exist as frequency and patterns of energy flow.

Whereas the aura is a field of energy, it is also composed of emanations that are rays of light vacillating in the space around us. Old paintings of

Christian saints and Hindu deities often depict both the halo of light and fingers of flame around the head of the image. The first time I saw these emanations was in a yoga class in the late 1970s. I was in a slightly altered state of awareness when, with an empty mind, I gazed at my yoga teacher and saw blue light radiating from him. The light did not appear as a blanket of brightness, but was made of individual emanations, separate fingers that contained structure not seen in a ray of light. The emanation looked like fiberoptic filaments undulating like the arms of a sea anemone. I call them filaments of light.

The filaments of the aura are very fine emanations, thicker in diameter closer to the body, finer and more ethereal further away. Changes in thickness occur in bands that are called the layers of the aura. The thickness of the filaments in each band is an expression of the band's frequency: The lowest frequency band is closest to the body; the highest is farthest away. There are seven primary bands, but as with primary colors, there are many variants. Each band or layer resonates with a specific frequency and contains explicit information for a person's physical, emotional, mental, and spiritual function. The width of each band changes as a person focuses on different aspects of growth.

The aura is the template for our physical sojourn. Thoughts, beliefs, and attitudes appear as geometric patterns that connect filaments from different layers. These patterns direct what we perceive, how we feel, and how we use our energy. They broadcast who we are to the world and attract our life circumstances. We attract circumstances that resonate with our patterns regardless of whether the pattern is limiting or expanding, therefore making them self-perpetuating. We can creatively interact with the aura by becoming aware of our subconscious patterning and making conscious choices for something different. Meditation is a great tool for accessing this process, and exercises are part of the discussion in Part II. Additional information on how these patterns are created and how they function can be found in *The Path of Energy*.

The Traditional Chakras

The aura receives information from the environment, transmitting it to the body-mind through energy centers called chakras. Chakras are wheel-like vortices that receive and express subtle energy. They are anchored in the core of the body and positioned along a central line of energy, often called the Hara line, named by author and energy intuitive Barbara

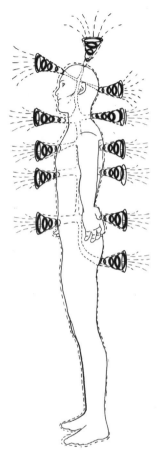

Illustration 3.1: The Chakras Front and Back

Illustration by Wayne Mason

Brennan.[4] Chakras project into the layers of the aura via front and back emanations (see Illustration 3.1). In the Hindu system there are seven main or major chakras; in the Tibetan there are 10. In both, there are as many as 21 minor chakras in places such as the palms of the hands, the soles of the feet, and in the joints.

Each of the main chakras opens into a specific layer of the aura and receives the energy from that layer. Information carried on energy is metabolized and transformed into emotions and body sensations that inform us about our environment. This information is integrated and fed into our perceptions. Our responses are transmitted back out through the chakras into the aura, where they broadcast the compilation of who we are into the ambiance.

The locations of the chakras are as follows:

1. First chakra, the Base chakra, is anchored in the coccyx of the spine and projects in one direction only: straight down into the earth. In the Tibetan system there are two chakras in the area of the Base chakra.

2. Second chakra, the Sacral chakra, is located in the pelvic bowl below the belly button and above the pubic bone. It has front and back emanations. In the Tibetan system it is called the Secret Place.

3. Third chakra, the Solar Plexus chakra, lies above the belly button in the V of the rib cage and has front and back emanations. It is called the Navel Wheel in the Tibetan system.

4. Fourth chakra, the Heart chakra, is located in the center of the chest with front and back emanations. It is called the Heart Wheel in the Tibetan system. In the same system, located at the top of the sternum between the fourth and fifth chakras is another called the Fire Wheel.

5. Fifth chakra, the Throat chakra, is located in the middle of the throat, projecting front and back. This is called the Throat Wheel in the Tibetan system.

6. Sixth Chakra, the Third Eye chakra, is located between the eyebrows in the center of the head, with front and back projections. In the Tibetan system there is a chakra between the sixth and seventh located at the level of the forehead called the Wind Wheel.

7. Seventh chakra, the Crown chakra, is located on the top of the head with one projection opening upward.

Many people who are energy intuitives see additional chakras located off the body that are propelling soul evolution. Although there are more, of the two most common, one is between the knees, called the Earth Star chakra, and the other is above the head in the outer layer of the aura, called the Solar Star chakra. To me, the Earth Star chakra connects to the spiritual essence in physical form; the Solar Star connects with the physical essence in spiritual form.

Chakras are described as wheels because each one is divided into segments, and the entire assemblage rotates as energy is either received or transmitted. Some systems picture the segments as flower petals, some as wheel spokes, and some as rays of light. Whether a petal or ray, the emanation leaves the chakra and flows into the body, becoming internal channels of energy called *nadis*. There are said to be 70,000 nadis that feed the body on a cellular level. Each chakra has a different number of divisions signifying its frequency. In Hindu pictures the Base chakra is a flower with four petals, whereas the Crown chakra is a lotus with 1,000 petals.

The Body Sounding Chakra Model

I experience the chakras as having centers where light filaments are concentrated. The arrangement is similar to the stamen in the center of a flower. I call these filaments chakra fibers. They are denser and have more substance than the light filaments of the aura. Whereas light filaments in the aura maintain the templates of our physical, emotional, mental, and spiritual aspects, the specialized filaments of the chakras have two key functions.

Chakra fibers are both sensors and anchors. As sensors, they contact, examine, and perceive the world around us. They respond to our attention; where we put our attention is where our fibers explore or anchor. When our attention is fixed, our fibers act as stabilizers, keeping us grounded and attached to our personal perspectives. When our chakra fibers are free we have more free attention for exploration. If too many fibers are free, we lack grounding and stability. When too many are anchored, we become stubborn and stuck in our beliefs. Balancing freedom and stability is a constant dance. When a chakra is closed down, it protects itself by coiling the fibers in the center of the chakra, limiting free flow of energy.

Whereas both major and minor chakras are involved in energy exchange, the main chakras reflect levels of consciousness. They are windows into the soul. The seven traditional chakras interact directly with the neuroendocrine system as physio-energetic centers. Information gleaned in these centers is transmitted to the nervous system and endocrine organs, conveying awareness to the mind and eliciting a body response. Each chakra is associated with an endocrine gland and a nerve plexus, and transmits frequency that is depicted as a color, tone, and expression.

Many systems teach that each chakra governs a specific aspect of the soul's development. The Body Sounding Chakra Model is holographic: Each chakra participates in the development of all aspects of the soul. Each chakra represents a unique perspective or vantage point that contributes to total awareness, and provides a particular set of skills to growth and expression. The goal is to gain a totality of awareness and expression as opposed to ascending through degrees of awareness.

The chakras are portals of perception: gateways of consciousness offering essential information for being a fully functional human. Becoming fully functional and clear of distortion requires awakening to spiritual impulse. This impulse flows into each chakra along the Hara line from which the chakra emanates. According to Brennan, the Hara line is a solid pole of intentionality that runs vertically through the center of the human body, connecting upward to the sky and downward to the center of the earth. The Hara line is the foundation of the human energy system. It is associated with human intentionality and the soul's mission for this life, containing a person's inner Divine Core and providing the spiritual impulse.[5]

Each chakra is fed from the Hara Line, but energy also flows between chakras via three main nadis in both an upward and downward direction (see Illustration 3.2, The Nadis Connect the Chakras.) The flow between chakras allows for integration of perceptions and also provides one chakra to support another. In this system, as one chakra grows and changes, all chakras do, and the results are reflected in the aura as changes in bandwidth, color, and density. Also, geometric patterns that represent thoughts, attitudes, and beliefs may become more fluid, change shape, or dissolve altogether.

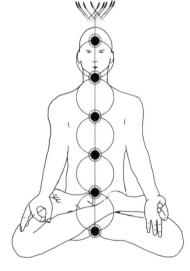

Illustration 3.2: The Nadis Connect the Chakras

Illustration by Wayne Mason

In most models, personal development is achieved through a step-by-step progression from the Base chakra to the Crown, implying that as physical beings we are striving for spiritual awakening. Once the energy rises to the Crown, it travels back down, bringing spiritual vitalization to each chakra. Rudolf Steiner and Meredith Sowers-Young (creator of the Stillpoint method) propose that the energy flow begins in the Crown chakra and descends, implying that we are spiritual beings seeking physical expression.

In the Body Sounding Model, energy ascends through the Base chakra and descends through the Crown chakra simultaneously, meeting and passing in the Heart chakra. The Heart chakra is the seat of the soul, the throne of a person's spiritual essence. It holds the balance between spirit and form; it is the center of transformation, transmutation, and transcendence. In Hindu teachings, the symbol for the Heart chakra is the six-pointed star. It is created by two overlapping triangles, one pointing downward (spiritualization of matter) and one pointing upward (raising matter to spirit). The center allows access to holographic awareness.

Describing the energy system in terms of layered bands and centers of exchange does not provide an accurate portrayal. It doesn't convey that the system is dynamic, interactive, and alive. When visualized, it is extraordinarily beautiful. Vibrant colors explode and recede, moving through geometric forms while light filaments undulate in resonance with surrounding vibrations. The system is in constant flux: perpetual motion responding to internal and external stimuli. It is an animated, exciting, ever-moving mosaic of light.

Working With the Body Sounding Model

In the Body Sounding Model, each chakra contributes a unique vantage point: a specific type of perception and ability that applies to all stages of development. For instance, the ability to manifest is seen in many models as either a function of the third chakra or the first chakra, and if a person is having trouble manifesting, he or she works to clear those chakras. In this model, each chakra contributes a specific insight to the function of manifesting, and if a person is having trouble, he or she needs to investigate the whole system. There is no set order for this exploration; each person begins where he or she feels drawn.

Here's an example: A man wants to manifest a new career. He is inspired by the good he wants to provide to humanity (Heart center), and energizes his inspiration by connecting with his creative passion (second chakra), which he uses to develop his vision and blueprint for the new career (Third Eye). He then connects his vision to the highest good of all and divine timing (Crown), and activates his personal mastery (Solar Plexus). Communicating his vision into the world (Throat), he begins to marshal resources (Base) and put his plan into action. His success and ability to respond to challenges are a reflection of how well each chakra functions. There is no hierarchy. If the man has difficulty making his dream a reality, he must access his perceptions in each area through his emotional matrix, as we'll see in Part II of this book. In this system, challenges are opportunities: They allow us to observe self in action and to uphold our intention.

The Chakra Portals

The chakras are portals of consciousness; they are viewpoints into other dimensions of reality. Each one adds to the depth of our awareness. Emotions generated in the chakras are reflections of our thoughts, beliefs, and attitudes. They represent how we energetically process the events of our life. Ideally, chakras function dynamically, opening and closing in response to stimuli and the need for growth. In reality, each of us functions better in one or more chakras than in others, depending on the issues being addressed. For example, a person might function highly in his Heart chakra when dealing with relationships, yet have a hard time keeping his Heart chakra open when examining business goals.

The following descriptions are an opportunity to explore your own system. You can approach it as an exercise to explore how well you function and perceive through your chakras.

Crown

The Crown chakra connects to Universal Consciousness, the all-encompassing hologram of existence. Its vantage point rises beyond interconnection to recognize that we are one. The Crown chakra perceives through Gnosis: immediate, inner knowing. It provides the ability to see events in light of the highest and best good for all, and expresses divine purpose and timing. When things don't seem to be working out, this chakra reflects higher purpose and reminds us that everything has a proper time and place. This chakra maintains alignment to life purpose.

When open and functioning, this person might:

- Be able to look beyond appearances to underlying truth.
- Be able to sense the flow of events and time actions accordingly.
- Express patience, confidence, and presence.
- Be able to embrace the whole of a situation or person.
- Recover easily from disappointment or failure, putting it into a higher context.

When imbalanced, a person might:

- Force issues and rely on the energy of the Solar Plexus chakra of personal power and will to get things done.
- Be judgmental, especially with regard to social issues, politics, religion, and world affairs.
- Lose sight of the greater good when making goals and pursuing plans.
- Become easily discouraged by obstacles.
- Have a hard time finding meaning and purpose in life.
- Feel spiritually disconnected.
- Have an excessive need for an authority figure and desire to hand over responsibility to someone higher up.
- Desire to have spiritual authority over others even to the point of wanting to be worshipped.

Emotions and Expressions—Balance can express as:

- Feelings of bliss and ecstasy.
- Peaceful acceptance of the contradictions in life.
- Taking personal responsibility.
- The desire to act as mentor and guide for others.
- Satisfaction in accomplishments.
- A quiet sense of purpose.

Emotions and Expressions—Imbalance can express as:

- Deep depression, loss of focus, and hopeless despair.
- Illusions of grandeur/God complex, or worthlessness.
- Taking on more than can be accomplished.
- Feeling that nothing is ever good enough.
- Lacking direction and purpose.
- Denial of spiritual reality.

Third Eye

The Third Eye chakra connects with Creation Consciousness, and its vantage point is the constructs that organize life and life events. It perceives through insight, seeing inherent blueprints and design. It is able to visualize structure and what is needed to bring an idea into reality. Insight is direct communication with the essence of people and events, and often opens psychic perceptions. Decisions are easy because the organizing principle is clear.

When this chakra is open and functioning, a person:

- Is able to create goals.
- Is good at conceptual organization.
- Is quick to see how things work and what needs to be done when something is broken.
- Can see interconnection and synchronicity, observing and interacting with the flow of life.
- Can receive guidance from psychic perceptions.
- Understands what motivates other people and can see what isn't working in her life.
- Understands his or her own motivations and is able to self-reflect.
- Can make fast decisions based on profound insight.

When this chakra is imbalanced, a person might:

- Have trouble grounding and manifesting ideas.
- Be easily confused by complexity.
- Want black-and-white answers.
- Force structures, rules, and regulations on others even when ineffective or inefficient.
- Lose sight of the organizing principle behind an effort or plan.
- Be easily frustrated by lack of planning.
- Overthink every decision.
- Be unable to move forward because all options look equally important.

Emotions and Expressions—Balance can express as:

- Tremendous mental focus.
- Enjoyment in solving problems.

- Ease in leadership roles.
- Happiness when creating things, including art, writing, organizing a corporation, designing architectural blueprints, writing music, crafting mathematical equations, creating scientific theories.

Emotions and Expressions—Imbalance can express as:
- Confusion, mental fog, frustration.
- Job avoidance.
- Resentment of others who have the position/ability they covet.
- Desire to tear structures down.
- Hypercritical of the way systems work, how society functions, and of community structure.
- Deep skepticism of things they don't understand.
- An inability to think outside the box.

Throat

The Throat chakra aligns with Clarity Consciousness, the consciousness of truth and intention. Its vantage point is that of the authentic self, the part of a person that speaks from the power of his own inner truth. It perceives through intuition. This chakra represents commitment to following the highest and best good, and to hold the intention of higher design. It has the ability to call forth what is needed to turn plans and ideas into action steps. The vibration it sends out alters existing structures and allows something new to be born. It clears the path for expression.

When this chakra is open and functioning, a person:
- Communicates clearly.
- Speaks from her true self.
- Is committed to truth.
- Expresses himself eloquently.
- Is able to bring ideas into reality.
- May enjoy public speaking.
- Has a strongly developed intuition.
- Can hold intent through any obstacle.

When this chakra is imbalanced, a person might:

- Have self-doubt.
- Do what others expect of her rather than what she would like.
- Pursue other people's agendas.
- Have trouble knowing or expressing his own mind.
- Be deceitful to get what she needs.
- Say what other people want to hear.
- Disdain self and others.
- Drop his plans at the first opposition.

Emotions and Expressions—Balance can express as:

- A straightforward, honest, and forthright manner.
- Heart-centered communication.
- Love of music and singing.
- Enjoyment of simple pleasure.
- An ability to laugh.

Emotions and Expressions—Imbalance can express as:

- Hostility, expressed as nasty words and mean communication.
- Frustration at plans never actualizing.
- Blame placed on others for the difficulties in one's life.

Heart

The Heart chakra aligns with Holographic Consciousness, and its unique viewpoint is to feel the divine essence within all. Its perception is empathy, and, through resonance, a person is allowed to feel what another feels. It provides the experience of being one with all while still seeing the individual interconnection between all life. It allows one to focus on the good in self and others regardless of circumstances and outcomes. It is the transition between the spiritualization of matter and the raising up of matter to sprit. Within the center of the overlapping triangles is a space of calm clarity that provides direct access to a person's spiritual center, highest self, and holographic awareness.

When this chakra is open and functioning, a person might:

- Tolerate differences of opinion.
- See the good in others in spite of their actions.
- Seek love as the highest expression of reality.

- Work to better society.
- Be concerned with justice, injustice, and cruelty.

When this chakra is imbalanced, a person might:

- Be hard-hearted and cruel.
- Build a wall around his or her heart.
- Lack an ability to see or feel from anyone else's perspective.
- Deny other people's experiences as legitimate.
- Have a strong belief in the presence of evil.

Emotions and Expressions—Balance can express as:

- Being calm, accepting, and inviting.
- Being centered in a crisis.
- Having highly developed integrity.
- Kindness.
- Being fair and truthful.
- Listening to others' views.

Emotions and Expressions—Imbalance can express as:

- Denial of spirituality.
- Harsh judgment of the conduct of others.
- The desire to punish wrongdoing.
- Contempt for partner and friends.

Solar Plexus

The third chakra is the center of self-awareness. The vantage point is personal perspective, and the perception is gut feelings. This center defines the difference between self and others. It creates boundaries and identifies personal needs, strengths, beliefs, and point of view. Through acknowledgment of the self, it provides the ability to assess and utilize one's own unique contribution and personal strength while identifying others' unique contributions.

When balanced and open, this person might:

- Be an entrepreneur.
- Be able and willing to take tremendous risks based on gut feelings.
- Trust his own perceptions over factual evidence.

- ❷ Make a good detective, scientist, or investigator.
- ❷ Seek to bring out the best in others.
- ❷ Mentor younger or less experienced people.

When imbalanced, this person might:

- ❷ Be unable to work with others.
- ❷ Believe she has the only correct path.
- ❷ Be at odds with the people around him.
- ❷ Refuse to acknowledge other people's contributions.
- ❷ Be excessively competitive or, conversely, avoid conflict at all costs.
- ❷ Refuse to share what she knows.
- ❷ Undercut friends to get the upper hand.
- ❷ Do anything to appear successful.

Emotion and Expression—Balance might express as:

- ❷ Confidence and self-assurance.
- ❷ Poise, presence, and personal power.
- ❷ Appreciation and gratitude to others.
- ❷ Helping others feel important and valued.

Emotion and Expression—Imbalance might express as:

- ❷ Arrogance and self-righteousness.
- ❷ Insecurity and lack of confidence.
- ❷ An insatiable ego.

Sacral

The second chakra is the seat of Creative Consciousness, different from Creation Consciousness. Its unique perspective is creative expression and its perception is inspiration. Through inspiration, the awareness that we are co-creators of reality is awakened. When cultivated, this awareness can energize all endeavors in life and provide the motivation for great accomplishment and personal dynamism, giving us the fire in our belly. The portal of creative expression allows us to see everything that exists as a conscious act of creation. Nothing is here by accident. Every life form, every object, every situation is designed. This awareness provides the inspiration to release creative vision and the passion to bring it into reality.

When open and functioning, this person might:

- Have dynamic energy to pursue his or her dreams.
- Respond to creative vision of the Sixth chakra with artistic skill.
- Be charismatic and able to motivate others.
- Have the ability to acknowledge others and inspire others to their best self.
- See the possibility in all situations.
- Have a wonderful sense of design, balance, and composition.

When imbalanced, this person might create his or her own difficulties. He or she might:

- Yearn for creative expression, but be unable to produce.
- Sell out his or her dreams or artistry for money or prestige.
- Refuse money and/or relationships in order to preserve an ill-defined creative independence.
- Be unable to see the manner in which reality and limitations are self-created.
- Have difficulty creating or maintaining fulfilling relationships.
- Be driven by yearning and unfulfilled longing and desire.

Emotion and Expression—Balance might express as:

- Passion, spontaneity, and free thinking.
- An engaging personality that can influence others.
- The ability to connect deeply in romantic partnerships.
- The ability to be an equal member of a partnership, romance, or group.
- A positive, outgoing manner.
- The ability to work through problems with creative solutions.

Emotion and Expression—Imbalance might express as:

- Being moody, pessimistic, and defeatist.
- Being critical of other people's creative efforts.
- Doubt of creative abilities.
- Sexual addictions or no sex drive.
- Being duplicitous in relationships of romance, friendship, and business.
- Apathy.

Root

The Root or Base chakra is connected to Survival Consciousness. It is aligned to the material world and is focused on what we need for physical survival: food, shelter, and enough money for basic needs. Through instinct, the Root chakra provides security and comfort. It has the ability to get things done and, when in alignment with the rest of the chakras, can move mountains to fulfill goals and ideals. It represents the foundation, providing nourishment, grounding, and abundance.

When open and functioning, this person may be:

- The go-to person to get things done.
- Adroit at commandeering supplies and materials for projects.
- Manager material.
- Financially stable and a wiz at budgeting money.
- The picture of healthy physique.
- Grounded and self-reliant.
- Always looking to grow and improve standing in life.

When imbalanced, this person might:

- Use food to fill emotional needs.
- Have a hard time making ends meet.
- Suffer physically, especially in the legs and low back.
- Be easily seduced by power, money, or prestige.
- Be unmotivated and unable to believe in self.

Emotions and Expression—Balance may express as:

- Being emotionally present, even-tempered, and slow to react to criticism.
- Being careful and pragmatic.
- Being happy and satisfied with life.
- Competitiveness.
- An ability to make and keep commitments.

Emotions and Expression—Imbalance may express as:

- Lust, greed, envy, and desire.
- Forgetting to bathe or take care of physical needs.
- Insomnia and anxiety.
- Apathy and reluctance to improve.

Chart 3.1 Easy-Access Chakra Guide

CHAKRA / Color / Tone	NERVE PLEXUS / ENDOCRINE ORGAN	Consciousness	Perspective	Sense / Derived from:	Ability
Crown / White or Violet / C with B	Central Nervous System / Hypothalamus / Pineal	Universal Consciousness	Highest and best good of all	Gnosis (inner knowing) / Direct download	Maintain alignment to your purpose
Third Eye / Cobalt Blue / C with A	Autonomic Nervous System / Pituitary / Pineal	Creation Consciousness	Divine plan behind and within events	Insight / Psychic perception, clairvoyance	Ability to see blueprints and make structures / Can perceive other people's motives and agendas
Throat / Sky Blue / C with G	Cervical Ganglia/ Star Ganglia / Thyroid	Clarity Consciousness	Authentic Self: personal inner truth	Intuition / Vibration / Clairaudience	Ability to hold an intention with commitment, to clear out the old and to call forth what is needed to empower plans

Heart Pink or Green C with F	Cardiac Plexus Thymus and Heart (as endocrine organ)	Holographic Consciousness	Divine Essence within other people and all life force	Empathy Resonance	Ability to stay connected with good in self and others regardless of circumstances and outcomes
Solar Plexus Yellow/Gold C with E	Solar Plexus Pancreas Adrenal cortex	Personal or Self-Consciousness	Personal power, willpower, and self-mastery	Gut feelings Mental and emotional processing	Ability to see your own and others' unique contribution and personal strength
Sacral Orange C with D	Lumbo-Sacral plexus Ovaries and testes	Creative Consciousness	Creative expression and passion	Inspiration Awakening	Ability to energize life through creative passion; fire in the belly
Base/Root Red C	Sacral-Coccygeal Adrenal Medulla	Survival Consciousness	Material and financial foundation	Instinct Inherent wisdom	Ability to get things done in material realms; logistical, practical skills

- ☯ Hypochondria.
- ☯ An over-focus on small details.
- ☯ Harboring resentment.
- ☯ Lacking commitment.

Meridians

In the Body Sounding Model, emotions and feelings are generated in the chakras as part of a two-way energy information exchange. Emotions are responses to stimuli that integrate information received on conscious levels with energetic information below our everyday awareness. Emotions interact with our internal landscape, feeding our perceptions and fueling our thoughts. Communication is a two-way street, and emotions transmit our responses and drive our behaviors and actions. In this model, it is through the meridians that emotions emerge as body events. Emotions, thoughts, attitudes, and beliefs are wound together in the interaction between our inner self and outer world.

Traditionally, the meridians are channels of life force called chi or ki in Chinese medicine. In Taoist philosophy, chi results from the interaction of two polar and complimentary forces that, through the Cycle of Transformation, create all the expressions manifest in nature. These forces are known as yin (the receptive force) and yang (the active force). In the Body Sounding Model, the interaction of these two forces creates the subtle energy matrix that maintains physical templates. This principle is illustrated in the human body via the Hara line, which connects Heaven (yang) and Earth (yin) to manifest the human energy system.

Taoist wisdom maintains that chi is transformed into five phases, or elements: Metal, Water, Wood, Fire, and Earth. They are regarded as five features inherent in everything and represent processes and tendencies. Twelve of the primary channels of energy are associated with key organs and are called the Organ Meridians. It is no surprise that they are divided into yin and yang partners, and express the processes and tendencies of the Five Elements, including emotions. It is said that specific emotions are generated in particular organs and transmitted through the corresponding meridians. Although there is no correlation that I know of between the organs that generate emotions and the chakras, nonetheless I propose that there is a link.

If the information in this chapter has been overwhelming, this is where it gets more personal. Meridians transmit emotions through a transformation cycle with yin and yang expressions. They are not static; they move from one state into another as a function of internal process. Here is a short summary of some of the traditional emotional correlations to meridians:

- **Metal** (lung/large intestine meridians): Represents substance, strength, and structure. Deals with what to hold on to and what to let go of. Traditional emotions are grief, sorrow, and sadness on one end of the spectrum, and courage, dignity, non-attachment, and strength on the other. Often issues revolve around how we hold our boundaries.

- **Water** (kidney/urinary/bladder meridians): Represents rest before starting another cycle of growth. Deals with ancestral energy and transmits emotions of fear or fright, which, through the cycle of chi transformation, becomes alert stillness, gentleness, and trust. Issues often involve coming to terms with fear through faith.

- **Wood** (liver/gallbladder meridians): Represents the beginning of growth and rapid change. It reflects anger, resentment, frustration, and jealousy on one end of the spectrum, and kindness, forgiveness, assertiveness, and focused will on the other. It often deals with the ability to plan and strategize and bring goals into form.

- **Fire** (heart/small intestine and pericardium/Triple Warmer): Represents the height of activity. Fire is dynamic and brilliant in its activity. The heart meridian is said to be the seat of the Shen, or spiritual center of a person. On the one hand are emotions of impatience, shock, anxiety, and dislike; on the other, love, joy, gratitude, compassion, and honor.

- **Earth** (spleen/pancreas/stomach): Represents balance and neutrality as the patient and nourishing mediator. The emotions are worry, pity, and overthinking, as well as fairness, openness, and empathy.

The best discussion of the emotions and the meridian system can be found in the book *The Joy of Feeling* by Iona Marsaa Teeguarden, MA, LMFT, the founder of Jin Shin Do® Bodymind Acupressure®.[6] This pioneering book, published in 1987, was years ahead of its time. In it, Iona brilliantly synthesized Eastern/Taoist philosophy with Western psychological theories. The breadth and scope of her work can't be overstated, and is entirely relevant in today's complex world.

Iona explores emotions along the spiral path of the yin-yang cycle of emotional transformation, explaining that there are no "good" emotions or "bad" emotions; all emotions are direct responses to stimulation, internal and external, that help us maintain balance as we handle complex situations. Finding and staying in one emotional state is not possible or desirable as situations change and evolve. Emotions help us navigate the landscape, formulating and energizing our responses to life.

As Iona said on the back cover of the 2006 printing of *The Joy of Feeling*, her book describes five aspects of the psyche, each of which "is related to one of the '5 Elements' of traditional acupuncture theory, and thus to certain 'meridians' (channels that transport Qi or energy), acu-points, and parts of the body. Integrating Eastern/Taoist philosophy with Western psychological theories, the author's 'Emotional Kaleidoscope' diagram of five emotional spectra (on p. 57) shows the interrelationship of nearly a hundred feelings and emotions. As illustrated by numerous case stories, the Emotional Kaleidoscope can be used to help guide the release of distressed feelings and encourage the natural movement from 'extreme' (stress-responsive) emotions to 'synergic' (harmonious) emotional states. By getting in touch with the body and listening to the bodymind, we can contact our wise, strong, and joyful core Self—our original inner nature, which directs the process of becoming that Self that we truly are."

The Emotional Kaleidoscope shows how emotions transform from one state into another. When we are balanced, synergistic emotions are generated that facilitate a flow of energy and information. When we are stressed by extreme situations, we feel *extreme emotions* that include grief, anxiety and fear, anger, "over-joy" or excitement, shock, concern, and reminiscence. As Iona said on page 56 of *The Joy of Feeling*, "These are normal reactions to stress, but they initiate extreme activity of the sympathetic nervous system and of the related organs and parts of the body; hence they are more yang or active states. These extreme emotions need to change back into the related *synergic states*, which include openness, resolution, assertion, joy, empathy, and sympathy. These 'synergic states' are feelings accompanied by bodymind relaxation or a parasympathetic response; hence they are more yin or passive states."

The Emotional Kaleidoscope demonstrates how emotional states naturally transform, moving in and out of each other. It is a dynamic system. Extreme emotions produce energy and galvanize action. Imbalance happens when we feel overwhelmed or unable to cope, and ignore these normal reactions to stress, repressing them with the help of physical tension. This can lead to hyperactive and hypoactive states of bodymind imbalance, and these *distressed feelings* can become chronic, influencing our perceptions and causing physical pain and dysfunction.

Iona defined "distressed feelings" as "states of psychological conflict [in which] the extreme emotions have not been released and transformed back into the related synergic feelings. Rather, stress has turned into distress." Although uncomfortable, distressed emotional states provide important clues about how we handle life, where we are stuck, or where growth is taking place.

For more information, read the *The Joy of Feeling: Bodymind Acupressure* or go to the Jin Shin Do® Foundation Website at *www.jinshindo.org.*

Summary

In the Body Sounding Model, Brennan's Hara line forms the axis of the human energy matrix. This matrix is made of both a field of energy and individual rays of light. It forms the template of our physical body and the medium through which we are connected to other points of life in the larger universal matrix. It receives and transmits information coded on flows of energy.

Chakras are processing centers from the Hara line into the aura. They receive external information and translate it into internal information in the form of emotions, gut feelings, instinct, and intuition. The chakras transmit internal information out through the aura, creating our presence. The meridians share a common pathway with the Hara line where they receive input from the chakras and conduct it through the body.

If this seems confusing and overly intellectual, the good news is that we don't have to understand all the details of how it works to be able to use the system. It is as natural and innate as seeing, breathing, talking, and walking. We use it all the time, in every minute of every day. The purpose of bringing it into awareness, intellectually and perceptually, is to be in command of our energy and the personal space around us; to be able to gather and use our energy to promote our path and purpose. This is personal power, and having it requires being aware of the habitual emotional responses that rule us.

What would it be like to be free of the immediate angry response we have when someone opposes our ideas; to be able to evaluate them without a backlog of past patterns? How would our life be different if we were free of the fear of other people's judgment and criticism, able to act from our authentic center? The challenge is to receive emotional information free of the non-functional patterns of the past, to extract the information we need and use the energy provided to create change. In this path of emotion is true empowerment.

Chapter 4
Emotional Science

Joe sits at his computer in a coffee shop. He is completely engrossed by the screen before him, oblivious to people coming and going. Suddenly, the hair on his neck stands on end and he feels an uncontrollable anxiety. Whirling around in his chair, he looks directly into the eyes of a man leering at him with raw malice. As Joe meets the other man's eyes, an electric shock shoots through his nervous system and he is instantly filled with physical energy.

How did Joe know the man was looking at him? What signal was strong enough to break through his concentration and spin him around? Where does energy interface with matter and transform an energy signal into instant physical preparedness?

In our model, the ill intent of the man was conveyed on an energy carrier wave. It was received by Joe's energy system with an emotional force of such magnitude that it pulled Joe's attention off his computer and into his surroundings. Before the information reached the emotional processing center in his brain, Joe was already reacting as the energy signal informed his intuition and triggered the release of adrenaline. Immediately a chemical cascade flowed through his body, tightening muscles, stopping digestion, and focusing his awareness into razor sharpness.

Not all scientists think that a subtle energy component to our biological makeup is ridiculous or doubt the role emotions play in our internal communication system. Scientific support exists in the experiments of neurocardiologist Andrew Armour and psychoneuroimmunologist Candace Pert, who, along with other pioneering researchers, give merit to an energy model of reality. They reveal that emotions are informational body events that have enormous transformational power.

The science presented in this chapter does not *prove* the existence of subtle energy, and the scientists quoted may not agree with the conclusions I've reached. There is no scientific proof that energy structures exist in the body or that there is an energy connection to emotion. Those who feel and experience flows of energy don't need convincing, and the scientific fraternity casts out their members who dare reach for new understanding. We explore the science because it helps us create models and notice patterns, which is the basis for how we learn. Also, it is fascinating. Ideas evolve and the constructs we create change. Just as one scientific experiment lays the groundwork for the next, the energy model presented in this book isn't meant to be rigid; it is a springboard for further growth.

The Feeling Brain

Like Joe, nearly everyone has had at least one experience of feeling someone's attention on them. A research study published in 1999 by Russek and Schwartz validates the ability we have to feel the presence of another or to sense when someone is looking at us, even if we can't see the other person. Subjects in the Russek and Schwartz study demonstrated a 57.6-percent positive performance in knowing when they were being looked at from behind for an extended period of time.[1] In Joe's case, there was added magnitude to the transmission: intense emotion.

In our model, subjects in this study were sensing the energy of a person's gaze and subconsciously processing the information into a conscious perception. If the natural ability to sense the presence of another person uses the same faculties as sensing a spiritual presence, then a Canadian study published in 1992 may reveal what part of the brain is involved in processing energy information. The study appeared in the journal *Brain Cognition* and concluded that experiences of intense meaningfulness, including sensing a spiritual presence and experiencing enhanced creativity, correlate with increased burst-firing in the hippocampus–amygdala complex of the brain.[2] More recent studies confirm that the hippocampus is also involved in experiences of déjà vu, the strange and eerie feeling of recognizing something despite encountering it for the first time, that were induced through electrical stimulation.[3]

The possibility that this area of the brain may be involved in energy awareness is especially intriguing because it is also the area involved with emotional experience. The hippocampus–amygdala deals with the development of perception, emotional processing, and memory. The same type of linkage that occurs between emotion and memory may well exist between emotion and energy.

In memory, events that occurred with little emotional content are less likely to be recalled than events coupled with strong emotion. This is easily demonstrated with the difficulty in recalling rote information, compared with the ease of remembering the plot of a movie that was deeply engrossing. On the other hand, extreme trauma has such emotional intensity it can block memory and also trigger the disabling physical reactions of post-traumatic stress disorder.

The accessibility of energy information also seems linked to the intensity of emotion. We tend to disregard energy information that arrives without an emotional urge. For example, I met my husband at a convention. It was 1991, and Colin was a speaker at the Omega Conference put on by John White, our current literary agent. During Colin's lecture on crop circles, I had an unusual experience and was curious to talk with him about it. However, I also really wanted to hear the next speaker. An internal battle ensued, causing me to repeatedly rise from my chair intending to go and meet Colin, only to sit back down to wait for the next speaker. Every time I sat, I became extremely agitated. Every time I stood to move, I was filled with energy and felt a sense of flow. As the battle escalated, the agitation when I was sitting became so uncomfortable, I simply couldn't remain seated any longer. Following the energy, I left the room for the most important meeting in my life.

Over time I've learned to listen and follow, no longer needing such intensity to hear the messages coming from the subtle energy flows around me—at least not all the time! Each of us is challenged to pay attention to random thoughts and the feeling sense that goes with it, such as a sudden urge to take a different route home. As we do we will find that we are missing traffic jams and understanding the world around us differently. As the link between emotion and energy becomes clearer, it provides a tremendous resource.

Into the Heart of Matter

If emotions are processed in the brain, where is the interface between energy and emotion? Are other areas of the body involved, such as the heart?

The connection between the heart and emotion is legendary. Aristotle believed the heart to be the seat of thought, reason, and emotion, and the Stoic Greek philosophers of the third century BC held that the heart was the seat of the soul. In Chinese medicine the heart is the throne of Shen, the physical abode of our spiritual connection to Source. In the chakra system, the Heart chakra is the meeting of Heaven and Earth, the transformational point between spirit and matter where lower impulses are transmuted into the desires of higher consciousness. To most of us, the heart is where we nourish our love and grieve our losses. For many, it is where we hold our identity.

Neurocardiologist Andrew Armour, in a HeartMath Institute publication, places the heart in the center of the emotion-energy matrix. Whereas the brain is the body's primary information-processing center, Armour's research reveals that the heart, too, is an informational-processing center. Information is sent to the heart from nerve ganglia throughout the body. The intrinsic nervous system of the heart receives, processes, and responds to information in concert with the brain as well as independently. In fact, the nerve complex of the heart exhibits the same mechanisms for memory that exist in the hippocampus of the brain, indicating that heart synapses produce a type of short-term recall.[4]

We expect the heart to respond to bodily information through changes in rate, rhythm, and vessel constriction, but Armour believes additional information is conveyed on the heartbeat. In a comparable manner to the nervous system, transmitting messages by encoding information in the gaps between neuron firings and thus creating patterns of electrical activity, he proposes that signals from the heart are transmitted through patterns of heartbeat intervals and electromagnetic waves.[5] The beat of the heart affects every cell, entraining the body to its rhythm and synchronizing activities between organs and tissue. Changes in a person's heart rhythm shift the energy state of his or her entire body.

Interestingly, the primary type of information conveyed through the heartbeat is emotional. Experiments have demonstrated that "cardiac input to the brain influences brain centers involved in perception and emotional processing."[6] In other words, information received in the brain from the heart forms our emotional experience—a fact of which ancient people seemed aware.

The difference between feeling anger and feeling happiness is familiar to us all. We can agree that our heart rate increases in the first case and decreases in the second. However, studies at the HeartMath Institute show that not only the heart rate changes, but so does the heart rhythm. Unpleasant emotions produce disordered heart rhythms with less synchronization in the nervous system and less physiological coherence compared with positive emotions.[7] No surprise that this can have health consequences, but it *is* surprising that studies have shown that emotional states can be passed between people via the heart's electromagnetic field.

Every organ in the body produces an electromagnetic field. Measurements taken with the EEG (electroencephalograph) and EKG (electrocardiograph) record the electric field of the brain and heart, respectively, and are used as diagnostic tools in medicine. The SQUID (Superconducting Quantum Interface Device) is used for magnetic field imaging of the heart, brain, and other organs. Measurements of the heart's electric field are claimed to be 60 times greater than that of the brain. The magnetic component of the heart's electromagnetic field is said to be even greater, as much as 5,000 times stronger than that of the brain. The electromagnetic field of the heart is so strong it can be detected several feet away from the body![8]

Studies reveal that information coded on the electromagnetic field of the heart can be transmitted with no visual, physical, or perceptual contact between one person and another. Research author Rollin McCraty reports that "evidence now supports the perspective that a subtle yet influential electromagnetic or 'energetic' communication system operates just below our conscious level of awareness...and contributes to the 'magnetic' attraction or repulsion that occur between individuals."[9]

Although we embrace technology that codes information on electromagnetic waves—such as cell phones, wireless computers, and so forth—considering the possibility that biology can use the same mechanism troubles many. Enter Luc Montagnier, a French virologist and 2008 Nobel Prize joint recipient for the discovery of the link between HIV and AIDS. In 2009, Montagnier stunned the biology research community with the publication of a study titled "DNA Waves and Water." His study with bacterial

DNA claimed to show that DNA produces extremely low frequency (ELF) electromagnetic fields, and the electromagnetic waves had the ability to organize nucleotides into DNA. Using water as a substrate, in the presence of ELF electromagnetic fields, Montagnier was able to induce nucleotides to organize into recognizable bacterial DNA even though the water no longer contained any remnant of the original DNA.[10] Like Galileo and even young Einstein, Montagnier was immediately cast into the arena of quackery by the same peers who had awarded him the Nobel Prize.

Studies such as these indicate the direction for the future. However, the science is still young and far from conclusive. We have only signposts to direct further investigation for those whose minds are open, but if we accept the possibility that electromagnetic fields propagate emotional information, our next question becomes: Where in the body does the translation from energy to emotion take place?

Physiology of Emotion

Standard neuroscience states that emotions originate in the brain; however, research by neuroscientist Candace Pert turned this idea on its head. In a research paper published in the *Journal of Immunology* in 1985, she provided the first evidence that emotions have a biochemical basis and are generated in both the body and the brain. Her research showed that emotions are carried on neuropeptides, chemical messengers believed to be created only in the brain and central nervous system. Further, she showed that neuropeptides could be produced by any cell in the body. Her article concluded that the molecules that carry emotion and their receptor sites are part of the network of communication between the brain and body.[11]

Pert's research validates the idea that emotions provide information. She also demonstrated that emotions are body events: They occur exactly where we feel them. Additionally, she came to believe that there is an energy component to emotions. As you can imagine, she, too, was thrown into the category of quack. Hers is a fascinating story.

Candace Pert is an internationally recognized neuroscientist and pharmacologist who has published more than 250 scientific articles on peptides and their receptors, and whose research was the basis for a Nobel prize awarded to the lab where she worked.[12] Her story is documented in her book, *Molecules of Emotion,* and began with her discovery in October 1972 of the opiate receptor, a receptor in the brain that responds to the opium drug.

A receptor is a site on a cell membrane that binds substances such as hormones and neurotransmitters. They are electrically activated in a type of key-and-lock system: Each receptor is keyed to one type of substance. When a receptor receives the substance that it binds, an electric charge is released into the cell activating chemical signals that represent the action of the substance. For example, opium can only bind and activate an opiate receptor. If the brain did not have opium receptors, taking opium would not cause an altered state of consciousness.

The discovery of the opiate receptor raised the question of why receptors exist in the brain for a substance that isn't produced in the body. The answer came from two pharmacologists, John Hughes and Hans Kosterlitz, who discovered that the body produces compounds similar to opium named endorphins, short for endogenous morphine-like compounds. The receptors that bind opium and similar drugs are actually endorphin receptors. Endorphins are well known for their ability to relieve pain and induce well-being. Few people today do not know that the high they feel from exercise, massage, or meditation is created by the release of endorphins.

The euphoria that endorphins produce indicates a biochemical basis for emotions. The natural place to look for molecules that carry emotional information is in neuropeptide messenger molecules, and Pert's experiments demonstrated that they are, in fact, the carriers of emotional signals. In addition, she discovered that most cells can generate neuropeptides and have receptors sites to receive them as well. In other words, cells throughout the body have the ability to generate and receive emotional information. She believes this exchange of neuropeptides is the basis for mind-body communication.

The average cell has thousands of receptor sites for neuropeptides; brain cells have millions, indicating the central role the brain plays in processing information. Nerve cells in concentrated complexes (ganglia) along the spine receive information generated in the cells and communicate it to the brain, and vice versa. These nerve complexes have a relationship with chakras in the traditional chakra system. In her book, Pert describes the first time she considered this connection: A man showed up in her office asking if she knew if there was a correlation between endorphins and the chakras. She states, "I had no idea what he was talking about, but, trying to be helpful, I pulled out a diagram that depicted how there were two chains of nerve bundles located on either side of the spinal cord, each rich with information-carrying peptides. He placed his own chakra map over my drawing and together we saw how the two systems overlapped."[13]

It seems that the energy that was received by Joe's chakras stimulated the production of neuropeptides in the nerve ganglia associated with each chakra. There is no proof of this theory; it is conjecture, but it is only through the posing of possibilities that question are investigated.

Into the Future

The field of New Science is full of strong pioneers breaking new ground in the arena of mind and consciousness. While Nobel-contributing scientists such as Candace Pert and Luc Montagnier became outcasts the moment they spoke of possibilities outside the accepted scientific paradigm, their light will continue to inspire open minds long after the old school has passed.

The Russek and Schwartz study cited earlier also evaluated the extent that a person's openness to some type of spiritual reality impacted his or her ability to feel the gaze of another. Not surprisingly, subjects with a higher degree of openness had a greater performance.[14] Simply by being open-minded we perceive more of what is happening around us. Ultimately it is our perceptions that guide the questions we ask and directions we take. We don't need science to open our minds; we only need to pay attention.

A final aspect of the Russek and Schwartz study revealed that positive results were the same whether a person actually looked at a subject or merely focused his or her *intention* on a subject. The evidence is mounting toward one important conclusion: When emotion and intention are combined, a tool for transformation is created.

Chapter 5
The Embodiment of Emotion

As information cascades through the energy system, it ultimately lands in our bodies. We don't need science to tell us that emotions are body events; we know they are because that is where we experience the pain or pleasure of our feelings. When we stub a toe, we don't consider whether the injury really occurred in the brain; we know it happened in the foot because that's where it hurts. So why do we consider that emotions happen anywhere other than in the body where we feel them?

The reflection of this basic knowledge is seen in the body metaphors we use in our language, giving us valuable clues to the translation of emotional information. Metaphors are only useful if they convey information we all relate to. For example, when a person wants to be "on the same page" with someone else, we understand the person wants to have all the same facts. If someone tells us we have to "put the brakes" on a project, we know we are moving too fast.

Body metaphors are especially useful because they provide information about common feelings along with the location of where they are felt. They speak of a shared internal and external awareness. Consider the following. If someone says:

- *I feel heartbroken.* We know the person is grief stricken and feeling it in the chest region.
- *I have the weight of the world on my shoulders.* We know the person has a lot of responsibility (and probably very tight shoulders!).
- *I have butterflies in my stomach.* We know the person is anxious and feeling it in his gut.
- *My stomach dropped when I saw him.* We know she is shocked, disappointed, or terrified.
- *I am galled.* We know the person is angry and feels the emotion largely in the upper abdomen.

Candace Pert explained that all cells can produce the peptides that transmit emotional information, and also revealed that the relay stations that gather and relate this information to the brain are the nerve ganglia along the spine, the same ganglia that are associated with chakras. Mystical traditions, science, and our experience are coming into coherence.

The location of an emotion is related to how we express or repress what we feel. At this point it might be a good idea to define the difference between emotions and feelings. Obviously they are intertwined, and perhaps even inseparable. I tend to use them interchangeably; however, I think of them differently.

I think of feelings as the sensation of emotions. They occur concurrently with body sensations such as tightness in the chest, tingling, butterflies, and so on. Feelings provide information; they relay the assessments made by our subtle energy system. How we feel about something or someone forms our perceptions. Feelings are the body's expression of energy information; perceptions are the brain's expression of our emotional translation mixed with intellectual reason. Perceptions represent balanced input between mind and body.

I think of emotions as the energy or force in what we feel. Emotions provide the expression of our feelings. They are the action that is motivated by the information we receive. Physical actions, behaviors, goals, choices, and attitudes represent how we react to our perceptions. Emotions and feelings are both linked to past events, the energy of which is stored in our tissue.

A suppressed emotion is the avoidance of feelings that we don't want to experience; a repressed emotion is the containment of the action associated with the feeling. Suppression attempts to limit what we feel, whereas repression attempts to control the result of how we feel. Feelings and emotions are so closely connected there is often no point in distinguishing them, but doing so is helpful as we increase awareness and create new approaches to life.

The Emotional Process

Emotions represent the embodiment of energy information. They are somatic events that provide direct translation of energy into conscious awareness. How we experience them creates both an intellectual and physical reaction, as the body metaphors in our language reveal. When we feel fear, we are given both the information that we are in danger and the physical energy to respond. Unimpeded, the information from what we feel is processed and the energy it generates is discharged in an appropriate action.

Imagine walking in an unfamiliar city and suddenly realizing the people who were around you have gone in different directions and now you are alone. You wonder if you are in danger, but immediately begin to assure yourself that everything is fine. However, the feeling of fear that sends shivers up your back and causes a dropping sensation in your stomach keeps you alert to danger. Observing a shadow emerging from the alley ahead, you turn and find you have a burst of energy that allows you to sprint down the street to safety. In this example, the feeling of fear provided useful information and the energy was discharged in immediate muscular exertion. There was a simultaneous processing of information and use of the energy generated.

Sometimes the fear we feel has been triggered by a past memory and no longer relates to present information. Because we were not safe on this street in the past, every time we walk down it, we feel fear. In this case, the same muscles that were used to run from danger are now used to repress an emotional response that is not appropriate to the situation. In this case, feelings are giving information about the past.

Feelings and emotions can often be overwhelming, and the body has mechanisms to dampen our experience and control our reactions. When we feel uncomfortable or painful emotions, the body responds in much the same way as it does to the pain of a physical injury: It tightens. When we strain a muscle in our back, or sub-lux a vertebrae, adjacent muscles in the area tighten around the injury, limiting movement and protecting the injury from further damage. This is called muscle splinting, and the same mechanism occurs with emotional pain. As you would expect, muscle splinting occurs in the body region where we feel the pain. For example, people who have lost a loved one will likely have muscle splinting in their chest region, where they experience the pain of loss.

When we feel disabling emotional pain, the body limits the intensity of the feeling by contracting the muscles around the pain and thereby diminishing our experience of it. This is a survival mechanism meant for acute situations. Each of us can imagine a time in our lives when the grief of loss was so overwhelming we felt we couldn't go on. The numbing effect of muscle splinting in that moment is lifesaving.

Muscle splinting is also a means for inhibiting dangerous impulses such as unacceptable emotional reactions. Every child is taught that they cannot hit other children, but what happens when the impulse to protect your corner of the sandbox must be curtailed? The same muscles that are used to express territorial protection by hitting, contract with the tension of holding the arm back to inhibit the response. The learned ability to control the impulse of anger is as important as protection from disabling pain.

While muscle splinting for physical or emotional reasons has survival value, when it becomes an ingrained response to life, chronic muscle splinting turns into muscle armoring and causes considerable problems, as we will see in Chapter 8. What we hold in the body becomes a subconscious force that directs our choices and limits our enjoyment of being alive. Eventually, the information of suppressed feelings must be processed and the energy of repressed emotions must be discharged to maintain a healthy response to life.

The tension of muscle splinting increases dramatically when physical and emotional trauma are combined. When a person is in a car accident, for example, the fear felt at the moment of impact travels along with the vector of force when the person's head hits the windshield. The force lodges in the body, and the energy, along with the feeling, is held in the body as an "energy cyst." This theory was developed by John Upledger, a doctor of Osteopathy.[1] Knowing that each cell can produce emotion, I find this theory to have considerable validity and clinical merit. Healing the injury can only progress so far until the energy cyst is contacted and the emotion processed and energy released.

Body Segments and Emotions

The physical mechanisms of suppressing and repressing emotions came into modern-day focus with the work of Wilhelm Reich, the father of body-centered psychotherapy. A student of Freud's, he received his medical and psychoanalytic training in Vienna in the 1920s.[2] His system is still in use today, as are the two primary offshoots established by his students: *Bioenergetics*, developed by Alexander Lowen, and *Core Energetics*, developed by John Pierrakos.

Observing that psychologically healthy individuals display high levels of vitality, Reich identified the source as the unimpeded flow of life-force through the body. He called this energy *orgone* and observed that it flows through the body in vertical waves. He related the waves to those of the sexual orgasm, which he considered essentially important to human health.[3] People who display a high degree of physical and psychological health and vitality are able to experience the pleasure of these energy waves without blocking the experience through muscular tension.

Reich also noticed that emotions and orgone are related. In the revolution of bodymind awareness throughout the past 50 years, it is commonly agreed that feelings of all kinds are heightened with influxes of energy. Diminishing unwelcome feelings requires limiting the flow of energy, or orgone, something Reich saw happening through the creation of a shell of muscular armoring. Says Ken Dychtwald in his book *Bodymind*: "This shell not only kept out harmful or painful stimuli, but also served to limit the experience of fearful and painful emotions from within."[4]

Armoring, Reich discovered, occurs in bands of circular tension that constrict to minimize what we feel and control emotional expression. He identified seven bands, called segments, that, when tightened, reduce the vertical flow of orgone. Each segment functions independently of the others, and constricting one segment does not automatically cause a tightening of muscles in the segments above and below. However, tightening the front, side, or back of a segment causes corresponding contraction in the remaining parts of the segment. For example, it is easy to tighten your chest without tightening your lower abdomen. However, tightening the chest automatically causes tightening of muscles in the upper back and rib cage. (Appendix B contains a chart of the seven segments.) It is interesting to experiment with how easy it is to isolate contraction of the different bands.

Tension in a segment can become chronic, negatively impacting psychological and physical health. Chronic armoring results in stiff movement, decreased function, and rigid thinking. Free-flowing orgone reveals itself in the brightness of the eyes, the healthy shine of the skin, open body language, and a positive approach to life. Identifying and releasing muscle armor helps to shift emotions at their source, freeing our energy and attention to engage creative living.

The seven segments Reich identified are ocular, oral, cervical, thorax (shoulders and chest), diaphragm, abdomen, and pelvis. The arms are included in the thorax and the legs in the pelvis. Reich's segments seem to resonate with both ancient and modern models. Although not exact, Reich's segmental bands have a strong correlation to the chakras. They also correspond to transverse planes of fascia, strong sheets of connective tissue that help regulate the vertical movement of fluids and energy. In *The Complete Guide to Acupressure*, Iona Marsaa Teeguarden also identifies nine Taoist horizontal energy rings around the head, shoulders, chest, diaphragm, and abdomen.[5]

Putting all this information together, it appears the circular bands of tension not only identify muscles involved in emotional expression, but also identify where psycho-emotional experiences are generated and/or processed in the body, information we will use in Part II.

Feelings and Beliefs

It is rare to be so clear of past conditioning that experiences are met as if new and impressions formed simply from the pleasure or displeasure of the encounter. Experiences stimulate memory, and feelings are a mixture of new information with past patterning. When our feelings and perceptions are in alignment with the beliefs and attitudes from our past, we are in coherence.

In a natural state, we process information from feelings as they arise and discharge the energy they carry in an immediate response. According to the tenets of co-counseling, if the energy is not released through action, the body discharges the excess energy through shaking, trembling, crying, laughing, sighing, yawning, and excessive sweating. Whether the feeling is of great fear or tormented love, the excess energy is discharged through the same mechanisms.

In today's world, we seem to have constant stimulation with little ability to either process the information or discharge the resulting energy. Unprocessed emotions become the basis for limiting attitudes and beliefs, and when the body is not allowed to discharge emotional energy, it remains locked in the body, where it becomes a trigger in future events and the basis for overreactions to seemingly minimal insults.

Here's an example: One day when my daughters were young, we were painting T-shirts with two of their friends, Ellie and Chloe, around 5 and 7, respectively. Chloe's T-shirt was amazing: She painted a large Earth on the front of the shirt, complete with continents and oceans. Right at the end of her painting, her brush slipped and one of the continents leaked into the ocean. Chloe was devastated. She came from a high-performance family and I could feel her shame at making a mistake.

When the other three kids ran out to play, Chloe stood in front of her T-shirt, which was lying on the floor drying. She was visibly upset, clenching and unclenching her hands while gritting her teeth and frowning. The girls' parents were arriving soon and I needed to clean things up. The impatient part of me wanted to send Chloe out to play, assuring her that it didn't matter; her T-shirt was still beautiful. On the other hand, the parent in me wanted to comfort her and tell her not to worry; no one would even see the mishap.

Both of these responses were an attempt to minimizing her feelings, which would stop the processing she needed to do around her perceived failure. Rather than push her, I sat down next to her and looked at her T-shirt with her in silence, sharing the moment with compassion for her disappointment. Within a few minutes she began to shake, then gave a huge sigh and turned to me with big smile before running outside to play with the others. When her parents came to pick her up, she proudly displayed her T-shirt.

If I had interrupted Chloe's process, her disappointment would have remained inside as a failure. Every time she looked at the T-shirt, all she saw would be the leaking continent. The rest of her beautiful accomplishment would remain unseen. Through time, mixed with other unprocessed failure, it would become part of a limiting belief such as "I'm not good at art," or "I'm not creative." Would one interruption of a process like this create a limiting belief? No, but if the same thing happened every time she tried to process a disappointment, it would. Eventually, the limiting belief would direct her willingness to engage creative activities, even directing her choice of career, style of dress, and so on.

Feelings that have become trapped in the body by muscle tension become subconscious forces influencing our actions and beliefs. After a while, instead of feelings and emotions instigating muscle tension, muscle tension begins to instigate emotions. It's simply hard to maintain an open, positive attitude when muscles are bound up, tight and hurting.

Body Language

Wilhelm Reich said, "Every muscular contraction contains the history and meaning of its origin." The beliefs we hold in our body are discernible through our body language. Furthermore, 90 percent of communication is non-verbal, and a person's impression of another is established within the first three to seven seconds of meeting; that's all the time it takes to read another person's body language.

The muscle tension used to avoid emotional experience and expression impacts our movement, posture, physical expression, and involuntary reactions. It isn't difficult to read. A child who is used to being hit withdraws from unexpected touch. His shoulders may be permanently drawn up around his ears and his head hung forward, eyes peering out from under furrowed brows. A spoiled child given no boundaries throws herself into situations whether she is wanted or not. Her chest and chin are thrust forward and her legs splayed in defiance.

The tension used to suppress old wounds or hold back expression uses energy that is withdrawn from engaging positive change. What if we could identify our subconscious patterns and release them, freeing the entrained energy for positive living? This is the focus of body-centered emotional process, and everyone would benefit from some such practice. Alexander Technique, Bioenergetics, SomatoEmotional Release, Jin Shin Do® Bodymind Acupressure®, Myofascial Release, Rolfing, Rubenfeld Synergy Method, and the Trager technique are but a few such disciplines.

What we think and believe about ourselves and the world lives in our bodies. Body language provides clues as to what might be secreted inside, and we can use these clues to contact and release old patterns. How we handled the experiences of our past helped us survive difficult situations. There is no judgment in what we find, only compassion and desire to grow. Following are some common emotional expressions and the tension that develops around them. Chronic tension is trying to cover expression, but in reality it freezes it. Energy is redirected, and whether our vitality is projected inward, outward, upward, or downward helps us read body language. Of course, each person is unique and individual; this list is only to help us identify how our body may be communicating.

- **Happiness:** Relaxed muscles with an open body. Energy will be evenly mobilized between inward and outward, core and periphery, and up and down. Eyes will likely be bright and engaging, accompanied by free and fluid body movements. The body will be responsive to stimuli.

- **Anger:** Flushed face or neck, snarling, bared teeth, clenched fists, forward leaning, tight shoulders and back, legs coiled for action. A chronically angry person may embody these expressions in a permanent effect of tension around these gestures. He might appear tight-lipped and closed down, with muscles coiled as if ready to strike. Energy will likely be upwardly mobile with focus in the chest, which may be expanded and armored. Eyes will usually be bright and the contact outward and challenging; the back and neck may be tight.

- **Fear:** Pallor, perspiration, dry mouth, varying voice pitch, muscle tension, trembling, fidgeting, and shallow breathing. A chronically frightened person will likely have inwardly focused energy, hunched shoulders, caved-in chest, and little energy flow into the eyes, arms, and legs. Arms will often be kept close to the body and legs held tight together. Head down, with neck stiff, this person avoids life rather than engaging it.

- **Sadness:** Lip trembling, absence of intonation in speech, and tears give way to chronic patterns of downwardly mobile energy. Eyes are energized with need, beseeching onlookers to care. This person will often have armor through the chest, which may be collapsed forward with overstretched muscles in the back. Arms and legs might be loose, un-energized, unorganized, and flaccid. Arms might be wrapped around the chest in an act of self-nourishment.

- **Guilt:** Flushed neck or face, avoidance of eye contact, grimacing, and sweating palms. Chronic patterns of eye avoidance shouldn't be confused with fear or sadness. Guilt often manifests with a put-on act of optimism that carries an angry edge as the person justifies the action causing the guilt. Energy might be outwardly mobile to deflect attention, with protective tension in the back, arms, and neck.

- **Shock:** Raised eyebrows, eyes wide, and mouth slightly open. Energy may be frozen and the person unable to respond to stimuli. Eyes can be vacant and the person might look right at you and never see you. There is neither flaccid nor excessive tension, as everything is simply frozen. The neck may be rigid, the face fixed, and responses seem rehearsed and unrelated to stimuli.

Summary

Because emotions are body events, our body is the gateway into our exploration. As we follow the clues our emotions provide, we can begin to access their information and release bound energy. In doing so, we uncover an innate awareness of subtle energy that we can use to make decisions and empower our goals. The attention that was absorbed in body tension is freed to engage the present. The path we will explore in Part II will show us how to contact and use the subconscious forces that direct our choices.

Chapter 6

Emotions:

The Interface of Energy

In Part I, we looked into the world of subtle energy through the lens of emotion, explored the energy system of the human body, and reviewed a part of the science that is helping us quantify our experience. We saw how emotions and energy are translated into body events that leave trails in our musculature, fascia, and even in our organs. Subtle energy emerges as the life force that animates and organizes, not only physical form, but also ideas, awareness, and consciousness. Emotions are the translation of this energy.

In the past decades, the treatment of emotions has shifted considerably. Continuing from Victorian times through the 1950s, emotions were contained and suppressed. Boys were taught that feelings were a weakness and were admonished to keep a "stiff upper lip," creating bodies full of tension; girls were trained with "sugar and spice and everything nice," learning that anger was unacceptable. Then the pendulum swung in the '60s and '70s, moving so far in the opposite direction that an "anything goes" attitude developed. "Follow your feelings," originally an encouragement of

75

self-acceptance and self-trust, became a dictum to ignore the consequences of actions, leading people into irresponsible and potentially dangerous behaviors.

Emotions are not unique to humans. From bared fangs to wagging tails of delight, animals exhibit a range of emotional expression that is recognizable in its resemblance to our own. After the devastating tsunami in Indonesia on December 26, 2004, stories began to circulate about the behavior of animals along the coast. Approximately one hour before the tsunami hit, people reported "bizarre" animal activity. Elephants started wailing, and some broke free of chains to head to higher ground. Dogs refused to go out for their daily beach walk, and snakes, rodents, nesting flamingos, and even bats were reportedly seen fleeing the coastal area. Although 150,000 people perished in the ensuing disaster, relatively few animal carcasses were found.[1] Do animals pay attention to senses we have stopped using? Does the ability to tune in to subtle cues have a neurological basis?

Some humans take great offense at being compared to animals, believing humans are separate from other species on the planet, even though 98 percent of our genes are the same as those of the Great Ape. For many there is a raging debate as to whether animals even feel emotions at all. Research by neuroscientist Candace Pert into the biochemical basis of emotion reveals that "the same, simple physiology of emotions has been preserved and used again and again over evolutionary eons and across species."[2] Clearly, emotions must have survival benefit, and learning to understand and use their lost language can only take us forward.

The same swing of the pendulum that divided the mind and emotions introduced tension between science and personal experience. We all have intuition: We feel the body respond to people before we know who they are, know that a lost friend we haven't heard from in years is on the other end of the ringing phone, or feel someone watching us from behind. However, we have been trained to trust science instead of our intuitive capacity, turning science into a religion. Even the most rigid scientist must recognize the role emotion plays in inspirational leaps of thought that lead to the resolution of long-standing enigmas.

The pendulum is moving toward a more balanced approach, with the mind and emotions working together, and science helping to explain what we feel rather than telling us our experiences are impossible. The task now is to come to the table with all aspects of ourselves present: to engage reality with mind and reason as well as instinct, gut feelings, and heartfelt emotion, to receive the input of emotions in the present moment as an energy interface.

PART II
THE LANGUAGE OF OUR CORE

In Part I, energy was followed through energy structures to emerge as emotions linked with neuropeptides, body segments, and feelings. In Part II, emotions are explored as an integral aspect of the vehicle that carries our consciousness, illuminating the path to our core self. Using tools of awareness to traverse the gateway of our bodymind, we listen to the messages from our core. Emotional wisdom requires being willing to feel all of our feelings, not just the ones we like. There will always be times of pain and challenge, yet, as with happiness, painful feelings are transitory. The question is: How will we respond?

Illustration by Mark Johnson

Chapter 7

Consciousness, Everyday Emotions, and Transcendent Emotions

A soft, squirming bundle is placed in Shaun's arms and he looks for the first time into the face of his newly born child. His heart is on fire and his chest expands as he swells with love. Simultaneously his natural instinct to protect his family is heightened and he suddenly feels an irrepressible desire to impart all that he has learned to the soul in his arms. Shaun's feelings place him at the pinnacle of his personal power. He is fully engaged in the moment, energetically expanded, and his awareness is sharp. His motivation allows him to overcome any difficulty.

Lisa is transfixed by the data from her experiment, fully immersed in the unfolding scientific discovery before her. Fascination and excitement focus her attention and shift her brainwaves into gamma wave pattern. The outside world disappears; time stands still as she is suspended in the present moment. Nothing exists except the fundamental question she is exploring. Lisa's all-encompassing awe and curiosity have resulted in an elevated state of mental focus, allowing her to delve into the mysteries of the universe.

Dave is walking down the street when he notices a man working beneath a car on jacks. Suddenly the car crashes down on top of the man. Before his mind can engage the problem, Dave is acting. His spontaneous compassion provides immediate direction and releases extraordinary energy. In what seems like a single leap, he crosses the road and, with superhuman strength, lifts the car off the man while another person pulls the man out from underneath. After the man is safe, Dave collapses on the ground with muscles shaking and heart pounding.

Emotions combined with intent are the creative force we wield in life. They are powerful magic, transforming the ordinary into the extraordinary. Their magnetic influence anchors us in the present and connects us to the innate wisdom of our body. Emotions are the messengers of our core self. When we consciously engage them and marshal their force, they help direct our life and fuel our authentic dreams.

However, emotions are wild magic. They can wreak havoc, unleashing uncontrollable anger, inciting irrational action, and sending us careening down empty or destructive paths. They embed in our tissue and direct our attitudes and beliefs into worldviews, unconsciously limiting our ability to learn and grow. Yet even the most seemingly destructive emotion has a mission, and, with discernment, we can receive its gift and turn its potent force into life enhancing-action.

In the expanding awareness of subtle energy, an emotional revolution is underway. As people begin to feel the flows of energy within and around them, the connection between energy and emotion is revealed. Reading, integrating, and using our emotional energy is an awakening: part of an expansion of consciousness. At the same time that science is discovering the biology of emotions, people are experiencing the power emotions have to discern and shift energy. They are realizing that emotions are the key to living as a spiritual being in a physical body. The shift we are experiencing now is moving the subconscious into conscious awareness and creating actions for a changing world.

Emotions and Consciousness

Emotions have a distinct yet largely unrecognized link to consciousness, possibly because both are so difficult to define. The term *consciousness* is often used interchangeably with *self-awareness*, although there are really two aspects to consciousness: It is both a personal attribute and a collective overarching principle of sentience called *universal consciousness*.

Personal consciousness is awareness of our motivations and the forces that drive us, including our perceptions, experiences, and how we see ourselves in the grand scheme of life. Universal consciousness speaks to a deeper, more fundamental reality consisting of the totality of all that is. Although our senses identify reality as being made of independent pieces, universal consciousness considers reality as one indivisible, interrelated whole. This concept is supported in metaphysics, quantum physics, philosophy, and religion, as author and researcher Dean Radin outlines in his book *The Conscious Universe.*[1]

We can imagine universal consciousness as the organizing principle that is vibrating the subtle energy matrix into the patterns of physical reality, the vibration within String Theory discussed in Chapter 2. People's individual points of consciousness are nodal points in the matrix, all interconnected and interrelated.

Current scientific thinking views consciousness as a hologram. Holograms are uniquely able to hold, manage, and access huge volumes of information with lightning speed. This is accomplished by storing information in the interference patterns between two or more waves. Actual bits of information are not found in any one location, but are located in the patterns between all locations. Every part of a hologram contains all the information possessed by the whole. If a holographic picture of an image is cut in half, there are not two halves of the picture, as when an ordinary photograph is divided the same way. With holographic film, each half contains the entire image. If the halves are divided again, each piece still contains a smaller, but intact version of the original image. This concept has changed scientists' view of nature, consciousness, the universe, and the functioning of the brain.[2]

In a hologram, the nodal points of personal consciousness are not only interconnected, but they also have access to the entirety, an important concept for human spirituality. Each person contributes his or her personal perspective to the whole and has access to the collective experience. Rupert Sheldrake describes the sharing of collective information as an energy-field effect of consciousness called the *morphic field.* Access to the information stored there is obtained through resonance.[3]

Becoming aware of the larger context is an expansion of consciousness found by going within and harmonizing with the rhythms of the universe. This is often described as bliss, a state of oneness with all life.

Where Spirit Resides

Humans have an overriding desire to understand our relationship to the universe. We seem to be wired to desire connection with the larger whole. Biologically, neuroscientist Candace Pert describes the opiate receptors in the brain as mediating a "bliss response," which she describes as divine union. Interestingly, the greatest concentration of opiate receptors is found in the most advanced part of the brain, the pre-frontal cortex, where reasoning and decision-making occur. In an interview with *6 Seconds*, an organization specializing in emotional intelligence, Pert says, "Scientists can never ask why; they can only ask 'what' and 'how.' But we know that the vibration in these receptors mediates, or leads to the whole organism feeling bliss." Further, she explains that endorphin vibration is the "bliss of union and divine union" that people are designed to want.[4]

In addition to our biology, our energy structures also seem preset to desire the experience of universal consciousness. In Chinese medicine, organs have both a physical and an energetic function. The heart is said to be the throne of our Spirit, or Shen, which is connected to the larger spiritual reality called the Tao. Staying in balance with our Shen keeps us in harmonious flow with the Tao, which our system requires for health. The chakras also have an inborn directive through the force of kundalini, lifting our awareness through the chakras to reach universal consciousness at the Crown chakra.

The Body Sounding Model presents the heart chakra as the central energy center and source of our spiritual power. Research at the HeartMath Institute shows that the nerve ganglia of the heart form a coordinating and relay center for emotional information generated throughout the body, and, as stated in Chapter 4, research has demonstrated that the heart has a much larger electromagnetic field than of that any other organ, including the brain.[5]

Through the Heart chakra, the universal consciousness of the Crown is integrated with Earth wisdom of the Base chakra, connecting us to universal consciousness while retaining our awareness as individuals. Further experiments at HeartMath suggest that people exchange emotional information through the energy field generated by the heart.[6] This suggests that it is through the Heart chakra that we are linked with other people and connected with the subtle energy matrix. It is our nodal point in the collective consciousness, our place of resonance with the larger reality.

The spiritual energy residing in the heart center is commonly referred to as the *core self, authentic self*, or essence. The core self is the seed of our spiritual awareness and, stripped of all our masks and pretensions, is our true nature, guiding us through the illusion of separateness. Our core self carries our life force, which is constantly seeking to expand and grow. Emotions are messengers from our core about our path and the subtle energy world we live within. Although all of our chakras connect with the world around us, it is through the heart that we find alignment with our core. When we do, our inner impulse and outer actions are congruent, creating powerful, expressive action.

Emotional Frequency

Every connection we make to the world has an emotional linkage. Emotion is an innate quality of consciousness. The range of emotion we experience is the control panel of our perceptions. If everything around us is frequency, emotions can be considered receivers, modulators, and transmitters, opening reality to our exploration. In the same way the eyes receive the frequency of 428 Terahertz and the brain translates it as the color red, our body perceives the signature frequency of an emotion as a specific complex of feelings and body sensations. We tend to ascribe one feature to each frequency; 428 Terahertz is red and that is its entire significance. We do not consider that other qualities may also be conveyed. Is it possible that 428 Terahertz also conveys an emotion? Does it carry a perception? Or is it just red? Our emotional reactions to color suggest they do convey something more. Red is used in restaurant décor to stimulate appetite and is used in danger signs because it activates rapid response by raising blood pressure and pulse rate.

These questions raise radical ideas. Many will consider the answer anthropomorphic. Science tells us reality is devoid of emotion—that it is governed by laws that are rational and precise. And then through quantum physics we find that the laws are more complex and entangled than we thought. Suddenly emotion may be more than the evolutionary blind alley of an antiquated sensory system. Perhaps it is our gateway into consciousness. I do not say this lightly or even easily. I came to this awareness over time and, as did the Taoist philosophers, through observation of nature.

This idea had been gathering force in my subconscious mind for some time before it arrived as a conscious awareness. It came through an interaction I witnessed with my two horses, Gabriel and Emerson. The boys are inseparable friends, something I thought of largely as herd instinct even though I recognized the caring they had for each other. One day when I called them in from the pasture for dinner, they didn't run up as usual. I went searching for them in the lower pasture and discovered that Gabe was badly hurt. He was unable to put any weight on his left front leg. I haltered him and tried to encourage him up the hill. He steadfastly refused, as even the slightest touch of his hoof to the ground clearly created excruciating pain. Each attempt of mine to encourage him left him more agitated, as he wanted to please me, but simply could not. Leaving the horses, I headed back to the barn to call the vet.

When I reached the top of the hill, I looked back and was shocked at what I saw. Assisted by Emerson, Gabe was climbing the hill. Standing along Gabe's left side, Emerson had placed his right shoulder flush with Gabe's left. With every step forward, Gabe leaned into Emerson, transferring the weight off his left foot onto Emerson's shoulder. In this way Emerson acted as a crutch for Gabe, and the two slowly climbed the hill.

Witnessing the compassionate intelligence of Emerson's assistance to Gabe brought me to tears even as it internally elevated me. I felt part of a larger sentience, one mediated by compassion, and I was lifted on an enormous wave of life-force. Humbled in recognition of the arrogance of my unconscious assumption of the emotional supremacy of humans, at the same time I swelled with pride to be part of the magnificence of the universe.

When written about from an ordinary level of awareness, the description of this event sounds melodramatic and perhaps sappy. One must be transported to the same state that the event inspired in order to enter the experience. It is the change of state that allows the expansion of perception. This is how emotions impact our conscious: They change our state of being and therefore change our perceptions and how we engage the world. The information we receive is conveyed on currents of emotion that alter the flow and frequency of our energy field and impact our interactions with others. Each experience builds to create the lens through which we experience life.

After the event with the horses helping each other I began to see the interactions within nature with new eyes. In every instance I saw emotion. Exchanges between people, people and animals, our mind and our inner voice—all occur on waves of emotion. Consider an exceptional sunset. Our admiration and awe provide the context to enjoy it. Emotions connect our inner and outer experience.

The Emotional Landscape

Annoyance, acceptance, despair, joy. Alongside our other senses, emotions are ever present, painting the landscape within which we live. They provide meaning, revealing our priorities and values, directing our path, and motivating our actions. Despite popular opinion to the contrary, emotions contribute to our reasoning and intelligence. There is no aspect of life they do not touch.

Although emotions have been with us since the early part of our evolutionary journey, they are often overwhelming and confusing. We don't seem to have learned how to use them with mastery, and usually people resist the idea that we can use emotions at all. Some discard them as weakness; others revere them as a means of attaining bliss. Few seek to master the information they contain and use their energy to enhance their quality of life.

Typically, emotions are divided into positive and negative, which is an expression of how comfortable or uncomfortable they are to feel or to behold in another person. However, every emotion, no matter how challenging, has function and usefulness. It can be difficult to see the function in an emotion such as despair, yet it has the power to unmask our delusions. Equally, every emotion, no matter how enjoyable, can become excessive and cause harm. Overjoy, for example, can cause us to lose our common sense and engage in risky behaviors. Chapter 11 looks more deeply into emotions and their functions, providing a compendium of emotional translations.

One reason emotions are classified as positive or negative is because of the effect they have on our health and well-being. Some, like joy and happiness, create coherence in our energy field, synergy among organs, and flow in our interactions with others. Long-term enjoyment of such emotions results in better health, more fulfilling relationships, and a greater degree of synchronicity in life events. Other emotions, such as anger and fear, generate chaos in the energy field. Although they galvanize and focus our resources to overcome short-term difficulties, when present for extended periods they impair our health and diminish our enjoyment in life.[7]

Although it is natural to think of emotions in terms of their comfortability, it is more useful to classify them as ordinary, everyday emotions or transcendent emotions. The distinction is tenuous and often hard to see, yet the fine line is present and important.

Everyday Emotions

Everyday emotions come and go in waves of intensity, creating the ambiance of events. They occur in the body and arrive accompanied by body sensations that are felt in specific regions. The region of the body where the emotion is felt is related to the chakra and segment it was generated in, as discussed in Part I. As we react to an emotion by expressing or repressing it, body tension extends into other regions. For example, grief is first and foremost felt in the chest. As we struggle to dampen the feeling, our chest region tightens in a segmental ring, and as we try not to express the emotion in tears, our throat, jaw, and face become tight as well.

Emotions arise to fulfill specific functions. When the function is fulfilled, they recede. As Fritz Perls, cofounder of gestalt therapy is alleged to have said, emotions have a life span that includes a birth and a death, a beginning and an ending. When we are able to fully process them, emotions arise and disperse according to a need. The vast majorities of feelings come and go with little lasting impact. A small minority impact us greatly: Some save our life, others inspire us, and still others break our heart. These are the ones that imbed to create our worldview.

If our worldview is the lens, we could say our state of being is the focus adjustment. As we move through different emotional states, our state of being fluctuates, bringing our worldview into focus. Depression, for example, is a state of being in which our physical energy is low, our emotions are restricted to a small range of feelings, and we feel spiritually isolated. It is a self-perpetuating cycle: Our state of being impacts how we perceive and our perceptions impact our state of being. In time this state of being becomes the lens of the worldview and then even happiness is only experienced in light of its general lacking.

A list of everyday emotions would take many pages and would describe every nuance of our experience. It is like a palette with all possible shades of color upon it. Some consider only a small handful of emotions to be "pure." The rest are combinations made with shades of many emotions mixed together. Emotions are complex. When an emotion is suppressed or repressed, it will emerge as a similar, safer emotion that can dissipate some of the charge. Here is a small sampling of the range of everyday emotions:

acceptance, amusement, anger, annoyance, anticipation, anxiety, apathy, appreciation, apprehension, assurance, avarice, awe, balance, belligerence, bereft-ness, bitterness, boredom, calmness, caring, certainty, closeness, competitiveness, conceit, confidence, confusion, contentment, courage, cowardice, defeat, delight, depression, desire, despair, detachment, disappointment, discovery, disgust, elation, embarrassment, enmity, envy, enthrallment, excitement, exhilaration, expectation, fear, fondness, friendship, frustration, fury, gladness, gratefulness, greed, grief, guilt, hate, happiness, hesitation, humility, hope, hopelessness, hubris, indignation, indifference, insecurity, jealousy, joy, kindness, like, longing, loss, love, loyalty, modesty, pain, paranoia, passion, patience, peace, pity, pleasure, possessiveness, pride, rage, resentment, reliance, relief, resignation, resistance, respect, sadness, safety, security, satisfaction, shame, surprise, sympathy, thrill, tolerance, wonder, yearning

When ordinary emotions are not fully processed, they live past their usual lifespan. They continue in our bodies as cellular memory and become the muscle tension of our body language. Unprocessed emotions develop into unconscious attitudes and beliefs influencing how we perceive events and organize new information. They control our state of being and therefore our worldview. Here are the salient features of everyday emotions:

- They arise in response to an event. This can be internal, such as a thought or inspiration, or external, such as an interaction with another person.
- They impart information and energy.
- They recede when the information is processed and the energy is dispersed.
- They become part of our body memory when they are unprocessed.
- Unprocessed emotions require muscle tension to suppress/repress their energy and can cause fatigue, muscular aches and pains, and illness.
- Unprocessed emotional information turns into conditioning and habitual responses, which become our predominant emotional response.
- In time, predominant emotional responses create our worldview.

☯ The information from our emotions is largely unconscious; the challenge of expanding our consciousness is to bring this process into our awareness.

Transcendent Emotions

Transcendent emotions are ones that elevate us from the mundane world. They uplift and inspire, making us want to show our own greatness and look for the best in the world. Many emotions, such as joy and awe, can inspire and uplift us; however, their effect is usually temporary. Soon after the inspiration passes, we return to our normal perspective. It takes repeated exposure to instill lasting change, and even then, with enough negative reinforcement we return to our embedded beliefs. Transcendent emotions, on the other hand, change us, and, therefore change our state of being and worldview all in the blink of an eye. Once we are shifted, our reactions are never again the same.

Salient features of transcendent emotions:

☯ They elevate us above separation and conflict.

☯ They put us in a state of receptivity to the sacred in life.

☯ They open the Heart chakra.

☯ They shift our level of awareness and state of being.

☯ Even with an onslaught of challenges, the worldview they inspire remains intact.

☯ They can be cultivated with a disciplined practice such as meditation.

☯ They contain all-embracing information.

☯ They aren't relegated to the life span of ordinary emotions.

☯ They don't eliminate ordinary emotions. The ebb and flow of emotional exchange continues; what changes is how we receive them and respond.

☯ They invoke the willingness to see people in their best light and to hold them in a vision of wholeness.

Virginia University professor of social psychology Jonathan Haidt, one of the speakers in the internationally recognized TED forums, a nonprofit think-tank for spreading new and worthy ideas, specializes in the study of what he calls *self-transcendent emotions*. They are defined as emotions that lift us out of self-interest, orienting us toward something more important than our usual concerns. He identifies three: elevation, admiration, and compassion.[8] I add three more: unconditional love, gratitude, and devotion, while accepting that there are still others.

Admiration may seem a strange choice for transcendence, as we typically think of it in regard to admiring someone's skill or accomplishment. *Chambers English Dictionary* adds that it is the act of admiring with "wonder, together with esteem, love, or veneration...."[9] Haidt suggests that admiration energizes us and inspires us to our own excellence, claiming that it "draws people out of their ordinary state of consciousness [and] involves feelings of transcendence...."[10]

I was unconvinced, but as I wrote this section, a synchronic event occurred. My husband interrupted me, wanting to share a clip he just watched on the Internet. It turned out to be a perfect example of the transcendence of the emotion of admiration. The YouTube video was of the 2011 audition of Emmanuel Kelly for the TV reality show *The X Factor*. Emmanuel was born in the war zone of Iraq. He and his brother were found as infants in a shoe box in a bomb-riddled park. They were suffering from injuries including missing limbs.

The brothers were raised in an orphanage until they were taken to Australia for surgery, where they were adopted. Although Emmanuel's story was moving, it was his performance that evoked transcendent admiration. Stepping to the microphone, this 17-year-old boy with every reason to be filled with anger and hatred sang "Imagine" by John Lennon. Not only was his voice lovely, but the depth and purity of his emotion touched everyone. While the judges tried to hold back their emotions, the audience did not. They wept, cheered, hugged each other, and were changed. The admiration he inspired offered his listeners hope—not hope that there could be a better world, but hope that a better world already existed. He was one person changing the world through inspiration.

I find admiration occurs concurrently with the elevation that Haidt describes as a "warm, uplifting feeling that people experience when they see unexpected acts of human goodness, kindness, and compassion. It makes a person want to help others and to become a better person himself or herself." He locates this emotion as "a warm, glowing feeling in the chest."[11] My experience watching Emerson help Gabe up the hill is an example of this. Elevation lifts us high enough to witness the sacred. Can you imagine how different the world would be if we acknowledged the sacred in ourselves, each other, and all life, and acted as though it mattered?

Compassion, gratitude, and unconditional love barely need mention, as they are already much discussed. Compassion is the unifier, allowing us to share in the suffering of another in order to lift the burden. Unconditional love is the connector. It is love of such depth that it is unchanged by circumstance, reciprocity, distance, or actions. No matter what occurs, the love for another is unchanged. People often think that unconditional love means never being angry with another or saddened by their actions. Actually, everyday emotions continue; they just don't change the deeper feeling. Our love for our children, for example, has ample room for impatience or frustration while never touching the underlying connection. Gratitude is the door opener. It allows us to give and receive freely, inspired by the simple joy of the abundance of life. It is the opposite of entitlement.

Devotion is an emotion we rarely think of except as religious devotion. It is action: ardent, selfless dedication; the act of committing oneself to a higher path. It can involve service to humanity, planetary wellness, or a single individual. Devotion is inspired by admiration, elevation, compassion, and unconditional love, forming their completion in an act of fulfillment.

Transcendent emotions play a key role in harnessing the wild magic of emotions. Embracing a broader perspective shifts our reactions toward what we feel. For example, imagine being in a discussion with someone who suddenly and aggressively attacks your point of view, acting as though his or her disagreement gives him or her permission to disrespect you. The rising of your anger informs you of the violation of your boundaries, and with no conscious action on your part, energy in your aura is focused in the perimeter to strengthen them. At the same time, energy floods the chakras of the Solar Plexus, Throat, and Third Eye, bringing clarity and conviction to your response.

In the past, your conditioning would have you tearing the other person down in an attempt to win and thereby maintain your sense of dignity. Now, your new perspective bypasses your past patterns. Dignity resides in you, not the other person's impression of you. The clarity in your energy field allows you to respect the other person even while you hold your ground. It allows you to seek wholeness rather than separation, and instead of spiraling into a shouting match, you and the other person reach an understanding.

Your anger plays an important part in marshaling your resources and sharpening your intent. Avoiding anger would not have helped you; at the same time, letting anger control you would have taken you into the same past patterns. You would have given your power to the other person, letting him or her determine how much dignity you carry.

Transcendent emotions free us from the habits of the past. Our perspective is altered, and its effect continues long after the inspiring experience has passed. It allows us to reach inside the body and find the missing key whose absence keeps us locked in the past. Transcendence implies being lifted out of our body, but in fact, the opposite is true: It is going so deeply within that we connect with our essence and join the stream of universal consciousness. Haidt notes that brain areas related to internal regulation and body sensing are more active when experiencing transcendent emotions.[12]

Using our emotions with skill and mastery means being free of past conditioning, and able to recognize and experience our emotions from a heightened state of being, as did Shaun, Lisa, and Dave. This can only happen when we are aware of and responding to our body. Inside the body are the tools of emotional mastery.

Chapter 8
Inner Tools for
Emotional Mastery

Mastering emotions is a simple three-step process: Discern the message, direct the energy, and take heart-centered action. The steps are straightforward; clearing the path to reach them is the challenge. The meaning within our emotions is hidden under layers of conditioning, and the manner in which they direct our energy is obscured, making it difficult to use them constructively. Consequently, emotions arrive as an unconscious force working beneath the surface of our choices and challenging our ability to manage their impact.

Because emotions were once considered remnants of a past instinctual intelligence, we are tempted to reject their input as unreliable. However, emotions don't exert their main influence in the older, reflex-oriented areas of the brain. Rather, they are essential to the pre-frontal cortex, the reasoning area where self-awareness is found. This area is also called the Seat of Self-Consciousness.[1]

As the last chapter showed, to use emotional information with mastery we need to be in charge of our state of being. This is a challenging catch-22, because most of the time our state of being is determined by our emotions. However, we do have tools that put us in charge: mindfulness, meditation, visualization, and intent.

These tools are discussed so frequently that they are often overlooked, especially because they take discipline to accomplish and require willingness to be uncomfortable in what is uncovered. There is also the misperception that it takes enormous effort and that results are achieved only through time. Actually, even the smallest effort yields results that each day build on the last. Stopping after only one day is still a positive gain.

Using these tools turns the flow of energy coming from our surroundings into a storybook. They reveal our greatest ambitions, and open our heart and mind to the fulfillment of our dreams.

Mindful Awareness

Mindfulness is a practice of disciplined awareness in which we pay attention to and acknowledge internal and external events as they arise. Thoughts, feelings, observations, experiences, and sensations are witnessed in the moment. Through observation we begin to connect external events with feelings of subtle energy in our body and the emotions they evoke. This is often referred to as "being in the body" or "being present." It is the opposite of everyday awareness, in which we ignore the sensations and feelings of the body, and most of what is happening in the world around us, as we strive to complete tasks, obtain goals, think about and label our experiences, and move material objects from one place to another. Mindfulness is the art of "being" in a world obsessed with doing. Through observation, the incessant internal dialogue of the mind is stilled.

In the Taoist philosophy of Chinese medicine there is a saying that blood (physiology) follows chi (energy), chi follows the mind (attention), the mind follows the Shen (spirit), and the Shen follows the Tao (the entirety of all that is). This means that our physiology responds to the movement of our energy, and energy is directed by our mind. When the mind runs in the circles of everyday awareness instead of following spirit, our attention is locked in conditioned patterns and the flow of internal chi is disrupted.

As our mind and chi are directed into the past or the future, the body responds as though those events are occurring now. Imagining a confrontation with our boss, for example, causes our body to respond as though we are in that conflict: Muscles tighten, adrenaline flows, and argument points solidify into righteousness. When we agonize over the details of a break-up with our lover, our heart constricts in grief, our chest muscles tighten, and we sink into desperation. Present emotions become confused with emotions from past situations and their meaning is tangled. Balance needs to be restored so the mind can return to following the dictates of our spirit and our emotions can inform us of the present energy reality.

Mindfulness provides a practice to break the cycle. Each breath, each sensation, each thought, experience, emotion, and impulse is attended to. Rather than damping down the energy flows of the moment and responding to people and events from patterns of the past, mindfulness encourages being present as life unfolds. If you have never tried the practice of mindfulness, here is a sample exercise.

Mindfulness Exercise

1. As you sit and read this, take a deep breath, inhaling all the way into your abdomen. Feel your chest expand, your ribcage widen, and your belly drop. Focus on the feelings within.

2. Take two more such breaths. As you breathe in, widen and expand; as you breathe out, let go of tension.

3. What do you notice? Comfort/discomfort? Ease/dis-ease? Resistance? Boredom? Relaxation? No need to change a thing; just notice what is present even as you read these words.

4. On your next exhalation, hold your breath for a small fraction of time. Can you feel your heart beat? Where? In how many places? Where does it throb? Where does it whisper? What is the quality, rate, rhythm, feel? Can you hear it? Continue breathing. What sensations and emotions arise as you notice your heartbeat?

5. Focus on your seat: How does the chair you are in feel to your muscles? Where is the pressure exerted in your buttocks and legs? What does your spine feel like? No need to change; just notice.

6. What does your skin feel? Is there a breeze? Do you feel cool, warm, damp?

7. What do you hear? What thoughts are going through your head? What is compelling you?

8. Can you go deeper?

In the practice of mindfulness we are not seeking to change as much as we are seeking awareness of what is.

Present Time

Present time refers to having one's attention on what is happening right here, right now. Our energy is free to explore the variables of life as they reveal themselves. Emotional information is easily received and we are able to decipher it free of past conditioning. The present moment is the point from which action flows; the center of our personal power. With mindfulness, we stand in our center, aware and awake, perfectly poised for action with access to everything we need.

In contrast, the mind in everyday awareness is engaged in constant internal dialog, commenting on everything we see, do, and think. The dialog is rarely insightful or original. Most of the time it is simply a series of judgments. We like this; we don't like that. The incessant babble writes the script we live by. Expectations determine not only how we interpret events, but also what we are able to perceive. Our past conditioning becomes our present experience whether it is relevant or not. We see what we are programmed to see. When two people witness an argument, they rarely report the same version of events. Each person pays attention to different details, is struck by different points of view, and draws different conclusions based on past programming.

Past conditioning is not all bad; it is a normal part of how we learn from our experience. However, when past events are not fully processed, the patterns that become engrained are not based on full perceptions. Once embedded, the past overrides new information and no longer serves our growth. Many of our patterns originally arose to protect us from pain and keep us safe. They are not our enemy, and in fact we might want to thank them for the role they played in helping us survive.

However, protective patterns of childhood become limiting patterns of adulthood: The abandoned child becomes the aloof adult; the child condemned for his mistakes becomes righteously angry in adulthood; neglect makes for greed. Most patterns originate in survival, keeping our core safe until we are ready to grow. Mindfulness asks the question: Are we ready to grow? Can we leave the internal dialog, quiet the mind, and move closer to our essence?

Attention

The primary instrument of mindfulness is attention. When combined with intent, attention is the most powerful tool we have. Where our attention goes our energy flows, creating a force that generates the circumstances of our life. In everyday awareness our attention flits from thought to thought, sending our energy down one path after another, changing so rapidly that our attention has no lasting focus. Over time we forget and don't realize the force we are wasting. Mindfulness allows us to focus the direction and impact of our attention, regaining its power.

Each time we invest our attention in a favorite dilemma, we reinforce it along with the beliefs we developed about ourselves and the world. Changing our attention and interrupting old patterns is an active choice; it doesn't happen unless we make it happen. The natural tendency is to use our energy along the same pathways, activating the same neural networks and reliving the same dramas. Producing a different outcome becomes harder each time we return to a habitual response. Refocusing our attention on the sensations of the present moment breaks the cycle.

Solving our problems does require thinking about them, and mindfulness does not espouse ignoring issues. It suggests paying attention to them in a different way. We are encouraged to suspend our internal dialog and to feel what is happening in our body even as we problem-solve. This creates an opportunity to resolve unprocessed events.

Focused attention makes staying in past patterns an actual decision rather than an unconscious habit. We choose to stay in old ruts for many different reasons; it is comfortable and we know what to expect. More importantly, we know what is expected of us: We don't have to extend ourselves and become vulnerable as our growth.

Mostly, we stay stuck because the memories and imaginings are charged with energy; each time we relive them our system is stimulated. In time we forget how to energize our system any other way. As we become more embroiled we lose connection to our core self and thereby lose the motivation to charge our system through upliftment. Upcoming chapters address how to change this. The practice of non-judgment is a place to start.

Non-Judgment

Non-judgment is meeting the world from the energy field of the heart. It is resonating with the essence within all life. When we connect through the heart-field we are motivated by compassion. We see bad behavior in light of the pain that generates it. At the same time, we don't have to condone bad behavior or try to mitigate the consequences it brings; we simply accept that this person is part of the whole.

When we extend non-judgment to ourselves, we are more able to accept responsibility for our actions. We are less likely to hide behind lies or strike out at others. We are more able to look at our patterns and evaluate whether or not they are helpful. Non-judgment allows us to see information free of conditioning, seeking the best choice for the present situation.

Our judgments are often attempts to please an imagined critic who sits on a throne inside comparing us to others and pointing out everything we are doing wrong. Although we envision this critic as the outside world passing judgment on our actions, it is our own unfulfilled expectations that plague us. It is the voice of past patterns, family conditioning, and desire for recognition and approval. To make ourselves feel better, we turn the spotlight of judgment on those around us. When the inner critic is in control, access to real emotion is reduced and our information supply curtailed.

Often people think that non-judgment means not having a perspective, opinion, or preference. Actually, it simply means not condemning that which we do not choose. Discernment and judgment are not the same. Whereas judging closes down information, discernment reveals information. Discernment is the ability to read information and make choices based on what is most beneficial, *according to our perspective*. We are no longer tied to being right or wrong; we are simply exploring choices.

When we judge an emotion, thought, or sensation as being good or bad, it separates us from the experience. Immediately we seek control, trying to elicit more of the "good" emotions while suppressing the "bad" ones. The other side of suppressing what we feel is expressing what we don't feel. We hide the emotion we judge as bad and express an acceptable alternative. For example, we may be angry with someone, but act as though everything is fine, producing distance and coldness. Or we may be hurt by something but are afraid of being vulnerable, so we behave as though we're angry instead.

We become the Great Pretender, and the face we present to the world is not who we actually are. Eventually the fortress around our feelings breaks down and the anger we feel is expressed in disproportionate rage, the hurt in unfathomable rejection of someone we love. The greater our pretenses, the farther away we move from our authentic core. As long as we are accommodating the voice of our inner critic, we miss the voice of our passion and mission. We miss the greatness of our spirit.

The bottom line is that judging our feelings doesn't change them; it only makes them less available. The feelings and messages are still present under the surface, directing our reactions and waiting to be acknowledged. Accepting what we feel invites our emotions to reveal themselves. We don't need to be run by them; we only need to feel them and hear what they have to say. Then we can use discernment to plot our course.

Judgment is part of an old paradigm, one that believes in separation and absolutes. In this scenario things are either good or bad, and we accept and embrace the good, judging and expelling the bad. We extend this duality into our own identity, embracing the higher self as good and condemning the ego as bad. However, they are both part of who we are; neither can be expelled and each has a function.

For example, the vast majority of geniuses are censured and ridiculed by their peers on first presenting a paradigm-shifting discovery. Without strong egos to champion them, these ideas would not prevail and we would still be in the dark ages! Without a strong ego, we continually try to satisfy the voice of our inner critic: We will say and do anything to please others. A weak ego needs constant support, acting in outrageous arrogance simply to prove itself good enough. Trying to expel it doesn't help. What we need to do is heal the ego and restore its function, using it in balance with the rest of our bodymind.

There is a different concept gaining ground: the paradigm of oneness consciousness. This is not new; it is an ancient idea supported by today's science. It is the model of holism that looks at all things as different aspects of one whole. It is expressed in the ancient yin-yang symbol of a circle with two swirling halves: The circle is the whole; the yin and yang halves are polarities embodied within. Neither polarity is better than the other. Both have distinct functions useful for specific ends, and both are necessary for creating the world. In Taoist philosophy, we move between the two polarities as situations require. The symbol represents dynamic balance, movement in response to external conditions, including the natural cycles of the Earth.

Illustration 8.1: Yin-Yang Symbol

Mindful Exploration

Throughout the rest of this book, mindfulness will be used as an access point to our emotional wisdom. We will employ it to experience old patterns in new ways, to create balance, direct our energy, and find our joy. Here is a simple example:

1. Let your mind go to a problem, worry, or past event that troubles you. At first, allow your mind to repeat the same worn track of your internal dialog. As you relive the experience, fully immerse yourself in every part of your memory: Smell the room, hear the sounds that were around you, and feel the ambiance until you notice you are becoming bored.

2. Now notice your body. Meet each observation without comment or judgment. Simply accept it.

    ☮ What is your muscle tension like? Are you tense or relaxed? How does your jaw feel? Your shoulders? Your hands?

    ☮ Feel your eyes: Are they projecting into the room like steel? Are they hard, soft, welcoming, desperate, kind?

    ☮ Feel your skin: What sensations do you notice? Tingling? Skin crawling? Itching? Burning?

    ☮ Notice your breath: Is it shallow, rapid, and constricted, or deep, slow, and full?

    ☮ Which chakra are you most aware of? Is the energy streaming, coiled and constricted, empty, or full?

    ☮ What is the energetic connection to the people you are with in your mind? Are you pushing them away, latched on, completely closed off? What is their energy with you? Are either of you stealing the other's energy?

    ☮ As you notice your body, fully engage your feelings. What lies underneath the rage? Fear? Unhappiness? What other feelings are present? What is the feeling of the hoped-for outcome of your imagining?

    ☮ Is there a belief about yourself, the other people, or the situation that is driving you?

3. As you pay attention to the body-sense that accompanies the memory, you may notice that your feelings about the memory start to change. As this happens, you have a choice: You can begin to break

the cycle and follow the changes you feel, or you can choose to reinsert the old pattern and stay locked in the past.

Meditation

Much of the information we receive from emotions occurs underneath the radar of our conscious minds. Whereas mindfulness brings us into awareness of emotions, feelings, and sensations, meditation unlocks inner realms to discern their meaning.

Meditation changes our state of being, and therefore our perceptions and how we receive them. Such shifts are quantified by changes in brainwave patterns that are associated with specific states of awareness. Choosing to meditate is choosing to elicit the same effects as transcendent emotions, and the more time we spend meditating, the more permanently we are altered. Recent research shows that long-term meditators have changed the actual structure of their brains—something thought of as impossible not so long ago. Now science is discovering that the power of our attention impacts the neuroplasticity of the brain and that emotions are primary players. The implications are enormous.

Brainwaves are electromagnetic emissions from the brain that are generated by the oscillation of neurons as they communicate with each other. They are measured on the electroencephalograph (EEG). Different brainwaves have been correlated to different states of consciousness. Until the 1990s, brainwaves were categorized into four basic wave ranges: beta, alpha, theta, and delta. More recently a fifth range, gamma waves, has been added. Here's a quick rundown on brainwave ranges measured in hertz (Hz), or cycles per second. The lower the hertz, the slower the frequency.

- **Delta** waves: 0.5–4 Hz. This is such a slow frequency that it is rarely encountered outside of deep, dreamless sleep. It is one step above brain dead and represents a very low energy state. There are no mental images or awareness of the physical body. Very deep meditation can be experienced here as a point of stillness.[2]

- **Theta** waves: 4–8 Hz. This occurs in sleep and with some types of hypnotic self-programming. When it occurs in meditation, the person feels unconnected to his or her body and may experience the self as an energy field.[3]

- **Alpha** waves: 8–12 Hz. The alpha state is one of deep relaxation and mental alertness while maintaining body awareness.[4] Alpha waves are associated with the moments between wakefulness and sleep, a state called *hypnagogia*. Alpha is considered the gateway into the subconscious and is involved with lucid dreaming, out-of-body experiences, visualization abilities, and inspired insight.

- **Beta** waves: 12–40 Hz. This is normal waking consciousness of high alertness used for problem-solving, planning, organizing, and so on. Stress experiences happen in this range.[5]

- **Gamma** waves: 40–100 Hz. Although this level of awareness is thought to begin at 24 Hz, 40 Hz is considered optimal for producing the effects associated with gamma waves. These waves synchronize all the areas of the brain, harmonizing the brain's activity and binding information from different areas together into perception. Says April Benasich, professor of neuroscience at Rutgers University, "It is the glue that binds perceptions, thoughts, and memories."[6]

The state elicited by transcendent emotions is the same as the powerful Gamma brainwave state achieved through meditation. In the gamma range, neurons are firing in harmony and brain activity is rhythmic and coherent. Consciousness is elevated with the occurrence of sudden insight, acute mental focus, and heightened cognition. The gamma range is also associated with feeling deep compassion, bliss, and a sense of oneness with the universe. For the first time research is building a bridge between heightened mental function and elevated emotional states. This new and important research is the result of a study that included the Dalai Lama and eight Tibetan monks at the University of Wisconsin.

Gamma waves are induced by the type of meditation practiced by the monks. The study, headed by neuroscientist Richard Davidson looks at what effects gamma waves may produce and what part of the brain is active during gamma wave emission. He used functional magnetic resonance imaging (fMRI) to view the eight monks' brain activity while they meditated in gamma wave states that were verified by EEGs.

In earlier research Davidson had identified the left-prefrontal cortex as the brain region associated with happiness, positive thinking, and emotions. The current study found that the monks' brain activity was also especially high in the left-pre-frontal cortex. The study states, "Mental activities such as focus, memory, learning, and consciousness were associated with the kind of enhanced neural coordination found in the monks. The intense gamma waves...have also been associated with knitting together disparate brain circuits, and so are connected to higher mental activity and heightened awareness as well."[7]

The results could imply that by inducing gamma waves, meditation creates an emotionally and intellectually coherent state. The study also states, "Mental training through meditation practice can itself change the inner workings and circuitry of the brain."[8] Other studies agree. Researchers at Harvard have found that meditation affects the structure of the amygdala, the emotionally receptive area of the brain.[9]

These findings are exciting. Those who meditate already know the power the practice has to bring new awareness to old problems. In meditation, emotions are received in context of a heightened state, which allows us to receive, process, and use their information and energy more cohesively. By engaging meditation, we are choosing to change how we perceive. In effect, we are choosing a different set of feelings and responses, shifting our emotions at their source.

The research also reveals what type of meditation most easily induces gamma waves. Most of us learn to meditate by concentrating our attention on a single focus, such as listening to a tone, observing an object, or following the breath. When we are absorbed completely enough to still the inner dialog, this type of meditation induces alpha or theta waves, and, with practice, delta and eventually gamma waves. However, the monks in Davidson's experiments enter gamma states of awareness by focusing their attention on the transcendent emotion of unconditional compassion. They immerse themselves in the feeling of being available to help others, and in so doing shift their state of consciousness. Given the results of this experiment, it seems that not only does the state of consciousness change, but the vehicle of consciousness, the bodymind changes as well.

Meditation, especially based on transcendent emotions, helps shift the brain out of conditioned responses into a mindset that can touch our spirit. It is the best tool we have to access our inner wisdom and essence, and experience heightened awareness, supersensory perception, and transformation. Says Aaron Hoopes, author of *Zen Yoga: A Path to Enlightenment Through Breathing, Movement and Meditation*, "At its core, meditation is about touching the spiritual essence that exists within us all.... The spiritual essence is not something that we create through meditation. It is already there, deep within, behind all the barriers, patiently waiting for us to recognize it."[10]

Simple Heart Meditation

1. Sit in a calm, comfortable place.

2. Take several deep, cleaning breaths: inhaling light, exhaling tension.

3. Focus your attention on your Heart chakra in your chest region. Notice the radiance of the heart-field. How far out does it extend? What is the quality of it?

4. Notice everything you can about your chest area. Notice the muscle tension, posture, ease, and comfort. Without needing to change a thing, with the next several inhalations, use your breath to give your Heart chakra an internal massage.

5. When you are ready, remember events that inspire you to compassion. Maybe it is the tsunami in Japan or the slaughter of dolphins. Rather than sinking into despair, choose to hold intent for the willingness to help. Inhale unconditional love, acceptance, and compassion into your heart and exhale it out to the world. Do this for as long as you like.

6. Without censure, notice your thoughts. It's okay that resistance, doubt, and judgment creep in. Simply acknowledge them and choose to release them with the next exhalation.

7. Continue breathing in compassion on the inhalation, breathing out resistance on the exhalation. With no expectation of anything, be in the feeling of your heart-field.

8. Sink into the feeling until you are ready to meet with your day.

Visualization

Visualization is the practice of constructing images in the mind's eye. It's used hand-in-hand with attention and intention to direct energy. As we focus our attention on a visual image, we direct our energy into its creation. Moving energy in the mind's eye directs the energy in our body and energy field, interacting with energy in the universe. Once we have discerned the message in our emotions, visualization directs the energy into constructive outcomes.

Visualizing is totally natural. It is a constructive use of the body's responsiveness to our thoughts, allowing us to prepare for events by practicing them in our mind's eye. As we see ourselves successfully performing an activity, our body develops the neural pathways that support it. Athletes, actors, and even CEOs use this technique to perfect their performance and obtain their goals.

Some people believe that they cannot visualize; however, they are doing it all the time. Every time a memory is replayed or a daydream indulged, visualization is happening. People who say they can't visualize are often saying they don't believe that creating images in the mind has power. Research says otherwise.

Athletes use visualization to mentally rehearse before competition. Brain studies show that thoughts produce the same mental instructions to the body as actions. Using mental imagery improves motor control, attention, perception, planning, and memory. In fact, thinking through a gym workout even increases muscle mass!

Researchers from the Cleveland Clinic Foundation in Ohio investigated the possibility of receiving strength benefits from simply imagining the exercising of a muscle. Amazingly, the results were positive: Thinking through an exercise helped maintain muscle strength in a group of subjects. Measurements of the brain's activity while the study group was visualizing suggested that the strength gains were due to improvements in the brain's ability to signal muscle activity.[11]

Today, everyone from Tiger Woods to major CEOs uses the art of visualization to improve outcomes. I experienced the undeniable power of it with horseback riding. Although I have a lifelong love of horses, I am a marginal rider at best and, as much as I love riding, I have never been good at feeling the action of my trainer's instruction. Then I found the video *Riding in Your Mind's Eye* by Jane Savoie. It showed riders beautifully carrying out verbal instructions. Watching the riders provided a clear sensory feeling of the action. After watching until the feeling of it was clear in my own body, I closed my eyes and, in my imagination, performed the action on my own horse, repeating it until I could feel the same sensation as I had felt watching the video. My riding radically improved.

Visualization offers us the opportunity to feel the reality of what we are imagining. Immediately our body and brain change. Our perceptions change, and so does our energy. Our vibration attracts circumstances into our life. Using our feelings as our guide, we can unerringly move toward our goals. Success with visualization requires using all of our senses and emotions. Here is an exercise to practice.

Visualization Exercise

1. Sit in a quiet, comfortable location.

2. Relax while taking in three deep, cleansing breaths. Inhale relaxation, exhale tension.

3. Notice the feelings, sounds, impressions, and thoughts playing along your being.

4. Visualize the face of a person with whom you are at odds.

5. Notice how your body changes as you envision this person. Feel the tension in your shoulders, back, neck, face, and hands. Notice the depth of your breath, and the feeling in your stomach and throat.

6. Immerse yourself in the feeling of compassion; release judgment from your thoughts and soften your body. It is not necessary to think of a specific instance with this person to invoke feelings of compassion. Our bodies know instinctively the vibration of love, of compassion, and simply thinking it will evoke it.

7. With no expectations, intend goodwill toward this person. Smile at him and see him smiling back at you. See yourself beaming light from the center of your heart-field.

8. Visualize you and this person engaging in a happy activity together. See and feel it in detail. Notice the location, the ambiance, both of your facial expressions and body language.

9. Say goodbye and release the image. Notice your thoughts, feelings, and body tensions/sensations.

This exercise may not alter the disagreement between you and the other person, but nothing can shift as long as you are both maintaining hardness. With no expectations of changing the other person, you can now begin to act differently in how you engage him or her. You can let a new perspective precede you.

Intention vs. Will

Intention is how we consciously direct our attention. An intention to be mindful returns our attention again and again to the present moment. Intention directs our attention and therefore our energy to a desired outcome. It is how we consciously manifest events in our life.

Using the power of our will is another way we consciously direct our attention, but our will is very different from intention. Will uses the power of command. It focuses all of our energy on an end result, narrowing our focus to only one outcome. The mind latches on to the desired result with iron-like resolution, concentrating cords of energy from the chakras. The power of our will tolerates no doubt, no second-guessing, no input from any cautionary emotion. The energy of willpower is hard, tight, and constricted. It has room for few alterations in course.

The focus of will is the perfect energy for emergencies. Saving people from burning buildings, holding on to a child falling off a ledge, or performing open-heart surgery requires nothing less than complete commitment to a preconceived outcome. Commanding all the resources available to meet the demands of will is the only course of action in such situations.

Although the power of our will is amazingly effective, it is costly. It burns through our physical and emotional energy; it destroys bridges after they are crossed and creates casualties in its single-mindedness. Using will's power is bringing out the big guns. The trick is to make sure the situation is best served by this type of action.

Intention uses the power of surrender. When we intend a desired outcome we surrender to its completion. Energetically we connect and come into resonance with the outcome. Our energy field opens to the outcome as though it is already present. Surrender accomplishes its goals through allowing. It is doing without doing.

Intention is the perfect energy for manifesting the circumstances of life. It attracts circumstances rather than commanding them, allowing for input and inspiration. Intention magnetically draws the flow of our energy toward the envisioned future, whereas the power of will pushes it. Energy is like water: It is not easily pushed; it flows toward least resistance. When we create a compelling intention, the natural flow of energy is toward it. The trick, then, is to create an intention so compelling that when we completely surrender to it, our energy naturally and effortlessly flows to its creation.

In extreme situations, it is obvious when to use the power of will over that of intention. However, in everyday choices it is an art. There is no exact formula. Direction comes from reading the subtle energy of a situation, our emotional read of the ambiance, and discerning when we need the direct focus of our yang will or the allowing of our yin intention. Like the yin-yang symbol, neither is better than the other; both must be used in accordance with the necessity at hand.

Try this: The next time you are making a choice, first visualize yourself engaging it with your will. Then imagine engaging it with intent. In which scenario do you feel more flow? This simple exercise will produce immediate direction in most situations. The trick is remembering to use it.

The Toolbox of Our Presence

The tools in this chapter increase our presence—the overall frequency we emit based on our essence and our state of being. All aspects of who we are, are brought to the table. Our presence is an emanation; it is what we use to touch the world. It is unique. No one else attends with exactly the same perception, insight, or feel. Being fully present makes us emotionally available to ourselves and to the people around us. Our mind is not miles away in another place, in another time. It is right here, right now; available to learn, grow, and embrace life. Once again, balance is the key to creating presence.

In daily life our attention is drawn in many directions and requires an active choice to stay focused in the present. As with anything, it can be overdone. For example, we can become so focused on what is happening internally that we neglect the fullness of experiencing the person sitting next to us. Although the practice is meant to make us more available, it can backfire, making us less available.

As we learn the language of emotions we find deeper places within. Some will be welcome and some we might wish to keep hidden. The more we embrace the practices of this chapter, the more we will learn and grow. It is tremendously empowering and at the same time humbling. Staying conscious in each moment has to be chosen in each moment. Sometimes we succeed; other times we don't. Essentially, we are making the choice to be fully aware, awake, and alive.

Chapter 9
Balancing Our Emotional Instrument

We are spiritual beings—consciousness embodied in physical form. The body is the instrument and vehicle that carries our consciousness in the exploration of reality. As spiritual beings our physical bodies are wired to receive energy. The subtle energy field that organizes, motivates, and sustains us can be felt. It is not just an idea or concept; it is a palpable substance as well as an indomitable force. Energy awareness is an essential part of who we are and is central to receiving direction from our emotional information system.

As the head researcher at the Institute of Noetic Sciences, Dean Radin provides unique insights into the energy-field effects of our awareness and the link between energy and emotion. Throughout the past two decades he has conducted experiments into presentiment, the ability to sense that something is about to happen. In a series of double-blind controlled studies using heart-rate and skin-conductance monitors along with other physiological indicators, he measured people's responses as they were exposed to a wide variety of photographs. Some were calm pictures; others contained highly emotional images, both happy and sad.

It was expected that subjects would exhibit physical changes immediately upon seeing an upsetting or exciting picture—an effect that was well documented. However, the experiments showed that participants were having physiological changes three to six seconds *before* they were confronted with impactful pictures. The participants themselves had no premonition of what type of picture was coming, yet their bodies did. The repeatable results of four separate experiments demonstrated that the odds against chance were 125,000 to 1. The studies also revealed that the strength of the response was proportional to the intensity of emotion in the event. Radin describes the three- to six-second interval as the "bow wave" of an approaching future event.[1]

This study has many implications. The idea that event horizons have bow waves is indicative of an energy-field effect, consistent with my idea that events first impact us through the energy field of our aura. It also appears to validate my premise that emotions and energy are linked. Most importantly, it demonstrates that emotions are important to our capacity for energy awareness. The more emotion an event induces, the more energy it carries, providing a force that we can creatively direct with our intent.

Feeling the energy that streams through us is as natural as feeling our heartbeat or breath. It is as visceral as the feeling on our skin of sun, wind, and rain. We feel it because we have the capacity to feel it and miss it only because of conditioning. However, decoding the many signals requires clarity. Being willing to feel our emotions and to be present to the body are prerequisites to reading our emotional-energy system. Balancing and tuning the instrument is the next step.

Tuning the Bodymind

Bodymind is a term used to describe our physical/psychological vehicle. The term does away with the idea that our mind and body are separate entities working independently of each other. It reaches beyond the illusion that intelligence is a mental activity devoid of the body's input or that body events such as illness are somehow separate from the influence of how we think. In the bodymind, the body and mind are different, interactive aspects of one whole. Each brings its own form of insight into our consciousness and each contributes to the totality of our wisdom.

The *Merriam-Webster* dictionary definition of *mind* includes "the element or complex of elements in an individual that feels, perceives, thinks, wills, and especially reasons."[2] Because feelings occur in the body, this definition automatically includes the body as part of the mind. What is missing is the concept of subtle energy—part of the "complex of elements" that guides our thoughts and actions are the changes in the vibratory pattern of our energy field.

In this book our energy structures and their impact are included in our definition of bodymind. The first step in tuning our instrument is balance. The following simple meditation helps harmonize mind, body, and energy.

Harmonizing the Bodymind

1. Focus on the central point inside your head where you locate your thinking process. Imagine your breath as light. As you inhale, imagine light coalescing in this thinking area. Visualize your brain expanding with light, freeing up neuronal connections and allowing each cell to vibrate with insight and inspiration. Continue until your head feels awake, aware, and alive.

2. Release your focus and notice what you feel.

3. Now inhale, bringing light into your sacrum, filling the pelvic bowl that sits below your belly button. Sink your awareness into this area and allow even deeper relaxation. Imagine your pelvic bowl glowing and expanding with light, connecting you to your source of physical energy and instinct.

4. Release your focus and notice what you feel.

5. Now, switch your focus to your chest, where your Heart chakra resides. With each inhalation, invite light into your heart. Fill your chest cavity; let it grow and let it glow. Radiate into the space around you, filling your aura with heart-centered light. As you become light-filled, feel your connection to your core.

6. Release your focus and notice what you feel.

7. Releasing all expectation, inhale light into all three centers simultaneously. Imagine them interacting with each other, exchanging energy and yet remaining separate and distinct. Continue to breathe, observing the balance, harmony, and flow.

8. Release your focus and feel the space around you. Notice how far away from your body you can extend your senses.

9. When you are ready, continue with your daily activities, maintaining an awareness of the energy within and around you as you meet your day.

Body Awareness

Dean Radin's experiments provide evidence that the body registers emotions before we are consciously aware of them. Some psychiatrists agree. Psychiatrist/author Norman Rosenthal states in his book *Emotional Revolution* that "the first experience of an emotion may be registered in the body before it is experienced by the mind."[3] Consequently, increasing our body awareness increases emotional awareness and emotional intelligence.

The fact that the body receives emotional information before the brain is something we can all relate to. Most have had the experience of feelings that seem to come out of nowhere and have no meaning. They are usually accompanied by body sensations that also don't appear to have any physical source, such as experiencing a tingling sensation along the skin when nothing is touching us.

Imagine sitting in a café and suddenly feeling tightness in your chest that accompanies a sense of anxiety. A shiver runs down your spine moments before a shadow crosses your table and your anxiety turns to dread. This could be the scene in any horror flick, a useful device because we can all relate to the physical and emotional feelings associated with an ominous presence. Equally, many can relate to the sudden heightening of our senses just prior to meeting someone special. We are acutely tuned in to the bow waves of events, provided they carry enough emotional energy to trigger a response. The bow wave of a person we don't know who is just passing by isn't likely to produce any noticeable effect.

Intercepting and understanding feelings require being willing to feel them. Training in not feeling begins in early childhood, and, as discussed, there are usually very good reasons for this. However, expanding our awareness of life into the realms of energy requires being able and willing to feel. Emotions, along with thoughts, feelings, and experiences, are registered and stored in the body. According to Candace Pert, the body is the subconscious mind holding the patterns that govern our behavior and growth.[4]

Stored emotion is associated with muscle tension in the body segment where the emotion was generated. Emotions, thoughts, feelings, and experiences that are locked in our tissue become part of the body's structure and function, influencing muscular development and patterns of movement. In this way, body language reflects our personal growth, revealing how we feel and what we think. Wilhelm Reich, the father of body-centered psychotherapy, is alleged to have said, "Every muscular rigidity contains the history and meaning of its origin."

Mindfulness helps us focus our attention on the body clues of our hidden feelings. Being aware of muscle tension, breathing patterns, and physical sensations leads us into the emotional feelings stored in the tissue. Unfortunately, most of us spend little time consciously connected to our bodies. Have you ever found a bruise on your leg and had no idea where it came from? In order to create a bruise, the bump had to be significant, yet many will have been so engrossed in something else that it was either not felt, or immediately dismissed and forgotten. Increasing our body awareness increases our ability to perceive energy, provides greater access to the wisdom of our body, and allows us to use the power of our emotions.

All of the exercises in this book are focused on bringing the mind into the body. The simplest way to connect with the body is to pay attention to the breath. Following the breath as it passes through the nose or mouth, down the throat, and into the chest as the abdomen expands automatically brings us out of our heads and into our bodies, providing access to the much more fascinating vistas within. In the following exercise, we explore the patterns stored in the body. Using this simple method encourages body-centered awareness and allows us to move through the world with greater perceptiveness.

Increasing Body Awareness

1. Sit or lie quietly with eyes closed. Without changing your breathing, notice it: How deep or shallow, how fast or slow? How fully do you exhale? Inhale? How much does your chest expand? How much does your abdomen expand?

2. Bring your attention to your feet: As you inhale, imagine bringing your breath all the way into your feet. Take a quick inventory of your muscle tension and sensation. Do you feel empty or full? Expanded or contracted? Heavy or light? What emotion are you feeling? No need to change anything; just notice. Take as many breaths into the area as you desire.

3. On an inhalation, bring your awareness to another part of the body, moving from your feet to your shins, thighs, pelvis, and so on until you reach your head. On an exhalation relax the area and leave it behind. Feel free to move or stretch as you need to.

4. When you finish moving through the body, allow yourself time to float in relaxation. Free your mind and feel. Notice images, thoughts, emotions, and body sensations. Allow them to come and go with no attachment.

5. When you are finished, spend a moment in gratitude for this
    magnificent instrument before moving on.

*Body awareness not only anchors you in the present moment, it is a
doorway out of the prison that is the ego.*
—Eckhart Tolle[5]

Balancing Intellect and Emotions

The heart and mind often seem to give conflicting advice. People are
counseled to follow one or the other: "Don't be ruled by your heart" or,
conversely, "Let go of your mind and follow your heart." Different people
seem to believe that one or the other has a greater ability to discern reality. However, even the most emotionally based person relies on reason
and even the most rational scientist is motivated and focused by emotion.
Emotions and intellect are meant to be used in conjunction with each other.

Many times emotions are clear and precise in the information they convey. They arrive with such dynamic force that we don't doubt their importance. We use them to prioritize our decisions and organize daily details.
Other times, our emotions seem to counter what our intellect demands and
we are fraught with indecision. They can become so confusing that they
take us completely off center. Finding a path through is easiest when our
body, mind, and emotions are integrated. Studies show that intelligence is
a function of how well the brain integrates input from all the various areas,
including the hippocampus-amygdala complex of the limbic system.[6]

The previous chapter discussed the pre-frontal cortex as the reasoning,
intelligent part of the brain. A major feature in brain studies of this area
has included the role emotions play in our intellectual process, which is
highlighted when a person's pre-frontal cortex is damaged. In an undam-
aged brain, the reasoning processes of the pre-frontal cortex integrates
input from many areas, including those related to sensory stimulation, emotions, past experience, and additional centers of intelligence. It coordinates
this information to plan, strategize, and problem-solve. So what happens
when emotions are removed from this process? In his book *Emotional
Revolution,* Dr. Norman Rosenthal describes two patterns resulting from
prefrontal cortex injury that demonstrate the contribution of emotions: the
Phineas Gage syndrome and the antisocial personality.

In the Phineas Gage syndrome, injury occurs later in life after the brain has fully developed. Although the person's ability to perform well on intelligence tests remains the same as prior to the injury, his or her ability to stay engaged with life and to experience a full range of emotions is damaged. He or she often becomes rude, insensitive, and boastful, displaying a lack of emotional depth that interferes with relationships. Emotional changes result in an inability to execute planning and decision-making skills. He or she is unable to make even trivial decisions, doesn't learn from past mistakes, and consistently repeats actions that result in pain, loss, and suffering. Although adhering to the moral code learned prior to injury, he or she has limited connection with others and is unable to plan for future events.[7]

In the second example, the antisocial personality, injury to the prefrontal cortex happens as a young child before the brain has finished developing. This person displays many of the same characteristics as the person with Phineas Gage syndrome; however, he or she also fails to develop social norms.[8] It seems any moral code the person did not learn prior to the injury cannot be learned afterward.

These two examples show the relationship emotions have to facts and figures, providing the facts of life with context and giving them meaning in decision-making. Without this unity, we seem unable to prioritize, plan, strategize, or learn from past mistakes. When we have no context for information, we are unable to use it. This quality also allows us to connect with others in meaningful ways and learn the rules of social conduct. We are helped in learning social values, holding a vision for the future, and making ethical choices.

Difficult emotions that are unstable and result in rash decisions are likely the result of our inability to process them and integrate them with the rest of our intellect. Research conducted by Stanford neurophysiologist Karl Pribram concludes that the brain's ability to store and correlate massive amounts of information is due to its holographic nature. Every piece of information is infinitely interconnected with every other and stored as patterns of neural networks similar to the manner in which holographs store information.[9] In this model, gamma waves may be accessing the holographic properties of the brain when producing an acuteness of insight, mental focus, and emotional elevation. In addition, some find holographic awareness can be enhanced through balancing the left and right hemispheres of the brain.

In the 1960s, American psycho-biologist Roger W. Sperry discovered that the right and left halves of the cerebral cortex function very differently.

His research, for which he won a Nobel Prize in 1981, showed variances in the way information is processed from side to side. Generally, the right hemisphere of the brain is more visually oriented, processing form and structure. It is creative and able to see the big picture in complex inter-relationships. It is linked to emotion and intuition. The left hemisphere is orderly, literal, and articulate, handling complex, rapidly changing stimuli. It is good at discerning sequential order.[10] However, recent research suggests that left-sided functions, such as math, are better processed when both sides of the brain are equally engaged.[11] Used together, they enable creative problem-solving and connect short-term decisions to a long-term plan.

Although each of us uses one side of the brain more dominantly than the other, we switch back and forth many times throughout the day in order to approach different situations with the best skill set. People with better balance and integration are able to respond with creative, intuitive intellect.

Here are several simple exercises to balance the hemispheres of the brain. The first three were developed by Dr. Paul Dennison and his wife, Gail, creators of Brain Gym. They are widely practiced in a number of disciplines. The fourth uses the power of visualization.

Balancing the Two Hemispheres of the Brain
Exercise 1: Circle-Triangle

1. Draw a circle in the air with your left hand. At the same time, draw a triangle with your right hand.

2. When this becomes easy, switch hands and draw a triangle with the left hand and a reverse circle with the right.

3. Continue switching sides until you can do it easily on both sides.

Exercise 2: Cross-Crawl

1. Stand or sit and lift one knee. Touch your knee with the opposite hand

2. Drop your knee and raise the other, touching it with the opposite hand.

3. Keep alternating the lift of a knee and tap with the opposite hand.

4. Change speeds, slowing down into slow motion and then speeding up to a vigorous pace.

5. Try to do this with your eyes closed.

Exercise 3: Kidney-Hara Balancing

1. Make an L shape with the thumb and index finger of the same hand, and place your thumb along one side of your breast bone and your index finger on the other side of the breast bone under the collar bone. There are two indentations. These points are on the kidney meridian. Press into the muscles. The point might be sensitive, so press gently yet firmly.

2. Place the palm of your other hand over the hara, the area below your belly button and above your pubic bone.

3. Hold this position and breathe until you feel calm and focused.

Exercise 4: Color Balancing

1. Bring your awareness into your head and visualize the right and left hemispheres of your brain while paying attention to any sensations.

2. Imagine two rays of light above your head, one blue and one yellow.

3. As you breathe, inhale and imagine the blue ray filling one of the sides of your brain (whichever one you prefer). Continue breathing blue into this side of your head, swirling it over, under, and around every part of it, sending currents of blue into every nook and cranny.

4. Leave this side of the brain swirling in blue.

5. On the next inhalation, imagine the ray of yellow light swirling into the other half of your brain. Continue breathing yellow into all parts of this side until it is completely suffused.

6. Sit with each side fully its own color and feel how they are different.

7. Now, as you inhale, send color from one side to the other until both sides are green. Notice how this feels.

8. Next time, use red and blue, and make purple.

All of these exercises are useful when feeling mentally or emotionally overloaded, confused, or unfocused.

Honoring the Core

Emotions speak directly to our core and become the basis of our instinctual and intuitive perceptions. They are translations of frequency that arrive in our energy field and interact with the body and all its interwoven layers of energy. The core speaks the same emotional language, and when we are connected to our center, we are in dialogue with the conscious universe.

The core self is our spiritual and energetic center. For some, the core self is the soul; others call it the mind, as in Merriam-Webster's definition "the immaterial essence, animating principle, or actuating cause of an individual life."[12] The core maintains our authentic self, guiding our path and illuminating our particular purpose in life. There are five core impulses that strive to be nourished as we progress through life. Each impulse predominates at different times in life, and it is rare and wonderful to have all five balanced and fulfilled at once.

The five core impulses or basic needs that we strive to fulfill in living a meaningful and empowered life are similar but not identical to Maslow's Hierarchy of Needs. Core impulses are not necessarily developed sequentially. I have linked them with the five elements of traditional Chinese medicine (TCM) that govern the six pairs of energy meridians, as discussed in Chapter 3. Each impulse requires developing specific qualities and is motivated by a specific desire. Emotional reactions are messages from our core that direct our attention when one or more impulse is being ignored, impeded, or fulfilled.

1. **Physical Necessities:** Food, water, shelter, and safety are basic requirements of life. Without the basics it is very difficult to fully develop the other impulses. Obtaining physical necessities is an attribute of the Earth element, which governs the Stomach and Spleen meridians and nourishes both the body and the mind.

   ◑ The qualities that are developed in Earth are self-reliance and cooperation.

   ◑ The desire is trust.

2. **Standing:** Standing is our sense of belonging and right of self-determination. It relates to social recognition. Having our unique contribution received, recognized, and honored is central to our sense of belonging in our family and community. Standing is not about hierarchy; it is about honoring and being honored. Essentially it is the need to pursue our individual path within a community. Standing is an attribute of the Metal meridians: the Lung and Large Intestines.

- ❷ The qualities that are developed in Metal are self-worth and the ability to create and maintain boundaries.
- ❷ The desire is structure.

3. **Connection:** Connection encompasses the need for relationship, the longing to love and be loved. It includes romantic connection, links to our ancestral roots, and psychic connection. It also encompasses the yearning for inner union with spirit and the transcendence of bliss. Connection is an attribute of Water governing the meridians of Kidney and Bladder.
    - ❷ The qualities developed in Water are our ability to give and receive and our willingness to be vulnerable.
    - ❷ The desire is flow.

4. **Growth:** The drive to break new ground and develop our abilities to their greatest potential is an inherent quality of life. It fuels our ambition and determines our goals. The meridians of the Wood element, Gall Bladder and Liver, govern this impulse.
    - ❷ The qualities that are developed are resourcefulness and resilience.
    - ❷ The desire is expansion.

5. **Creative Expression:** Our most direct experience of the divine arrives through creative expression. It is as essential to our health and well-being as breathing and drinking. Creativity is not relegated to a specific area such as art, music, or literature; it is how we express the divine spirit in everything we do, including making a meal, establishing a household, or conducting an experiment. When we are in a state of creativity we are in the stream of universal consciousness. Creative expression is an attribute of the Fire element, which governs four meridians: Heart and Small Intestines, as well as Heart Protector and Triple Heater.
    - ❷ The qualities that are developed are inner beauty and inspiration.
    - ❷ The desire is integration.

We feel and access our core through the Heart chakra, which connects with the central line of our energy system. When we are centered, we are positioned in the center of our being, and when we are grounded, we are connected to our body and the Earth. Centering and grounding are fundamental in enacting the directives of the core.

Honoring the Core Exercise

1. Take three deep, cleansing breaths, inhaling diamond-like clarity and exhaling everything you do not need. Imagine your breath penetrating all parts of your body. Breathe all the way into every extremity, including the ends of your hair and out into your aura.

2. Take three more vitalizing breathes through your whole bodymind.

3. Focus your attention on the center of your Heart chakra, in the center of your body, in the center of your chest.

4. See it as a small spark of diamond-light, radiating in all directions. Feel its quality, tension, and texture. Does it have a color?

5. With your breath, imagine light from your spiritual source descending through your Crown chakra and connecting with the diamond in your heart. Inhale light into your heart, expanding its size and brilliance. Exhale and allow the radiance of your heart to shine out.

6. Continue building your diamond heart-light from your Crown.

7. Relax your focus and feel your Heart chakra.

8. With your breath, imagine bringing energy up from the Earth through your Base chakra, ascending through your body into your diamond heart. As before, with each inhalation let your heart-diamond grow in size and brilliance. On the exhale, allow the radiance to shine.

9. Relax your focus and feel your Heart chakra.

10. Connect Earth and Sky by inhaling energy in through the head, down through the heart, and out the Base chakra to the Earth, then breathing in through the Earth and out through the head.

11. Continue this rotation, building branches into the sky and roots into the Earth.

12. Feel yourself grounded and centered with your heart full.

13. Allow gratitude to elevate you.

Chapter 10
Deciphering Emotions

Rebecca is introduced to the CEO of a company that intends to invest in a new product her business has developed. The man is attentive, courteous, and generous in his praise, giving Rebecca ample reason to be hopeful, yet everything he says sends prickles of annoyance down her spine, causing her to bristle like a porcupine. For no reason she can understand, the man's confident smile and studied interest in her product make Rebecca anxious, and her anxiousness feeds her annoyance, which begins to simmer into anger. Rebecca's back is up, and the flood of energy into her system heightens her mental acuity and critical thinking.

Is Rebecca reacting to subliminal cues that remind her of a past boyfriend? Is her paranoia about big business disrupting an opportunity? Is her attachment to her idea resisting the input of another person? Or is she receiving subtle energy signals that this man intends a hostile takeover of her business?

The reason why Rebecca is reacting this way is not as important as the reactions themselves. If Rebecca is feeling anxious, her body is telling her that there is incongruence. Maybe this important CEO does have a hidden agenda, or maybe Rebecca doesn't really want an investor whom she has to please. Whatever the cause and whatever the final result, Rebecca's anxiety is letting her know that she should not make any commitments without more information. It is providing her with a clear message to slow down—if she knows how to decipher it.

Rebecca's annoyance and eventual anger provide additional information. She is being informed that this man is challenging her boundary. While this is happening, without her being aware of it or knowing why, Rebecca's anger is pouring energy into the boundary of her aura, protecting her from undue influence.

Politely declining to close the deal, Rebecca negotiates for a delay to consider her options. At first the man is annoyed and threatens to withdraw the offer, then becomes sickly sweet as he entices her to accept. His behavior confirms her suspicions and her resolve strengthens as she insists on a delay. As she leaves the meeting, Rebecca has a sense of lightening and is glad she didn't sign the papers on a deal that looked too good to be true. Although her emotions made her feel uncomfortable and unhappy, they may have saved her from making a very bad mistake.

How Emotions Function

Emotions are messages from our core. They guide our choices and direct us in the attainment of the five core impulses discussed in Chapter 9. They create physical changes that give us energy to act, and shift our energy flow to strengthen the action we need to take. To discern their meaning, we need to accept them, listen to them, feel their movement, and use their energy. As with Rebecca, before we are even aware of what they mean they are adjusting body chemistry and shifting energy flows. By the time the mind receives the message our state of being has been changed so that we are open to its meaning. Once recognized, the emotion will subside and the energy will naturally do what it's meant to do.

The first time I presented the ideas developed in this book was at a conference at the Mercy Center in Madison, Connecticut, in the early 1990s. Bernie Siegel was the keynote speaker, and I was one of four other presenters talking on a range of topics. When organizer Harwood Loomis asked me to speak, I was excited for the opportunity to present ideas about energy and the emotional language. The lecture was well received, yet I was not prepared for the difficulty of the questions afterward. I was beset with people wanting to know how to handle emotions that overwhelmed them. People suffering from depression, anger, and despair asked how to find the function in their feelings. I remember most vividly a man looking at me with pain-filled eyes and asking what the function of grief was as he struggled to deal with the loss of his lifetime companion.

Feeling painful emotions is not easy, and once we do, their discomfort will not magically disappear; however, when we understand the function, we can extract information and assist the flow to channel the strength of what we feel into the rectification the emotion is offering. The process for doing this is in Chapter 12.

As much as we might like, we cannot cast out painful feelings as folly; there are no mistakes in our biology. Avoiding what we feel means we miss important messages. Trying to avoid fear, for example, is not only impossible, but it also leaves us exposed to harm. Usually when people avoid a specific feeling, they are afraid of the message or force that it carries and fall into the trap of suppression. Suppressing an emotion does not get rid of it; instead, the emotion becomes an unconscious force.

Ruled or Empowered?

One of our fears about fully engaging emotions is that we will bounce from emotion to emotion in a state of constant reactivity and emotions will rule our mind. We fear emotional awareness will make us volatile and moody, swinging from highs to lows. Interestingly, it is the suppression of emotions that causes such swings, not the awareness of them.

Being clear of the ghosts that interfere with the reliability of our emotional information requires discernment and self-awareness, two attributes in short supply in today's hectic world. In the past, people waited years for a single opportunity. Today, every minute offers more opportunities for experiences than we can possible act on, and yet, unable to discern what will fulfill us, we still want more.

The power emotions have in directing our actions can cause extreme pain. Rash behaviors, angry explosions, and the emotional override of our ability to think can leave us fearful of engaging this essential realm. Afraid of the force of our emotions, we try to think ourselves out of what we feel. However, thoughts cannot change emotions. We cannot *think* our self in love with someone whom it would be advantageous to marry, or think our self out of love with someone because our family doesn't approve. Our mind can direct the force of our emotion, but it cannot talk us out of what we feel. We can submerge feelings and carry on as though they are not there, but, like a beach ball held underwater, eventually they will surface.

When we are afraid of our emotions, and attempting to think ourselves out of them hasn't worked, we might next try to suppress what we feel through "transformation." How many teachings exhort people to release their fear and transform it into love? This approach is another form of submergence: burying feelings and turning them into unconscious forces. Emotions cannot be fully released until they are heard and their message understood. To release the messengers before the message has been delivered would be abandoning our authentic self. Our spiritual directive does not allow this.

If emotions are the saboteurs that they are often accused of being, why do they exist at all? Why would nature select an attribute that is self-destructive?

When life is disrupted by out-of-control emotions, we have either lost the ability to read and use them, or are afraid of the message they carry. Consciously engaging emotions may involve completing processes from the past that got stuck, thus freeing the energy that is maintaining unresolved patterns. Whether clearing old emotions from the past or meeting fresh emotions in the present, fully feeling our emotions allows us to interface with them at their source.

Ghost in the Works

Emotions are a powerhouse of personal potential, and the compendium in Chapter 11 provides portraits of their function and use. However, before we look at what specific emotions mean and what they offer, it's necessary to understand some of the ways the messages from our core can be distorted and confused. Then it is possible to measure the reliability of their information.

Emotions are part of an elaborate system whose dependability must be maintained through self-care. Although the messages from our core are always true, they may not always reflect what we are imagining. Sometimes they are informing us of the present and sometimes they are revealing where we got stuck in the past. Sometimes they are detailing external happenings and sometimes they explain our internal limiting beliefs. Following are some elements that can impact our emotional wisdom.

Biochemical Disturbance

Biochemistry alters our emotional reactions. Our bodies are not machines and can be affected by imbalances in neurotransmitters (neuropeptides), hormones, and inflammatory reactions in the body. Biochemical imbalances can affect our moods, energy levels, state of being, emotional reactions, and even our thoughts. Some emotional states, such as clinical depression, require medical care to support healthy incorporation of the messages of emotions into our life.

Millions of interactions occur in one instance when an emotion is created, and they require basic building blocks to function properly. Neuropeptides that transmit emotional information are made from amino acids, which come from quality protein. Deficiencies in the nutrient precursors for making neurotransmitters such as serotonin, GABA, or endorphins can leave us unable to feel emotional well-being.

Hormones are also intimately connected with our emotions: Excess cortisol from the adrenal glands can cause agitation, anxiety, and rage. Lack of the thyroid hormone thyroxin may result in depression, apathy, and hopelessness. Hormones, neurotransmitters, and brain function all require nutrients to maintain physical balance. Without adequate levels of iron we can't think and have no muscle strength or energy. Iodine and tyrosine limit hormone production, and essential fatty acids are necessary for nerve conduction.

These examples remind us that our percipience depends on the food we eat. In short, to fully trust our body and what it is revealing through our emotions, we must take care of our vehicle. A balanced diet of whole foods, clean water, and exercise, and the avoidance of toxins, are essential ingredients to healthy function.

In addition, some emotions speak to us with physical sensations that mimic physical distress. For example, anxiety can present with sweating, heart palpitations, and chest tightening. To assume those symptoms are related to anxiety, however, may neglect a heart condition. Anyone who suddenly undergoes a noticeable change in emotional and/or physical function with no obvious cause needs to clear him- or herself with a medical check-up.

Manipulation

The electromagnetic field effects of the heart as described in HeartMath publications and discussed in Chapter 4 have some very interesting implications. The transfer of emotion from one person's field to another's helps us develop empathic skills and build understanding in relationships. It can also explain the formation of mob mentality: When emotion is sparked in groups of people, it transfers like wildfire through the assembly. From the ecstatic frenzy of religious ceremony to the riots of revolution, mob mentality can have so much force that it overrides common sense.

The manipulation of people via the emotional field is a common practice of groups with charismatic leaders, seen in cults, political and social movements, religious institutions, and self-help gurus. Many times, there is no intention to hurt or lead anyone astray; it's simply part of the transmission of a point of view.

When our emotions are not balanced by reason and directed with intent, we are easily manipulated by people and events that can lead us away from our truth. This happens between individual exchanges as well as in groups. As we saw in Chapter 9, the capacity to reason involves using the input from our emotional feelings and body-knowing, as well as our intellect to find meaning and direction. Internal balance is necessary to discern our path.

Should we suddenly feel confused and overwhelmed with another's point of view, the antidote is self-knowledge. "Know thyself" is one of the dictums of ancient wisdom and conveys protection from undue influence. Any time we feel our foundation swayed by a group or charismatic person, retreating into nature will help rebalance the bodymind, providing us the opportunity to reconnect with our core.

Past Trauma

As Candace Pert noted, our body is our subconscious mind and holds a record of all our past actions. Everyone has been involved in some type of trauma, whether a car accident, injury, physical assault, or painful emotional relationship. As discussed in Chapter 5, past trauma is stored in the body as muscle tension when the information in the event is not fully processed. The results are physical pain and dysfunction that can become chronic.

When trauma is trapped in the body, our impressions are locked in past perceptions of reality. They drive our behavior, direct our attention, and keep us from growing. Trapped emotions crop up anytime a similar event occurs and acts as a trigger. For example, a client of mine was hit by a car while riding her bike. At the moment of impact she felt both extreme rage and fear. Afterward, whenever she walked or rode her bike on the road and was passed by a car, she literally "saw red" and was temporarily blinded. Once the car passed, her sight returned. Each episode terrified her, as she had no control over the episode and was certain she was going to be re-injured.

Triggered emotion usually expresses in one of three ways: The emotion can be inhibited and drained of energy, it can be exaggerated and extra-charged, or it can arrive as a physiological reaction, as happened with my client. The body's discharge mechanisms are discussed in Chapter 5.

Emotional trauma reacts the same as physical trauma. In fact, the body doesn't discern between physical and emotional pain, and both are treated the same. One woman I worked with was sensitive to being looked at. As she got older, she became convinced that every time someone glanced in her direction he or she was planning to follow her home. She took elaborate routes to be sure no one followed her and lived with extreme anxiety. Her emotions were no longer giving her good information about her present safety. Instead, they were telling her where she was stuck in her past. As a teenager she had been stalked by an older man, and although she received therapy at the time and forgot the incident long before her paranoia began, the fear remained trapped in her body to return later in life, triggered by the death of her father, which left her feeling exposed and vulnerable.

When emotions are suppressed, repressed, or trapped in the body via muscle tension, we are disconnected from their meaning. Consequently, the emotional information we receive is unconsciously being measured against our past. To be fully present for the experiences of today, past trauma must be freed. Exercises and recommendations for safely releasing past trauma are found in Chapter 13.

Dissociation

Extreme trauma such as physical abuse can result not only in losing connection with our emotions; we can also lose connection with our body. When we are invaded and abused, it is often safer to disconnect from our body than to feel, especially when we are powerless to change the insult. This is a healthy survival strategy and probably is the reason we survive some of things that many of us have endured. At some point, however, we need to come home and reclaim our power.

When we are disconnected from our body, we can't receive the energy information that our body provides. This impacts our decision-making abilities, our centeredness, and our grounding. Unable to feel fear, we lose our warning system; unable to feel anger, we lose our ability to protect ourselves.

Energy exercises in this book and other resources are always helpful when we lose connection to our body. Professional energy healing sessions, emotional processing work, and body-centered psychotherapy are excellent tools.

Thought Forms and Energy Attachments

Our aura has electromagnetic qualities and carries an attractive force. When we hold fear and other unprocessed emotions in our energy field, the emotions are similar to little vibrating seed pods that attract like-energy. Anytime we have a thought the seed pods can attach to, they get bigger, creating energized thought forms. Consequently, our energy field can be filled with thought forms charged with emotional energy. When other people agree with the content of our thought forms, the energy of their emotions feeds our thought forms and our vibrating pods get larger. Because they live in our aura, they become part of the filter of our energy information.

Additionally, people can project their beliefs and desires into our aura, becoming attachments in our field. Attachments can direct our perceptions, senses, and thoughts, all contributing to manipulation. Grounding, centering, and creating boundaries are excellent ways to clear our field of energy attachments. A grounding and centering exercise is at the end of this chapter.

Stress

Stress causes considerable interference in our emotional system. Although stress can be a motivator for growth, it can also lock us into fixed responses. Stress initiates the flight-or-fight reaction in Hans Selye's General Adaptation Syndrome, leaving us charged with energy that has nowhere to go. Chronic stress causes us to respond to all stimuli with the same degree of overreaction, clouding the accuracy of our information. Another stress reaction is to freeze. In this instance our system is overloaded with stimuli. This is considered a shock reaction and literally does not allow us to receive information. Although these stress responses are adaptations for survival, as a daily strategy they cause us to use less than our full potential. When faced with stress, the use of the grounding and centering exercise at the end of this chapter can help rebalance and reset our system.

Attitudes and Beliefs

There are no dysfunctional emotions. However, when we suppress or repress our emotions without due process, they fester, and the patterns in our energy field reflect in our state of being. Emotions are intertwined with our attitudes and beliefs, and therefore even the most direct message must be carved from the matrix of our past experience, cultural expectations, and the unhealed parts of self that form the lens through which we receive information.

As we become more proficient at energy awareness, we come into contact with beliefs and attitudes we have adopted but are not part of our core expression and are limiting us in some way. They may have been imprinted on us from our culture or may be projections from family members and friends. The more connected we are to our core, the more able we are to measure whether the beliefs we encounter are expressions of our core self and then decide whether or not to release them.

Grounding, Centering, and Creating a Boundary

When we feel disconnected from our emotional information system, we can reconnect by grounding, centering, and creating boundaries. Grounding is being connected to the Earth, important because we are essentially electromagnetic circuits. Grounding increases our strength and energy flow, helping us stay balanced. When we are grounded we are more connected, responsive, engaged, and fully present. Centering is the ability to bring our attention to the core of our being where our authentic self resides. When we are centered we are connected to our inner truth and able to perceive more clearly.

The more grounded and centered we are, the greater our personal presence. The essence of who we are and the state of being we are in are reflected in our presence, the overall frequency we emit. It's the vibe people receive when they meet us. Our presence is our ambassador to the world, informing others of the quality and flow of our energy.

Grounding and centering also help develop our boundary, the place where we end and another begins. It marks our emotional, physical, and energetic space. We are interlinked with each other, and energy flows into, through, and among us all. We feel each other's energy and influence each other's energy flow. Concurrently, we are separate individuals with our own distinct energy that is patterned according to our vision, intent, and emotion. The challenge for our boundary is how to stay connected and flowing with others, yet maintain a border to protect us from the energy experiences we choose not to have.

Generally our boundary extends about three feet away from our body and aligns with the outer layer of our aura, although it can expand and contract as needed. It allows us to exchange with others with no confusion about where our space begins and ends. We use our boundary to open to energy with which we resonate and close to energy that is harmful to us, thus ensuring our ability to act from our center and connect to our source. Healthy boundaries allow independence of thought and action—exchanging with others without losing our personal identity, uniqueness, or autonomy.

The ability to use the emotional compendium of Chapter 11 will be enhanced by the following exercise.

Grounding, Centering, and Creating a Boundary Exercise

1. Put your right hand over your Hara (the area under your belly button and above your pubic bone) and your left hand over your heart.

2. Inhale and visualize energy flowing into your body through the top of your head.

3. Breathe this energy through your body all the way to the area under your right hand, your Hara. Let this area fill with light.

4. Exhale and imagine sending this energy out through your sacrum and deep into the Earth, sending roots into the ground.

5. Inhale and visualize energy rising from the Earth through your body to your heart under your left hand. Let this area fill with light.

6. Exhale and imagine sending this energy out through the top of your head as branches reaching into the sky.

7. Continue breathing through the branches and roots of your energy body while filling your core. Cradle the energy in your core between your two hands.

8. Continue and you will soon feel the clear, calming effects of being centered and grounded.

9. When you are ready, as you inhale, bring energy in from the Earth and Sky at the same time.

10. Exhale and send the energy out into the space around you, filling it with light.

11. Extend the light three feet away from your body and imagine a bright border demarcating your space.

12. Put your awareness inside this line and say, "This is me."

13. Put your awareness on the outside of this line and say, "This is you."

14. Do this several times until the boundary around you is bright, clear, and strong.

Our boundary exists all the time, whether we enforce it or not. Centering and grounding help us to be aware of the condition of our boundary and take steps to maintain it. Returning to the exercise as you work with the emotions in the compendium in the next chapter will help you feel how accurate the information is for you.

Chapter 11
The Emotional Compendium

All the tools to discern and translate emotions are now introduced. Deciphering emotions is relatively easy, as the language is natural and innate. We do it all the time, although this usually occurs below our level of conscious awareness. Essentially, emotions are revealing our energy interactions. They inform us of the impressions we are receiving from the ambiance: what our light fibers are exploring and anchoring to, what is coming toward us, and how we are responding. Being present for the exchange is the goal of emotional awareness.

The emotional interpretations presented in this chapter are based on my personal journey, 30 years of client facilitation, and studies of body-centered emotional processing. My first awareness of the positive value of even difficult emotions came through Jin Shin Do® BodyMind Acupressure®; however, the reflections I offer here are my own. I am not representing a school of thought or teaching.

Following are some common emotions, along with their meanings and energy flows. The compendium is presented in absolutes; however, it is really a series of reflections. Rather than blanket interpretations, these are thumbnail sketches to jumpstart the process of exploration, provoking questions for each person about how their energy is flowing and what their emotions mean.

As was stated before, every emotion, no matter how uncomfortable, has function, and every emotion, no matter how pleasant, can be excessive and cause harm. The nature of energy is to move, and emotional energy flows in the direction of function. For example, the energy that carries anger will immediately flow into our boundary. The energy that arrives with jealousy will immediately seek to strengthen our core. We can feel these shifts when we pay attention to our body in the midst of our emotions. With mindfulness, we can feel our boundary harden, our core enliven. Following the energy helps us know the message. If our boundaries need strengthening, then we are under some type of attack, perceived or real. If our core needs enlivening, then our self-value is shaky. Any answer we need can be found by following where our energy goes and what it does.

When we acknowledge an emotion and receive the message it carries, the intensity of what we feel recedes, although the energy continues to exert influence until its function is fulfilled. Once completed, the body returns to balance and we integrate the information. However, when we suppress a feeling, or repress its expression, we stop the process. Now we no longer have access to the meaning and must overlay past conditioning to understand what is happening. Because energy is meant to flow, if it cannot disperse, it continues to energize past patterns and continues to escalate. Instead of dispersing, it grows, making it difficult to know whether it is the situation that is escalating or whether it is our reaction that is escalating. When we accept our emotions and work with the energy changes they initiate, we can respond in the moment.

Whether or not our emotions are our allies depends on our willingness to engage them and our desire to improve the quality of our being. We all have access to the information presented in the compendium. We all have a body and we all have emotions; thus we all have admission to the information contained in the morphic field around us.

However, no one can discern the absolute meaning of an emotion for another person. Everyone has his or her own dialect of the emotional language. Special training and abilities are always useful, but not essential. I have met psychologists and psychiatrists who are well studied in emotions yet are completely disconnected from their own. I have also met psychics, channels, and empathics who receive through such a narrow lens that their information is for only a small group of individuals. In short, other people's insights are valuable, but they must be balanced against personal perceptions and sensibilities. It is part of the challenge of being human to learn how to use our vehicle and to decode the emotional language in our own way.

Whereas shades of meaning are unique to each individual, the larger commonalities of our emotions allow us to understand each other through the feelings we share. Much of the impact emotions carry is because they create the link between us. Every emotion comes with a message, a gift, a challenge, and energy to fulfill its function. The most important aspect in understanding and using emotions is to honor them. We don't need to change the energy flow or control how we feel; we need to listen and act accordingly.

The emotions chosen here are not "pure" ones; they are those that people question the most. A few of the more dynamic emotions are given in-depth treatment, and some include a list of additional features. Information about meridians is based on the five elements of traditional Chinese medicine (TCM); information about chakras is based on the Body Sounding Model. In most cases, the descriptions are short and accessible. Before reading the profiles, try this exercise.

Discerning Emotional Meaning Exercise

1. Pause before you read the description of an emotion.
2. Remember a time when you felt this emotion very clearly.
3. Pull a vision of yourself experiencing the emotion into your mind's eye. Look at your face, your muscle tension, your eyes. Observe every nuance of your body language and expression when you were feeling this emotion.
4. Step inside the memory and don the body language as a mask. Fully sink into the feeling of this emotion. Exaggerate it; make it as big as it can be. From the inside notice your muscle tension, your face, your eyes, your energy field.
5. Where is the energy going and what is its effect? What is the message in the feeling?
6. When you have gathered the information, remove the mask and step out of the memory.

7. Imagine you are standing in a waterfall of energy. Take an energy shower, allowing all the residuals of this emotion to fall away.

8. Now read the description and compare your experience. If it is different, don't throw either one away. Keep what doesn't fit on the side and use it for reference.

Anger

Inhibited: depression, apathy, resentment

Exaggerated: outrage, fury

Anger strengthens boundaries and defenses. Energy flows into the boundary of the aura when someone or something is attempting to invade, interfere with, sabotage, or steal something we care about, or when an injustice is taking place against self or another. Anger responds to our being threatened with protection, and to obstruction and injustice by sounding the alert to honor our needs and hold our boundaries. Anger provides the force to break through obstruction, right wrongs, and achieve our goals. The message of anger is: *Stand your ground; the issue is important and worth fighting for.*

The energy of anger naturally flows into our boundary and protects us from energy coming in while still allowing our own energy to flow outward. Neuropeptides stimulate the sympathetic nervous system, and adrenaline pumps throughout the body, providing physical energy for defense. Blood flow goes to the brain and muscles for fast processing and action. When we accept the anger we feel, our energy is channeled more fully into the aura and our safety level is increased, allowing us to control and use the force of anger constructively.

We are socially trained to repress and deny anger, turning it inward, where it drains our energy, which often leads to depression, apathy, and resentment. Repressed, anger leaves us feeling powerless, becoming a dormant inferno that bursts into flame at every small obstacle or difference of opinion. When disproportionate rage clouds our minds and distorts our reactions, anger can easily move beyond defending boundaries into invasion of other people's boundaries.

Entwined with judgment and enlarged through repression, anger can have an extremely destructive impact, and this is why it is so hard to allow anger to function. When we judge, we think that whatever is obstructing us must be wrong, bad, or even evil, freeing us from restraint so that rage can take over. We justify any extremes to prove our point or attain our goals, and are willing to annihilate another and feel good about it. However, it only feels good to annihilate another when we feel powerless ourselves.

The crux of what anger teaches is how to use our power. When we own our personal power we have no need to annihilate others and we don't take obstruction personally. We can stay connected to someone and care about the outcome for him or her even while we are angry. Our self-worth is derived from our inner conviction, not from winning or losing. We are able to use the force of anger free of the unprocessed past. Obstruction and the anger it brings allow us to reevaluate goals, regroup, and move forward in dynamic, heart-centered ways.

Additional Features of Anger

Energy Flow: The flow of energy during anger is outward into the boundary of the aura. To use anger constructively, we need to feel it, acknowledge it, and let it teach us how to stand in the center of our power. We need to allow the feeling of anger to flow through and into the boundary of the aura and at the same time stay connected to our core.

Segment/Chakra: The solar plexus segment generates anger, as exemplified in the metaphors "venting my spleen" and having a "belly full" of anger toward someone/thing. Expression usually happens through the arms, shoulders, neck, and face. The chakra of this segment is the third chakra of self-empowerment. Stretching and massaging involved segments while visualizing the brilliant light of the sun in the solar plexus help to access true power.

Element/Meridians: Wood/Gallbladder, Liver. The Liver meridian generates anger and the Gallbladder distributes it. However, Wood is governed by Metal (Lung/Large Intestine), which governs boundaries. If Metal is weak, then there are no controls on Wood and anger can be excessive. If Metal is over-controlling, Wood is inhibited and anger is repressed. Balancing all four meridians of these two elements can be helpful in constructively using anger.

Message: Something important is being obstructed: A boundary is being breeched, an injustice is occurring, and action is required.

Core Learning: The core impulse is standing and the learning is that we have everything we need; we are powerful spiritual beings.

Key Questions: Where is your power in the situation? What do you need to reclaim it?

Anxiety

Inhibited: dread

Exaggerated: hyper-vigilance

Anxiety establishes congruence. It warns us to take care; things are not what they seem. Energy is concentrated in the sensory fibers of the chakras, directing received impressions into the core, where alignment can be established. Much of the physical discomfort of anxiety comes from the sensitivity of these fibers. Grounding helps the fibers deal more effectively with the information they bring in and takes the edge off over-excitement.

The incongruence that anxiety recognizes may come from many arenas: We may be experiencing presentiment of interference or difficulty coming toward us; we could be picking up on unspoken agendas in romantic or work relationships, or information withheld from decisions we are making. Anxiety may also alert us to our own internal incongruence. Maybe we are doing something because it is expected and not because we wish to, or feeling one way while acting another. The incongruence between a project we need to complete and our fears that we are unfit to do the job can cause anxiety. The essence of anxiety is fear of the unknown combined with fear of the past impacting the future.

When internal or environmental incongruence is not processed, it becomes an inner agitation that keeps us in a state of hyper-vigilance and/or dread. Conditioned anxiety usually starts in childhood when children aren't given access to information that directly affects them. Parents may be protecting their child from upsetting knowledge such as parental illness, an impending divorce, or financial upheaval. The child may feel things are wrong but is assured that everything is fine, forcing him or her to suppress the incongruence between what he feels and what he is told. Consequently, shocks seem to arrive out of the blue. The pattern of anxiety can also arise when a child is raised in an unsafe environment. A parent with anger management issues may flare into rages disproportionate to the child's actions, leaving her unsure when punishment will arrive or for what reason.

Anxiety takes us to a present problem or a past event that we are unable to understand clearly. If we are willing to sit with our anxiety and follow it to the place of greatest agitation in our body, we can move into our core and discern the things that aren't what they seem to be. In general, anxiety dissipates when we have something concrete with which to work. When we suppress anxiety and accommodate or hide incongruence, it slowly eats away at confidence and creates health problems.

The crux of anxiety is that we are afraid that what we are, or something we have done—some mistake we may not even have known we made—will arise and ruin us. When heeded, its gifts are self-reliance, self-worth, and self-responsibility. The message is: *Right here, right now, we have what we need. When the future arises, we will meet it.*

Additional Features of Anxiety

Energy Flow: The natural flow of energy motivated by anxiety is inward to our core and outward through the energy sensory fiber of the chakras. Anxiety connects our awareness of external events with the discernment ability of our core. When we inhibit this flow, energy builds up in the sympathetic nervous system, stimulating fight-or-flight responses. Grounding and centering are the best ways to calm the excess of anxiety. (You can try the grounding exercise in Chapter 10.)

Segment/Chakra: The segments affected by anxiety are solar plexus and chest. To avoid feeling anxiety, these segments will be guarded with muscle tension. The desire of the body is to curl around the heart protectively and collapse over the solar plexus in a fetal position; thus the involved muscles become very tight. Chakras involved are both the third and fourth. To receive the information anxiety is relaying, place one hand over the heart and one over the solar plexus, and focus breath and awareness on the hara line of the body. The balancing exercises in Chapter 9 are helpful in dissipating excess anxious energy.

Element/Meridians: Anxiety is an issue of the Heart and Small Intestine meridians, which are governed by the Fire element. The Water element controls Fire, and if Fire is excessive, Water may be deficient. Because Water is aligned with the core impulse of connection, the remedy here may lie in developing stronger connections between the people in our life and stronger connection with our core self. Balancing these four meridians can help access the information in anxiety.

Message: Things are not what they seem. Honor your core.

Core Learning: The core impulse is connection and the learning is "I am enough."

Key Questions: What part of yourself are you hiding? What needs honoring?

Apathy

Inhibited: emergence of phobias such as agoraphobia

Exaggerated: indifference, lack of connection to people and life

Apathy provides protection. It tells us that something is so difficult, or hurts so deeply, that we must withdraw. Sometimes apathy advises that the degree of our investment in other people's lives may have overstepped boundaries. Similar to anger, the energy of apathy flows into our boundary, creating an impenetrable fortress and withdrawing our connections from those around us. Our attention is brought inward, where we create a nest for caretaking our feelings, thus offering time and space to reevaluate how we are expressing our connections. In safety, we are able to adjust the level of our attachment and decide whether to permanently release the attachment of any of our fibers that might be breeching another person's space.

Apathy advises a reevaluation of our investment in specific outcomes. The essence of apathy is fear of being hurt or rejected, or being ineffective in actions to correct an injustice or fight for something in which we believe. Rather than a sign of not caring, apathy is a sign of caring too much; of becoming overly invested to the degree of overstepping other people's boundaries. It can be an indication that more parts of our self are trying to be fulfilled in a situation than are possible. For example, we may be trying to establish our connection with another person by helping him solve a problem and, in doing so, over-investing in his actions. If he asks us to step back, we feel rejected and unvalued, responding first with anger or sadness and eventually apathy. Another example is being passionate about a lost cause: The purpose of our life is invested in our success or failure.

The crux of apathy is connection. Apathy asks if we can stay connected to something or someone with respect. Can we give without needing to be on the inside? The challenge of apathy is to love without attachment.

Additional Features of Apathy

Energy Flow: Apathy creates a wall around us, restricting outside input. Attention is pulled internally, chakra fibers are coiled inside, and a protective shield is placed around the heart. In this nest we are able to connect with our core and integrate the messages and teachings while our energy structures readjust their attachments to people, ideas, and events. We emerge cleaner, stronger, and freer.

Segment/Chakra: Apathy often presents as "putting it behind me," and the back is often guarded, which causes the armoring of several segmental rings. The Heart and Throat chakras are often constricted, withholding the desire to connect. Use the Honoring the Core exercise in Chapter 9 to help.

Element/Meridians: The Bladder meridian running up the spine provides protection from outside influence and strengthens the back. Governed by the Water element, Bladder and Kidney regulate flow. Water is controlled by the element of Earth (Stomach/Spleen meridians), and balancing the meridians of these two elements can be helpful in establishing harmonious flow.

Message: All life is interconnected: Energy cannot be created or destroyed. Allow your caring to change form.

Core Learning: The core impulse is connection, and the learning is to love for the sake of love with no attachment to outcomes.

Key Question: What are you overlooking in yourself that you are trying to find through others?

Boredom

Inhibited: depression

Exaggerated: dependency

Boredom informs us that our core needs are not being met. What we are engaged in does not create life-affirming energy. Boredom warns that we may be neglecting our spirit and creative passion. Its essence is engagement. When the creative parts of self are not engaged, there is no emotional jazz in life.

Boredom helps us when our energy fibers have become anchored and fixed, using all of our free attention. Sometimes our fibers are locked into other people or electronic devices, looking to them to set our direction and provide purpose and meaning. When we resist boredom, this fixed quality becomes even more pronounced.

Boredom seeks freedom from dependency. The natural energy flow of boredom is to our core and allows us to reexamine our core beliefs, desires, and creative passion. When we stop resisting our boredom and fully engage it, it moves inward, releasing energy fibers and freeing our attention for exploration.

The message in boredom is that energy spent in the direction we are going is wasted. To find our passion, we must reestablish the core in its rightful place in the hierarchy of our actions. We must also open our senses.

Boredom is often the result of not having our essence acknowledged. When who we are is not received, we withdraw and become internally depleted. We have no energy to support exploration and creative expression. Children are often punished by being given a "time-out" from stimulation and excitement, and self-punishment is the crux of boredom. Boredom informs us that life without creative expression has no juice. The challenge is to be courageous and move in the direction of our passion. Boredom pushes us out of the nest.

Additional Features of Boredom

Energy Flow: Energy flow is directed into the core for reevaluation of our path and purpose, and creative outflow. It frees energy attachments. The "brain dead" quality of boredom encourages us to use our feeling senses.

Segment/Chakra: In boredom, the pelvic segment will often be closed down. Wilhelm Reich and Alexander Lowen, fathers of body-centered psychotherapy, speak of this segment as creating the pump that generates energy, impelling it through the other segments. The chakra involved is the second chakra, which generates creative passion and has the potential to be awakened in the throes of boredom. To help move energy, place your hand over your lower abdomen while bringing your attention to this area, then visualize a spiral of energy unfolding into this chakra from your core line. You might also activate the muscles with a Feldenkrais exercise called "the pelvic clock," which can be found on the Internet at *www.emr.msu.edu/documents/rehab/pelvic_clock.pdf.*

Meridian/element: Boredom is often a deficiency of the Wood element governing the Liver and Gallbladder. Energizing Wood by increasing the balance with the meridians of the Water element (Kidney/Bladder) is helpful.

Message: Feel for the essence within self and all life for inspiration.

Core Learning: The core impulses being challenged are growth and creative expression; the learning is that awareness has meaning and purpose.

Key Questions: Where is our value? What do we value in life?

Contentment

Inhibited: depression

Exaggerated: complacency

Contentment is the experience of flow throughout the constellation of people in our life. It induces a vibration that brings harmony to all the cells of our body and feels like the purring of a cat. The vibration of contentment opens our energy structures and invites flow through our entire system. Through the resonance of vibration, all parts of self are brought into alignment—internally and externally. Contentment's message is that we are enough, just the way we are, and life is enough just the way it is. It may not be our idea of perfect, yet, nonetheless, it is. True contentment is a rare prize!

Contentment is our bodymind telling us that we have done a good job—that we are meeting core impulses and life is worth living. However, some of us have been conditioned to believe that we don't deserve happiness and contentment. As a result we are always striving for something more, something better, and don't allow ourselves to rest in the enjoyment of what we have accomplished and who we are. When we inhibit contentment, we are unable to enjoy the result of our creativity and passion. The message is to celebrate!

Although contentment is more a state of being than an emotion, like all emotions it can be exaggerated. This generally happens when it is mixed with fear of change. Then contentment turns into complacency or even superiority. In reality, complacency is a reluctance to engage the discomfort of change and growth, convinced that nothing can ever be as nice as what we have.

We can help establish contentment by honoring the beauty all around us. We can encourage energy flow with our breath through the center line of our body while using the Honoring the Core exercise in Chapter 9. Activate the transcendent quality of the emotion of gratitude. Contentment and gratitude are perfectly encapsulated in Louis Armstrong's song "What a Wonderful World."

Denial

No inhibition or exaggeration

Denial gives us space and time to come to terms with untenable realities. Denial protects the psyche from overload. Energy flows into our boundary, keeping out impressions and sensations that contradict what we have decided is acceptable. Energy fibers are firmly anchored in people, institutions, and opinions that reflect what we want to believe. In short, we surround our self with our own reflection, which allows in no new light, thus creating an impenetrable shield. Although it's highly functional for short periods as it protects the core, when denial becomes a pattern, it keeps us from growing and damages the core because present dangers are not addressed.

As with all emotions, shifting out of denial involves being willing to fully feel and engage it. What is denial trying to shield? What core belief is so important that we are willing to lose connection to the world to uphold it? What truth is so frightening we can't face it? Denial protects us while we find a better way to maintain our core than to uphold untruths. Denial shields us as we find the strength to let it go and mourn our loss.

Many people don't realize they are in denial because of its shielding power. Clues of denial include life patterns in which the outcomes of our action don't match our intentions, for example, believing our spouse loves us even as he or she is consistently inconsiderate, unkind, or abusive, or believing a boss cares about our wellbeing as he or she steals our ideas and takes credit for our work. Both situations may mask a truth we are afraid to face: that perhaps we are alone in the world.

If we suspect we are engaged in denial, we are ready to embrace denial and find a better way to establish our core. Thank denial for its protection and invite new perspective.

Depression

Inhibited: illness

Aggravated: despair

When we are depressed, our energy system is in collapse. Depression is often considered the opposite side of anger. When the energy of anger is either not able to break through obstructions or is repressed, it can turn inward against the self, resulting in depression. Whereas anger directs our energy into our boundaries, depression is a collapse of that energy into our center. There is little outward flow, and we are cut off from motivation and inspiration.

There is a difference between biochemically based depression, which is not addressed here, and depression derived from limitations being placed on our life. Although we are trained to fight against limitations and use our will to rise up out of depression, we often don't feel we have the energy to get up out of the chair, never mind take on the challenge of motivating our life. Although depression seems like an enemy, it does have function: It provides us with us with space for lateral growth. Depression slows down forward movement and gives us the time to look sideways at what we may be missing in our fight against obstruction: Are we ignoring loved ones, letting values slide for progress? Have we missed an essential feature along the way?

Depression feels like something is missing inside; we are lacking, and our failure to overcome obstruction is because we are not enough. However, depression provides time to recover from battle. It allows us time to withdraw and reevaluate, looking more closely at our battle wounds, victories, defeats, and investments. Have we reached beyond what we had the energy and means to fund? Are we going after what we want or what we think we should want? Depression may be asking us to reassess our resources and strategies. It encourages us to realize that it's okay to rest, reconsider, and reconfigure.

When depression is fed through continued reinforcement and failure (real or perceived), it turns into despair. Despair can be a message that we have lost an essential connection to our core. Time is needed to reconnect to what is essential in life, and to rebuild self-esteem. At this point, a helping hand and heart can provide a needed spiritual lift.

Inhibiting depression typically occurs through wearing a mask of pretense. Feelings that are too debilitating are hidden by endless activity, projects, causes, and rescues. We have a house full of abandoned cats that we have adopted, or 15 places we have to be in the same hour. Energy is generated through the power of will. Repressing the expression of depression requires hiding behind the mask of false happiness, pretending everything is fine when people are around and then succumbing to depression when alone. We may find the effort becomes so great that we avoid people and social settings, staying home with food or drink for comfort.

Like all emotions, depression must be felt and acknowledged before it can reveal its messages and strive for happiness.

Additional Features of Depression

Energy Flow: Collapsed into the core and stagnating.

Segment/Chakra: Depression often occurs with a collapse of the chest and armoring of the chest segment, as if to shield the heart from disappointment. All the chakras are drained of energy, primarily the Heart chakra and Base chakra. To help the body move the energy of depression and hear the message, lie on your back across a rolled towel or pillow placed under your ribcage just below the shoulder blades. Spread your arms out to the side and allow your chest to be popped open by the positioning of the roll. With the inhale, lengthen; as you exhale, widen. Be open in all directions as you fully embrace depression. Listen to the message it has for you.

Element/Meridians: The Galbladder and Liver meridians of the Wood element generate and govern both anger and depression. The Wood element deals with growth and reveals the association between obstruction and growth of anger and depression. These two meridians are concerned with strategizing, planning, and distribution of resources. They are the generals in the army of our bodymind. Balancing the Wood element provides immediate access to the issues that we are reassessing through depression.

Message: Look at what is around with new eyes. Regroup.

Core Learning: The core impulses are growth and standing. The learning is that we are enough.

Key Questions: What is the essence of what we want to bring to the world? What have we lost?

Desperation

Inhibited: suicidal ideation

Exaggerated: magical thinking

The function of desperation is to jump-start creative thinking. It tells us in no uncertain terms that old ways of doing things can't work this time. There are no more resources and no further answers on this path. Consider the desperation of the astronauts and ground support in the crisis during the *Apollo 13* mission when an oxygen tank exploded and subsequent damage meant certain death for the crew. Equipped with only what was in the space capsule, the astronauts had to find ways to adapt what was available in order to bring the capsule back to Earth safely. Imagine that the situation you are in is a space capsule: How can we use what we have available in a different manner? Emergencies require thinking out of the box, and that is what desperation can bring.

Energetically, desperation instills the courage to release our anchors. The sensation is one of freefalling, as suddenly freed energy fibers search for new ground. If we can stay with the feeling and give ourselves a little time, our energy will find different ways to anchor as fresh perspectives and new vistas open for our creative exploration.

When suppressed or repressed, desperation becomes a belief in limitation. It can become a predominant emotion such that we create one crisis after another to confirm our belief that there are limited resources and we won't be able to survive. There is enough energy in desperation to spark suicidal ideation, and people who are having such thoughts need to seek help to find the way through. When we sit with the feeling of desperation and allow events to change, creativity has an opportunity to emerge, and reveal the resources we have and how to use them in new ways.

Sometimes, desperation leads us to the realization that there is no way out. I have been with patients suffering from terminal illness who have been desperate for a miracle drug or procedure. And suddenly there is an incredible moment when the person is moved to acceptance and is filled with peace and courage, facing the unknown fully aware that this may be the end. Whether or not it is the end of life, desperation can indicate the end of the road. The question is: Do we have the courage and creative passion to face the unknown fully awake and aware? Desperation can open the door to courage.

Disappointment

Inhibited: false hope

Exaggerated: despair

Disappointment illuminates what is false in our life and salvages what is true. It helps us see our illusions, expectations, and projections. When things don't work as we want, when people let us down, when we don't pull the rabbit out of the hat, the disappointment we feel helps us take stock of what is true and what is false. Disappointment helps us recalibrate and salvage what has value. The essence of disappointment is truth.

Energetically, our attention is directed inward to strip away the floss and bring us to the bare, essential truth. At the same time, flow is sent into our boundary, helping us perceive through our energy senses, and disengage our attachments from situations and people who give nothing back. Disappointment asks us to evaluate our energy investments. Are they paying dividends? Are we looking honestly, or are we using denial to make things as we want them to be? We often invest in illusion because what is real doesn't seem strong enough or good enough.

When we are disappointed in people it can be because we expect others to operate from the same set of assumptions that we hold. When their behavior doesn't match our expectations, we are disappointed. If we understand the assumptions that motivate other people's actions, what they do might make sense to us. For example, a client of mine was allowing her son and daughter-in-law to live with her while they got a start in life. She was unhappy that the daughter-in-law didn't help more with the housework. "I shouldn't have to tell her what I need," she complained. "It's obvious and she should know. She just doesn't care; she's just a taker, a freeloader, and I worry what my son's life will be like. I guess I have to be tolerant and let them work it out." It took a lot of processing for this client to realize she had a right to ask for what she wanted.

When she communicated with her daughter-in-law, she learned that in the culture her son's wife came from, unbidden help was seen as an insult, suggesting the job wasn't being done well enough. With communication, the door was open to develop a relationship that could not take place when each was "tolerating" the other. This client then needed to face why she had labeled her daughter-in-law as a taker and freeloader. In processing the situation she realized that she always gave more than was required and never asked for help in order to not be seen as a burden. The core issue in her disappointment was her fear that she herself was not enough.

Disappointment asks us to own our fear. The message is to have faith and be open; the truth is better than a lie.

Additional Features of Disappointment

Energy Flow: Inward to the core.

Segment/Chakra: Solar plexus segment and third chakra.

Element/Meridians: Water/Kidney and Bladder. The key tension in Kidney and Bladder is faith vs. fear. Disappointment asks us to feel our fear so we can flow into faith.

Message: Find the essence within and be inspired; the truth is enough.

Core Learning: The core impulse is connection and the learning is to look beyond the surface to the truth.

Key Question: What is the truth that I am afraid to see?

Discouragement

Inhibited: false confidence

Exaggerated: despair

Discouragement is a rumble of discontent that reminds us of the joy that is possible in what we are trying to achieve. Discouragement helps us switch from the power of will to that of intention. When discouragement engulfs us, we are being encouraged to release the hard focus of will and surrender to the outcome that already exists. Rather than trying to force events to fit our desire, discouragement encourages us to yield to the flow of life that moves toward the outcomes we desire. This may mean letting go of hard and fast goals and embracing the feelings we are hoping that the goal will bring.

For example, perhaps you are trying to get a record deal because it will allow you to make money and gain standing while creatively expressing what you love, but are frustrated by one closed door after another. Surrender to the joy of singing and jump into the stream that is heading where you want to go. Let people know you want to sing, make business cards, and sing at every opportunity that comes your way: Sing on street corners, in churches, hospitals, and community centers. Say yes when asked to sing at karaoke clubs or birthday parties. Continue to do the things you need to do to pay your rent and put food on the table. Fulfill your intention by surrendering to the feel that you are in the flow of life and the current will take you where you want to go. Attract what you want in life by surrendering to it.

Energetically, discouragement frees our energy attachments from fixed outcomes, and if we allow, it opens the second chakra of creative passion.

Envy

Inhibited: resentment

Exaggerated: greed

Envy is terribly uncomfortable to feel and challenging to engage. Envy steps in when we feel reduced and invisible; it boils our blood and motivates our energy for change. The energy of envy flows into our boundaries, protecting us from injustice while simultaneously flowing to our core. It reaches deep inside with a single message: We aren't seeing ourselves truly. Perhaps we don't know our true worth and measure ourselves against the gains of others. Maybe we overvalue what we have to offer and don't believe others deserve what they have. Maybe we haven't seen before that those around us don't value who we are.

When allowed to flow, envy strengthens our core impulse for standing. Envy propels us to be seen in the world as who we truly are. First, however, we must see ourselves through the eyes of truth. Envy encourages us to take stock of what we are doing and what we deserve. If they don't match, what needs to change? Is someone trying to overshadow or undercut us? Do we need to move to another company, or do we need to accept that we have not been performing to our ability and what we envy in another can only be achieved through harder work?

Whatever the answers, envy inspires us to change. It asks that we look at our life honestly and, if we don't like what we see, look for the underlying truth. Envy steps in when we have forgotten who we are.

Excitement

Inhibited: anxiety

Exaggerated: over-excitement

The energy of excitement flows outward through the aura and the chakra fibers, enlivening our senses and freeing some of our anchors. It mobilizes our energy and assists action, allowing us to stretch in areas previously thought to be outside of our reach. Excitement provides freedom from old ways of thinking and doing things. It activates us, signaling that the time is now. Excitement is one of the ways we naturally charge our system.

When we remove the creative passion from excitement or inhibit it with limiting beliefs, excitement turns into anxiety. In anxiety the energy system is on high alert and the heightened level of energy coupled with a sense of foreboding causes extreme discomfort. This feeling can be instigated through excitement when it is inhibited through fear. Maybe we are afraid we won't get what we want or that we will be punished for being too happy. In this case, the energy of excitement continues to flow into our energy structures. However, without a goal or focus, the energy causes the uncomfortable feeling of anxiety. The message is the same: Look for the incongruence, this time between what you truly want and what you believe is possible.

Over-excitement indicates we are dealing with illusion. We have excited our energy with something that is not real and our body knows it even as our mind is running in circles, chasing one possibility after another. Because the excitement is not grounded in reality, it continues to escalate beyond what can be sustained. Eventual crash is certain unless the message of over-excitement can be received; what is not real here? Grounding and centering exercises can de-escalate the energy and establish our connection to our core so that we can see the incongruence.

Fear

Inhibited: anxiety, panic

Exaggerated: elevation

Fear is part of our warning system, notifying us of danger and giving us the energy to survive it. As with anxiety, we are on high alert with all of our sensors tuned to every nuance in the atmosphere. Along with the rest of our body, our energy system responds to the degree of threat, and as the severity of danger increases, more parts of our system are activated. Fear initiates a fight-or-flight response, and its usefulness can be easily seen when the danger is apparent, as in a burglary when you must act immediately. The energy of fear flows into the boundary to protect us while also energizing the first, third, and sixth chakras, giving us all the resources, insight, and power we need to meet the crisis. Fear sends a cascade of chemicals stimulated by the sympathetic nervous system that energize and focus the muscles, brain, and eyes while turning off the body's resting functions.

Although most of the time we resist fear, sometimes we actively seek it. The heightened response provides a body rush, making us feel more alive than we may have ever felt before. We are so effective and perform so well, we feel we can "leap tall buildings in a single bound." Many people, knowingly or not, evoke the feeling of elevation by engaging in high-risk activities such as bungee jumping over canyons or tightrope walking over Niagara Falls. However, using fear to inspire elevation can come with a price tag. We can burn out the adrenal glands and deplete our vital energy, not to mention kill ourselves. When we are exaggerating fear as a way of life, it is asking us to look at what is missing in our aliveness. Why do we need to face death to feel alive?

Another reason we might instigate fear is for the heightened focus it provides. In normal everyday consciousness we are absorbed in our thoughts and plans. We pay little attention to the energy information coming and going through our system. We rely on our gut feelings and hunches without thought of where they come from or what they mean. All this changes when we are enveloped with fear. Fear opens us to the energy part of our awareness: Every tingle of our skin has meaning; every impression carries significance. Fear allows us to be cognizant of more of our abilities and experiences.

Fear is a natural part of heightening everyday activities. Although seeking the benefits of fear might seem foreign, it is one of the internal resources that we rely on, especially when we can't generate enthusiasm for a job. Procrastinating at work until a deadline approaches, for example, initiates fear that provides focus and motivation to get the job done. When we fear losing our partner, focus on our love increases, inspiring greater commitment. When we feel little spikes of fear throughout the day, ask what intention or goal we are trying to achieve and channel the energy fear generates into the goal we want.

Most of what we have learned about fear is that it is a limiting emotion that we have to eradicate. What is really being referred to is the unconscious beliefs that are energized by fear. However, resisting fear only makes it larger. When we inhibit fear and try to suppress or repress it, the energy turns inward and becomes anxiety or panic. Instead, discern what limiting belief is at work and allow the energy that fear generates to shift the belief.

Here's an example: Although I love to teach, I have a terrible fear of public speaking. For a long time I tried to overcome my fear with affirmations, positive thinking, and other mechanisms for suppressing my feelings as I forced myself to speak in different venues. When the situation did not improve, eventually I had to take my own advice and listen to my fear. To do this, I imagined myself at the venue of the last big lecture that I gave and relived the feelings and visceral sensations I experienced. Then I followed the feelings inside my body to where they were generated: in my heart.

The sensation in my heart was a combination of suffocating pressure and tingling. As I allowed myself to feel it, I suddenly remembered being in fifth grade and standing before the class proudly reading a story I had written. When I finished, the teacher berated me, saying I could not possibly have written the story. Even though other children came to my defense, saying they had seen me writing, for some unknown reason the teacher persisted in her opinion.

The shame I felt followed me through all my school presentations, and, sitting with my fear, I realized it followed me still. I understood that my fear was trying to keep me safe and protect me from ridicule. The need for protection was based on my allowing my standing and worth to be determined by my fifth-grade teacher. Remembering all this, I paid attention to my body and felt the projections of her judgment in my solar plexus. They were like hot pokers.

To reconcile the situation, I visualized my teacher and explained that she had made a mistake. I used the energy that fear provided to pull her projections out of my gut and hand them back; they were hers to resolve, not mine. Then I thanked my fear for keeping me safe. The problem was never my fear; it was my unprocessed feelings of shame. I had to take back my self-worth to continue.

When we feel fear the first question to ask is: *What is the danger?* If the fear doesn't come with an obvious danger, we may be getting advance warning of a mugger down the street, presentiment of a car accident, or a nudge that it is time to move out of a risky investment. Never ignore fear. It always has something valuable to say. Sit with it, ask what it is providing, and use the energy to create change.

Additional Features of Fear

Energy Flow: Into our boundary, sensory fibers, and Base chakra.

Segment/Chakra: Fear is usually associated with the pelvic segment and the first, or Base, chakra of physical well-being. When fear is structured into our body, the pelvic segment will be armored. When life-saving fear is initiated, the pelvic segment is energized to pump energy into the legs to either stand ground or run. The pelvis also energizes the segments residing above and sends rushes of physical energy up the body. The first chakra connects with the power of the Earth to provide the strength we need and also reveals the physical resources we have at hand to meet the emergency.

Element/Meridians: The Water element along with its two partnered meridians, Kidney and Bladder, govern fear. The Kidney meridian generates physical energy and the Bladder meridian distributes it throughout the body. The path of the Bladder channel runs down the backside of the body from the head to the feet. If we decide to fight, energy is sent to back us up; if we decide to run, energy is sent into the legs.

Message: There is danger, real or imagined, that must be met.

Core Learning: All of the core impulses can be involved with fear.

Key Questions: What is being threatened, and where is the danger coming from?

Grief

Inhibited: despair

Exaggerated: despair

Grief is the recognition of loss. The loss may be related to an idea, a project, or a dream, but the most devastating loss is of people or animals we love. The hole we feel inside is real; it is the disruption of our energy structures as the fibers that link us to others are torn, ripped apart, and left damaged and leaking. Grief is the pain of injury to our energy structures, the disruption of flow in the constellation around us.

Anytime we make a connection with a person, idea, plan, or place, we form an energy link and add a station in our constellation. Like the dark energy of the universe, this constellation forms the staging for our life. Through it we are connected to everything we interact with, especially people. Our energy fibers link with them as theirs link with us. Energy flows inside this structure in a give and take of nourishment, stimulation, and love. When we lose someone, connections are brutally torn. Energy flow is interrupted, and we can be left with holes in our aura, torn fibers, and damage to our entire system.

The pain of torn muscles is a dull ache, the pain of compressed nerves is sharp and shooting, and the pain of damaged energy structures is grief. Like the pain of our other injuries, it has function: It gives us time to review, unravel, and come to terms with the paradoxes within all relationships. It keeps us still as we repair and reconfigure. The argent brilliance of this fiery pain is cleansing, clarifying, and fierce. Nothing can stand in its path. On the other side of grief is the greater strength of love.

Sometimes grief is so overpowering, the damage so severe, that we cannot sustain it all at once. In this case the muscles of our chest segment tighten and modulate the amount of feeling that comes through at any one time. Suppressing grief this way is a survival strategy. Prolonging suppression flat-lines our life. We lose not only the experience of grief, but also all the other emotions of the chest segment, including love, happiness, elevation, awe, and so on. We live on a plateau with no peaks and no valleys.

Grief is more bearable when we know it is a healing force, and use our attention to assist its flow into and through the damaged areas of our heart, soul, and psyche. Emotions rise to fill a function, then recede, and as the constellation around us shifts and our energy structures heal, the pain of grief ebbs. The loss never disappears; the pain simply retreats.

Additional Features of Grief

Energy Flow: The energy flow of grief is into the damaged areas of our energy field, our Heart chakra, and our core.

Segment/Chakra: The chest segment generates the emotion of grief and the muscles of this segment harden to create an armor of protection. The Heart chakra sustains the energy of grief, directing its healing force to restructure the holes in our energy constellation and into the core to nourish our Shen.

Element/Meridians: The Lung meridian generates grief and, together with its partner, the Large Intestine, regulates boundaries determining what to hold on to and what to let go. These functions are governed by the element of Metal, which maintains structure and order. When the Metal element is strong, grief will be able to flow throughout the structure of our energy constellation with healing benefit.

Message: Love is the strongest force in the universe.

Core Learning: The core impulse directly affected by grief is connection. The learning is that flow continues through loss: No love, no light is ever lost in the universe.

Key Question: How can you honor what you have lost?

Guilt

Inhibited: denial

Exaggerated: poor self-esteem

Guilt is the reverse of anger. Guilt tells us when we have overstepped another's boundary. It tells us we have obstructed another or caused an injustice. Guilt reflects the quality of our own boundary to show us that we have hardened to those around us. Consequently, the flow of guilt is into our boundaries, cleansing and restoring health while reconciling us with those we have hurt. Some say that guilt is a useless emotion that only wastes our energy. Actually, guilt provides the motivation to make apologies and rectify our mistakes. Guilt is the counterpoint to arrogance and superiority. The discomfort of guilt lets us feel the pain we have caused for the purpose of learning. It restores self-pride.

Sometimes guilt arises over things that no one cares about except us. We feel guilty for eating a bar of chocolate or buying a new pair of shoes. In this instance, guilt is responding to the inner critic that judges our life.

Our guilt is rectifying what we want with what our critic judges is right. We listen to the critic because of conditioning, and the guilt we feel motivates us to restructure our beliefs. In the past, authority figures like parents and teachers may have used guilt to manipulate our behavior and we may carry old messages that are not true. If we can ride the feeling of guilt, it can help reveal the projections we carry from others and provide the force necessary to remove them and hand them back.

Happiness

Inhibited: longing

Exaggerated: mania

Happiness is feedback from our core that we are in flow. It is the awareness that everything in our past has come together perfectly in our present to create the future that inspires us. Our system is charged and ready to go. People, plans, and actions are in alignment. Not only are we satisfied with the present, we are excited by the future and assured of its outcome.

Happiness is often the reward for a job well done and the promise of satisfaction in future jobs. It is the acknowledgment that what we have worked for and attained has value. The fulfillment of any core impulse provides happiness; however, it is relatively short-lived unless the achievement is coupled with the core impulses of connection and creative expression. For example, we can be very happy about the purchase of a new house, yacht, or piece of jewelry, or can be delighted with the attainment of an award at the local country club. However, unless our feelings are aligned with connection to the core and creative expression, happiness will be short-lived.

Happiness is one of the ways we charge our system, and it is natural to strive for its attainment. When happiness is suppressed, it is usually because we are afraid of the inner critic and judgment from those around us. When it is exaggerated, it is done to elicit approval and admiration. When happiness is allowed to flow, it brings us into the center of the currents in life that are heading where we want to go. When happiness arrives, surrender to the flow. Laugh, celebrate, and enjoy the moment.

Hatred

Inhibited: resentment

Exaggerated: loathing

If anger is our response to invasion of our boundary, hatred is our response to invasion of our core. When our core is threatened and the foundation of our life crumbles, hatred is the weapon we command. It is the nuclear bomb in our defense arsenal. When we wield its focused, destructive power we are promising annihilation. Hatred has the ability to immediately marshal all of our resources and focus our intent. It is resourceful, self-reliant, determined, and implacable. It will find a way not only to ensure our survival, but also to prevail. The problem with nuclear war is that there are no winners.

The energy of hatred forms a fortress around our core, cutting us off from all external input. It strengthens our internal and external boundaries, performing surveillance, scouring our energy field for projections, attachments, or hidden bombs waiting to explode, and clearing them away.

One of my patients learned that her husband betrayed her by sleeping with her best friend. It's an old story, one we have heard many times before, but no matter how many times it has happened, when it happens personally, its devastation is complete. The hatred my client felt flooded her with strength and dignity. It immediately closed off her aura and strengthened her boundary, shielding her core from the wreckage of her shattered life.

With heightened mental focus and acuity, she moved with single-minded determination to protect her assets. In one massive explosion, all the projections lodged in her energy field were expelled. She could have succumbed to collapse, but she didn't, largely due to the empowerment of her hatred. On the other hand, some of the actions she perpetrated, driven by the strength of her feelings, revealed a part of herself that she never knew existed. She never imagined herself as someone who would read another person's e-mail or stalk her husband's mistress, yet she did both these things. When the crisis was past and survival was assured, she had to face the hidden demons within.

The crux of hatred is reflection. It takes us to the center of our own darkness and asks that we see our reflection in the obsidian mirror of our soul. If we are willing, hatred can illuminate everything within us that believes in separation. It can help us rebuild our life on more solid foundations that reflect and protect the beauty of our soul.

Inspiration

Inhibition: hopelessness

Exaggeration: illusion

Inspiration happens when our core receives support. Inspiration is one of the ways we charge our system and fuel our dreams. If we can create an inspiring future, we will find the energy to fund it. When we need refueling, we can do so with inspiration. Admiring the actions of others, finding spiritual connection, and stimulating any of the transcendental emotions of Chapter 7 are all ways of being inspired.

Jealousy

Inhibition: cunning

Exaggeration: aggression

Jealousy is a close cousin to envy, and its message is the same: We are not seeing our self clearly. Whereas envy is related to the core impulse of standing and focuses more on social or career status, jealousy is related to the core impulse of connection. It relates directly to our connections with the people in our life, examining how we treat them and how they treat us.

The benefits of jealousy are many. Although it can be a reflection of our lack of self-regard, it can also be our body alerting us to betrayal, or a reminder not to take the people in our lives for granted. In all cases jealousy asks that we evaluate how we are seeing our self in regard to our relationships. Are we being arrogant and taking our partner for granted? Are we being blind, using denial to shield us from the pain of betrayal? Do we undervalue our self so that every connection our partner makes with another, however innocent, threatens us?

The energy of jealousy is hot and smoldering. It can burst into an eruption with little provocation. When allowed to flow, it pours into our boundary, strengthening it while assessing the quality of the energy attachments we share with our partner. It seeks to repair damages and restore connection. It looks for interfering energy attachments that may be trying to separate us from our partner and disengages them.

Jealousy conveys that we have lost connection to our own value and possibly to our partner as well. Jealousy asks that we look at what we are taking for granted, and remember who we are personally and who we are as a couple. It helps us defend what is rightfully ours. When true love is threatened, beware, usurper: Jealousy is a formidable opponent!

Joy

Inhibited: sadness

Exaggerated: over-joy

Joy is the result of living from our core. When we are in joy we are flowing in authentic expression and from connection to our spiritual essence. Joy is not the happiness, contentment, or satisfaction of meeting external goals; it is the absolute ecstasy of fueling our life from our source. It is the reward for all we must endure to be who we are in a world constantly trying to mold us into a perfect consumer, employee, lover, offspring, product, and so forth. Joy and bliss are the results of living with transcendental emotions.

When we inhibit joy we move into depression, sadness, discouragement, or any of the emotions that indicate we are disconnected from our authentic self. When we are afraid of losing joy, we move into over-joy, which is an investment of energy in a state of illusion. We know we are in over-joy when we have to search for ways to energize and maintain our high. Joy comes with no effort beyond conscious living. It does not require manufacturing. The danger of over-joy is that it pours our energy into illusions, which foster bad decision-making. While in over-joy we may engage in risk-taking behaviors, hook up with partners who are users, get involved in cults, or find other ways of moving away from our core. Ironically, the emotion that best expresses the delight of the core removes us from its center in over-joy. The message in over-joy is: *Relax. It's okay to be on the journey. The process and the end result are the same. Enjoy it.*

Additional Features of Joy

Energy Flow: Energy flows from our core in a radiant burst throughout our body and energy system, and then beams out into the world. People in joy, glow.

Segment/chakra: The segment that generates joy is the chest segment and the chakra is the Heart chakra. The segment is wide open with an expansive chest, loose muscles, and free-flowing energy. The body language is open and welcoming. The Heart chakra radiates love.

Element/Meridians: The element that governs joy is Fire and the meridians are the Heart and Small Intestines. If fire burns out of control, it can consume us. Water controls fire, and maintaining a balance between expressing our core (fire) and connecting with our core (water) will keep the flames burning brightly without depleting our ability to continue growing.

Message: Enjoy the process.

Core Impulse and Learning: The core impulses at work with joy are creative expression and connection. The learning is that from our center we have it all.

Key Question: How can our joy provide service to others?

Love

Inhibition: loss

Exaggeration: dependency

Love is the glue that holds the universe together. In its elevated state it is unconditional, and when we engage it fully, love is the closest experience we have in human form to the bliss of divine union. Interestingly, neuroscientist Candace Pert explains that when we are in love we produce more endorphins, the molecule associated with the experience of bliss. She states that bliss coincides with a sense of universal connection and concludes that we are designed to seek this experience.[1]

The flow of love is all-encompassing. All parts of self are brought into higher vibration, and the world literally takes on a different hue. Some say that because we cannot sustain love, love is not real. However, the universe is dynamic; things ebb and flow, shifting from state to state. Love is the driving force. Love is always present beneath everything that we do. As an emotional experience, love tunes us in to the deeper levels of reality and awakens us to the energy flows within and without. Love opens our intuitive percipience more than any other experience. When we allow love to flow, the energy of the universe opens. Love is the sublime source of all the energy we need to charge our system. When coupled with a goal, vision, or dream, all things are possible.

Love promotes growth. We are human, and maintaining pure connection to love is elusive. Our conditioning and unmet needs become superimposed over the experience of maintaining love, inhibiting our ability to feel and express. Inhibited love creates disillusionment and asks that we return to truth. With disciplined thought and attention, we can use the strength of love to see through the false images we have created in our mind and use its force to remove them from our energy field.

When we cannot receive or express a true experience of love, we manufacture its visage. We might pour our self into other people in order to feel the connection we seek, overwhelming them in the process. We might hang on possessively to someone who does not love us, believing he or she will come around. These are attempts to meet unfulfilled needs and keep our system charged. In the end, we cannot fully love another or receive another's full love until we love our self. This doesn't mean gratifying our self-importance; it means meeting our self with compassion, non-judgment, and acceptance. When we bring love to self, we open the door for loving experiences and even open to our true mate.

Obsession

Inhibited: frustration

Exaggerated: possession

When obsession with a person, idea, or situation rules us, we are trying to charge our system through an addiction. It indicates that we have forgotten how to naturally recharge or are not able to maintain a charge once we have it. Perhaps we have holes in our energy structures that allow energy to leak, or we throw away our energy on people who give nothing back. Obsession is a way to keep energy flowing in a system that leaks. Its message is: *What are we not honoring in self?*

When we find ourselves obsessed with reliving the most painful experience of our life or are stalking our lover's old partner, we need to assess the level of energy we are generating through these activities. We need to look at what we are trying to honor. Does the pain we've been through honor our valor? Does seeing our lover's old interest honor our commitment? Is our obsession with celebrities honoring our equality?

In the exaggeration of obsession, the only way we can stay charged is to energetically possess the person we are obsessed with. We cover the person with energy attachments and siphon their vitality. We become energy vampires. There is only one message here: We have everything we need inside our self. When the constellation of our internal energy is not supplying our energy needs or not maintaining our energy, we have stopped honoring our core and obsession is the messenger. Use the energy of obsession to reconnect. The Honoring the Core exercise in Chapter 9 can be very helpful.

Passion

Inhibited: discontent, manic-depression

Exaggerated: manic euphoria

Passion inspires action. It clears and cleans our intentions, goals, and limiting beliefs. Passion is the result of connecting with the core impulse of creative expression and surrendering to what we find. We are uplifted, energized, and motivated.

When inhibited or exaggerated, passion feeds delusion. Inhibited, passion turns inward, creating discontent with life. Nothing is good enough; nothing compares to our grand passion. Passion can be so extreme that it becomes a state of manic-depression in which there is no energy to motivate any action, including living. The delusion is that life is not worth living. When exaggerated, passion turns into manic euphoria, an illusion of superhuman capabilities. Believing in invincibility, we may walk in front of cars without regard, spend our life savings at the casino, or engage in some other form of self-exaltation. Although this sounds like bipolar disorder, it is not the same, as bipolar disorder has a physiologic basis.

The core impulse being fed is growth, and a tree is the perfect metaphor for balanced passion. The deeper the roots of the tree, the higher the branches can reach. The message of passion is to reach for the stars while staying firmly planted on the Earth. Grounding and centering exercises are essential when channeling passion. When passion is out of control, the message is to ground the energy of the core impulses. Like an electrical circuit, our energy system must be grounded in order for the circuitry to work.

Sadness

Inhibited: depression

Exaggerated: anxiety

Sadness is a close cousin to grief. Although not a hard and fast rule, grief is primarily related to the losses of connection we experience externally, and sadness is related to the losses of connection to our core. Every time we move away from a core value or authentic expression of a core impulse, we experience sadness. The main difference between grief and sadness is that with grief, what we have lost cannot be returned. When people die, we can honor their memory and stay connected energetically to their essence—even commune with them in meditation—but we cannot bring them back. The loss of connection to our core, on the other hand, *can* be reestablished. Deep within sadness there is hope.

The flow of sadness is inward to our core, seeking to reconnect us to the authentic experience we desire. When we feel obstructed in living from our core, we move into depression. When we fear we will be punished if we express our core, we move into anxiety. With reduced energy, sadness insists that we retire inside for reconnection. It slows us down and forces us to sit in our feelings until we resolve them.

Sadness asks what is lost and promises that it can be restored. Its message is hope. It is natural to want to avoid feeling sad, and we can hide in denial for a very long time, using alternate ways of charging our system. Eventually, however, sadness will re-emerge, and we will return to its message and take advantage of the time, out it provides to find our authentic voice.

Additional Features of Sadness

Energy Flow: Into the core.

Segment/Chakra: Sadness is another emotion of the chest segment, and energy here will be collapsed over the heart. The Heart chakra seeks to bring energy home to nourish the Shen, our spiritual essence.

Element/Meridians: Heart and Small Intestines governed by Fire nourish and sustain the Shen. Feeding and protecting our fire helps maintain our connection to our core.

Message: Honor our spirit.

Core Impulse and Learning: The core impulses at work with sadness are the desire for connection with our spirit and its creative expression. The learning is that walking someone else's path can never bring joy.

Key Question: Where is our joy?

Shame

Inhibited: embarrassment

Exaggerated: self-hatred

Of all the emotions, shame can be the most difficult. It is a cousin of guilt, and in its pure state acknowledges that boundaries have been overstepped and mistakes have been made. Shame is evoked when we harm our self or another. Facing our worst mistakes and owning them is one of the hardest progressions of growth, which is the core impulse motivating shame. Whereas guilt brings rectification and self-pride, shame reduces us to the bare essentials of who we are so that we can rebuild from the foundation of our true self. The energy of shame drops us into the first and second chakras, pulling in our fibers and reconditioning them. It invites us to let go of all pretenses and accept that we are human.

Shame is one of the most powerful emotions we have. Small doses are enough to create huge internal and external change. Unfortunately, shame is often used to manipulate us, especially as children, and it can be crippling. Shame that comes as a projection from someone else carries that person's self-hatred. It is an attempt by the other person to alleviate his or her own discomfort by causing us to share it. The message in shame is that the worst has already happened. You are loved in the universe.

Additional Features of Shame

Energy Flow: Collapsed into the Base chakra.

Segment/Chakra: Shame is generated in the pelvic segment and second chakra. This segment and chakra relate to sexuality, and shame is often focused on the sexual impulse. The sexual impulse is life-affirming, and this segment is usually guarded with all impulses curtailed. Reaching for life, having relationships, and growth are restricted until the message of shame is heeded and the body brought back into balance.

Element/Meridians: Shame is often a form of self-blame and falls to the Liver and Gallbladder governed by Wood. It reflects a deficiency of energy in Wood. Nourishing the Wood element with Water can help restore proper balance.

Message: You have survived your mistake, and there is light at the end of the tunnel and a loving hand to greet you.

Core Impulse and learning: The core impulse is growth and the learning is that we are not born knowing everything and there is no owner's manual to teach us how. We will make mistakes and some of them will be bad ones. We are still lovable.

Key Question: Are we allowed to make a mistake?

Wonder

Inhibition: boredom

Exaggeration: delusion

Wonder is vast, inclusive, and uplifting. It flows into our chakras and expands us, opening the boundaries of our aura. It clears our head of disbelief and awakens our true potential. It instills an awareness of our individual place in the limitless scope of the universe. In wonder we are open, far-sighted, and clear. We perceive connections and see how the events and people around us fit together. It opens our heart, connects us to our core, and increases percipience.

When wonder surges out of control, we become lost in illusion, seeing everything that glitters as gold. As adults we spend an enormous amount of time and energy trying to foster childhood wonder in larger-than-life productions, but the effort can never fully create the desired effect. Wonder in this sense is a game of smoke and mirrors. However, even here there is function as we learn to become discerning.

Wonder is an effortless suspension of belief whose gifts are the ability to see old things in new ways and to imagine the impossible. The expansion wonder provides helps us see through the glitter of delusion to true gold.

PART III
ENGAGING EMOTIONAL AWARENESS

In Part III we begin the process of engaging the power of our emotions. As we tap into the energy level of our emotions and access their messages, life opens in new and unusual ways. When we align with the flow of life force, life instantly has more depth and meaning, and we feel greater fulfillment and empowerment. Most importantly, we live from our authentic core and experience our interconnection with the spiritual essence of reality.

Illustration by Mark Johnson

Chapter 12
The Four-Fold Process
for Emotional Mastery

Take a moment to explore. Relax and bring your attention into your body. Let your mind calm and then imagine a few people whom you know. One at a time, bring a full picture of each person into your mind's eye. If emotions appeared as colors with shapes, densities, and textures, how would the space around each person look? How crowded is it? How much flow is there? How much clarity? Take your time to explore each person, observing without judgment. Using the same technique, picture the space around yourself. What is the quality of your energy field? Flow? Clarity? When you are ready, take three deep breaths: Inhale clarity; exhale self-absorption. Fully feel the present moment. Notice your body, your breath, your thoughts. Now return your attention to your energy field. What do you notice? Your observations are a small example of what lies ahead in the Four-Fold Process.

Using the information and energy within our emotions is a natural skill—one many people have forgotten how to access. Too often we are overwhelmed by our emotions and are at their mercy as they drive our

169

behavior and send us in directions we don't want to go. The Four-Fold Process reconnects us with our innate ability to listen. Once heard, the intensity of our emotions subsides, along with their ability to drive our behavior. When we are fully present in our body, and listening to the emotional messages sent from our core, we claim our personal power.

The Four-Fold Process provides a framework to explore the non-ordinary reality within our emotions. Interacting through the medium of energy allows past conditioning to shift and open. The Process uses practices introduced in earlier chapters such as mindfulness, active imagination (listening), and visualization (moving) to open a new paradigm. In the old paradigm we have no control over our emotions: They arrive, create an impact, and recede as the stimulus fades. The only choice we have is to suppress, repress, or express them. The new paradigm allows the possibility that when emotions arrive, we choose how we will entertain them. Consciously or unconsciously, we build emotions with our thoughts and interact with them through their energy. The Four-Fold Process provides tools for conscious exchange.

The Four-Fold Process

Using this Process will not diagnose or treat psychological or medical conditions. Many emotional conditions are best addressed through professional treatment. Although this Process can be used to support emotional health, it is not a replacement for medical care.

The Four-Fold Process consists of making a choice to shift, receiving the information our emotions are transmitting, directing the energy they generate, and creating heart-centered action. The Process is simple yet surprisingly effective. For many, the following outline will be enough direction to be able to use it; however, the rest of the chapter further clarifies each step. Examples for use in emotionally charged situations or for creative opportunity are found in chapters 13 and 14.

1. **Shift Awareness.** Changing how we interact with our emotions starts with making a choice. Clearly stating this choice initiates a shift from everyday awareness into that of the mindful witness or observer, which involves identifying with our core and strengthening our boundary.

2. **Receive Information.** Emotions have a purpose and need to be acknowledged. We interact with an emotion by fully feeling it,

locating the place in our body where the feeling resides, and engaging it by acknowledging the emotion with gratitude and openness. The information contained within will make itself known through images of active imagination and/or sudden thoughts or realizations. We may be able to link the information to a limiting belief or past condition.

3. **Direct the Energy.** When an emotion is felt but not listened to, the energy builds internally and causes agitation. As soon as the emotion is acknowledged, even if the information it carries is not fully understood, the energy moves. We can assist this by focusing our attention on flow. Release our energy from the past and send it to the desired outcome with our attention and visualization. This can be as easy as repeating the word *flow*.

4. **Create Heart-Centered Action.** We are connected to the matrix of life through the chakra of our heart, and actions generated from this area are expressions of our core self. To create heart-centered action, access a transcendent emotion and *feel our connection to the world through the fibers of the heart*. This will seem completely foreign to many people, and others will understand it exactly.

The dance of emotions, energy, and actions is going on all the time at a subconscious level. Successfully using this method is making the subconscious, conscious. Although the steps are simple, it takes mental focus and practice. The tools of mindfulness, bodymind balancing, and visualization (as discussed in chapters 8 and 9) are the skills that make emotional mastery possible.

Many people are stopped in the exploration of their feelings because they have been trained to believe that doing so is an act of self-absorption. But whereas collapsing into emotional patterns is self-indulgent, emotional mindfulness is not. In fact, paying attention frees vitality and releases our attention so that we are more available to those around us. Using the Four-Fold Process to listen to what we feel connects us to the larger world through our heart-center. It brings us home.

The process is especially helpful in investigating and moving emotions we can't seem to shift. Perhaps we had an argument and can't let go of the residual anger. Maybe we broke up with a partner and can't shift the pain, or suffer chronic anxiety, depression, or anger. Additionally, when we are embroiled in emergency situations, our emotions arrive with urgent force and we often struggle to maintain presence of mind. Chapter 13 will explore modifications to the Process that help intercept the force of highly charged emotions.

Sourcing Emotions

One challenge in discerning emotional information is knowing how much of what we feel is a reflection of present-time information and how much is influenced from other events. Sometimes, emotions reflect the people, events, and conditions around us. Sometimes they reveal past patterning, and sometimes they presage events that have yet to happen or are transmissions from people who are far away. Knowing the source of an emotion is part of discerning its message and determining a response.

Present-Time Emotions

Present-time emotions are usually easy to decipher. For example, we are angry because the new security regulations are invasive (boundary breech), the bank refuses our mortgage application (obstruction), or a friend believes a lie about us (injustice). We are afraid because we heard an unusual sound in the basement, feel guilty because we blew up at our coworker, or are ashamed because we hurt a friend. Present-time information is clear: We can see what needs to be done and usually know how to do it.

Sometimes extreme situations occur that overwhelm our emotional circuits. Emergency emotions such as terror and rage arise in response to life-threatening conditions (or conditions perceived as life-threatening) and generate energy for instant action. The power of these emotions can override the mind with the immediacy of fight, flight, or freeze reactions. Maintaining the presence of mind to know when and how to assist these types of emotions can mean the difference between surviving a life-threatening situation and not. Presence of mind does not require avoiding or repressing emotions; sometimes screaming in rage or fear is absolutely necessary. With awareness we are helped to follow our instincts and gut feelings, to see and seize opportunities.

Working with the Four-Fold Process in ordinary situations will set the stage for applying the principles in extreme situations. When the Process becomes second nature, we will have more resources available to overcome challenges and employ the modifications that will be discussed in Chapter 13.

Past Emotional Patterns

Past emotional patterns govern our conditioned responses and often occur below the level of awareness. They arise in the face of present-time situations, but occur with unnecessary force. Whenever we overreact to a situation—when the strength of our reaction is out of proportion to the stimulus—we know we are being triggered by engrained patterns. Instead of learning about what's happening here and now, we're learning about where we are stuck in the past. For example, when a woman decides her new boyfriend doesn't love her because he forgot their one-month anniversary, she is probably not responding to the situation, but to a past abandonment. A one-month anniversary doesn't have significance enough that forgetting it produces those feelings by itself. Something deeper is being triggered.

Noticing when we are overreacting helps to determine what part of the information is related to the past and how to respond in the present. For example, the boyfriend's apparent lack of care was an opportunity for the woman to observe and release past conditioning. The resultant clarity would allow her to receive real-time information about the boyfriend's true feelings. It is impossible to get an accurate read of someone's intentions, feelings, or agenda through an overlay from the past.

We do not need to relive the trauma of events to heal. Sometimes we need to process the information about the event; other times we need to recognize what the emotion is trying to accomplish and release it. This came home to me when recovering from a very traumatic horse accident. I spent years processing different parts of the accident, trying to resolve the residual pain in my body. Then, during a bodywork session, I realized what my energy had been trying to do: stop the horse! The energy of that unfulfilled action was locked in my tissues. I used visualization and in my mind completed the action and stopped the horse while the therapist assisted my shoulder. This allowed the energy trapped in my tissue to flow. The release of pain was remarkable!

Here's an example of how the Four-Fold Process assists psychotherapy: Kim has a challenging relationship with her aging mother and is seeing a therapist to heal childhood traumas that are influencing their relationship. As Kim's responsibilities for her mother's well-being increase, she finds she is reluctant to engage in activities that bring her mother pleasure. When plans are made for her mother to meet with friends, go to the movies, and so on, Kim is annoyed by her mother's obvious enjoyment and finds ways to disrupt events. Sabotaging her mother's pleasure upsets both Kim and her mother.

Breaking the pattern is the focus of Kim's psychotherapy sessions; however, she also needs a method to shift dynamics as they occur. Using the Four-Fold Process allows her to disengage her energy from the past and re-attach to the present. Using the Process, she is able to intercept her actions, replacing the unconscious desire to sabotage with heart-centered support. Kim continues therapy for healing past traumas and uses the Process to move beyond her patterned responses in the moment.

Past emotional patterns are also reflected in our emotional state of being. Long-term emotional states such as depression, apathy, anger, disappointment, and so forth, indicate that the energy of past emotions is locked in a limiting belief. Identifying the limiting belief and releasing the energy it holds creates an opening for something new.

Transference

We are energetically connected to everything around us; strong emotional connections mean strong energetic connections. When we are deeply attached to another person, we are open to the energy of his or her thoughts and emotions. Consider Jill and Mike. Jill is washing dishes when she begins thinking of a problem at work and becomes very anxious. Mike is sitting at the table chopping vegetables when he suddenly feels an anxious gnawing in the pit of his stomach. Instinctively he thinks of Jill. Looking up, he notices her body language and asks if she is all right. As soon as Jill acknowledges her upset, Mike's anxiety recedes, although his caring does not.

Transfer of emotional energy happens even when two people are in distant places. It occurs quite regularly, though we aren't always aware of it. The emotions we pick up from others are simply part of the undercurrent that ebbs and flows through the day. Couples in love notice the exchange more often, partly because the force of love is a powerful connector. Have you ever had the experience of suddenly feeling waves of love wash over you, followed by thoughts of your lover? Chances are you were receiving his or her heartfelt emotion.

When a child, partner, or friend is going through difficulties we can become submerged in his or her emotions without being aware of their source. When an emotion rises quickly and unexpectedly, unrelated to where we are and what we are doing, it is often an indication that we are picking up transference from someone else. If so, grounding the energy, and sending love and support to the source of the feelings, even if we don't know who it is, will be received by the person and be helpful.

Here is a simple method of discerning whether an emotional reaction belongs to us or to someone else. It is similar to the boundary exercise in Chapter 10.

Discerning Transference

- Follow the feeling inside your body to where it is originating. Fully engage the sensations.

- Stretch your arms straight out in front of you.

- Turn your palms back towards your body and say, "This is me." Pulse your palms toward yourself while repeating the words "This is me." Notice if the feeling recedes, stays the same, or grows. If it stays the same or grows, the emotion is probably yours.

- Next, keeping your arms extended, turn your palms away from your body. Say, "This is not me." Pulse your palms away from yourself and continue to repeat the words. Notice whether the feeling recedes, stays the same, or grows. If it stays the same or grows, it is probably coming from someone else.

- You may need to repeat the process several times to experience a strong enough difference to indicate whether the feeling belongs to you or to someone else. With practice you will only need to ask the question and you will feel the answer.

Future/Past Transmission

This category, similar to transference, is usually considered psychic in nature. However, both components are part of the exchange of energy that is happening all the time. In transmissions from the past, the emotion of an event imprints itself on objects or in the Earth. Sensitive people feel the emotion. Have you ever gone into an old house, cemetery, or historic battleground, and felt a certain vibe as you walked around? Maybe you felt uneasy, or perhaps you suddenly felt angry, frightened, or deeply depressed. We can distinguish between an emotional imprint and other sources of emotional information by walking into a different room or going outside, then grounding and noticing if the mood shifts. Maintaining energetic boundaries helps remove unwanted emotional transmission.

In addition to the past, we sometimes pick up the bow wave of upcoming events. As explained in Dean Radin's experiment discussed in Chapter 9, the stronger the emotional content of the possibility on the horizon, the more pronounced the presentiment. Interestingly, when people are picking up on the future, they usually know it. We say things like "Something good is coming; I can feel it around the corner," or "I've got a bad feeling something awful is going to happen." We seem to know instinctively that the anticipation or aversion isn't about our present surroundings, past conditioning, or transfer from another person.

Going Deeper Into the Four-Fold Process

The intelligent use of emotions and energy is innate; The Four-Fold Process simply slows events to bring energy interactions into conscious awareness. With practice, both the effort and the steps disappear as the exercise becomes automatic and instinctual.

The basic tools for energy awareness are provided in Part II of this book. The practice of mindfulness allows us to switch into the neutral observer, which creates space between the arrival of emotions and our response. Grounding, centering, and developing presence are essential skills in maintaining connection to our core while we investigate our feelings. Maintaining a strong boundary not only keeps us safe, but it also creates the neutral space we inhabit while exploring. The use of active imagination allows us to interact with the images from our bodymind, and visualization is a tool for directing energy. Some people consider active imagination and visualization as the same, but I distinguish active imagination as a tool for listening to and dialoguing with the bodymind, and visualization as a tool for creating action. The distinction makes direction clearer.

The Process is a method for gaining self-awareness. It can be part of a regular practice of personal growth or used when we are distressed by emotions that won't shift. Emotions that hang on after the event are perfect instances to use this Process, as are chronic emotional patterns that limit us.

Step 1: Choosing to Shift

The desire to interact with our emotions indicates a choice to shift awareness; making a declaration brings it into consciousness and affirms our personal power. The shift we are making is from everyday awareness to that of the inner witness or observer. Self-awareness is always split between the two. Everyday awareness is the voice of inner chatter, usually the critic who judges everything we think, say, and do, or the victim who feels oppressed or mistreated by the events of life. The observer-self is the mindful witness discussed in Chapter 8: the neutral part of awareness that is able to discern the broader picture. Shifting our awareness from the perspective of one to the other is an expression of how we identify our self.

Everyday awareness identifies who we are through our emotional, mental, and physical state. But although we enjoy thinking, feeling, and experiencing, we are not our thoughts, feelings, or body. We are infinitely more than that. Mindful awareness identifies with the infinite more: It identifies with the core self, and our experiences are seen in context of a cohesive whole. As the mindful witness, we can step back from our emotions to observe their meaning.

Shifting awareness can be the most difficult challenge of the Four-Fold Process, especially when we are in the midst of highly charged emotions. Pre-programming the shift with some type of signal can be helpful. For example, whenever we practice mindfulness, if we press our thumb together with one of our fingers, the action will create an association and become automatic. In a charged situation, the automatic signal awakens the mindful witness. People oriented to sound may want to create a single word or mantra that, when said, elicits a similar response. The entire process is quickly personalized as we each create the method that works for us.

Step 2: Receiving Information

Psychic powers and/or empathic abilities are not required to understand the messages in our emotions. All we have to do is listen to our body. Every emotion is felt in the body segment where it is generated. To hear the message: Fully feel the emotion, follow it to the place in the body where it is generated, acknowledge it by naming it, and then listen. The information in the Emotional Compendium (Chapter 11) is an example of what can be discovered. Breaking down the components makes this step clearer.

Feel and Follow. There is a difference between the feelings of an emotion and the secondary feelings associated with expressing or repressing the emotion. For example, when engaged in an argument, the secondary feelings of controlling anger might be muscle tension in the shoulder and jaw, and mental frustration. The actual anger might feel like a core of sizzling molten lava roiling in the center of the solar plexus. Focusing on the shoulders, on the muscle tension, and the frustration is focusing on the attempts to control the molten core. Focusing on the molten core in the body is where the information lies. We access it through the feelings in the center where it is being generated. Feelings might include discomfort, tightness, emptiness, vibration, charge, pulsation, or just heightened awareness.

Here is an exercise to practice feeling and following:

Feeling and Following Exercise

- Randomly pick an emotion from the compendium in Chapter 11 and remember a time you felt the emotion. Recapture the feeling. Create an image of how the emotion feels and where in the body it is felt. What color, density, form is it? Let the feeling grow, and follow it. What force does the emotion produce?

- Then read the description in the compendium of the energy function and compare it to your energy experience.

- Do this process with a few of the emotions from the list, then feel and follow some emotions that are not in the compendium. You might be surprised at how easy it is to follow an emotion to its center.

Acknowledge. Acknowledge the emotion by naming it. This is important because it tells the bodymind that the emotional message is being heard. Eliciting a transcendent emotion such as gratitude opens the flow of information.

Listen. The body (and the subconscious) speaks in metaphors and images. Active imagination allows an image of what the emotion feels like to emerge. Examples: the tight knot of frustration, the boiling cauldron of anger, the underwater feeling of overwhelm, and so on. The more exact the image, the clearer the information. Also, allow metaphors to describe the feeling. For example: *I feel like I was hit by a truck*; *I'm tied up in knots*; *I'm walking in quicksand*; *I'm in over my head.* We may also hear the messages from the body as a sudden compulsion to action, or a dawning realization and knowing.

All emotions are capable of providing direct and immediate knowing. Sometimes we understand the message exactly. The vague feeling of unease, when followed inward, becomes a precise cord of agitation that provides a message in no uncertain terms: *Leave the place we are in immediately. Go and check the pot on the stove. Call home.* Another example: the unexplained sense of anticipation we feel when followed inward becomes a longing that reveals suppressed love for someone we thought of as only a friend.

On the other hand, sometimes emotions don't seem to have any real meaning. Chronic feelings such as free-floating anxiety seem to be unrelated to a message. Usually chronic emotional states carry messages from the past that are attached to trauma or limiting beliefs. The fear of putting in a job application might seem like a simple fear of rejection or judgment, but sitting with the feelings might take us to a childhood humiliation and the belief that we are undeserving—that we will never have what we want. Following these types of emotions into the body can reveal their source and allow us to redirect the energy they carry.

When the meaning in our emotions is obscure, getting to the core may require further digging. In this case, asking a series of questions and listening for the answers can be helpful. The natural response to this suggestion might be to say, "If I knew the answers I wouldn't need to ask the question." However, the body is the subconscious mind and holds a record of everything we have experienced. The bodymind knows the meaning of what we feel and where it's coming from. Asking questions while focusing on the body affords an opportunity to hear the message more clearly.

As before, use active imagination to pay attention to images, metaphors, sudden realizations, and the physical response that accompanies them. When we get a true answer, our system is strengthened and energy pathways are opened. The resultant movement of energy causes physical sensations. Incorrect answers weaken the system and close energy pathways. When we see an image, receive an impression, or have an idea that arrives with the body sensations of energy moving, we know we are in the right ballpark. Here are some of the more common body sensations associated with moving energy; however, each person will develop his or her own energy language.

- Upsurge of vitality.
- Tingling, skin crawling, or a feeling of air moving across the skin.
- A sense of opening, flowing, or internal loosening.
- Hot flashes or chills.
- Goosebumps or hair standing on end.
- Internal vibration.
- Butterflies in the stomach.
- A sense of being dropped or falling.
- Heart racing, pounding, or palpitations.

Dowsing and muscle testing are other methods to confirm answers. Dowsing consists of using devices such as a pendulum or dowsing rods. The energy of the correct answer is transferred from the bodymind through movement of the device. Muscle testing demonstrates the opening of energy flows with the strengthening of muscles. Although these methods are still reflections of the bodymind, some people find the answers are clearer when externalized. (Two easy methods to use are explained in Appendix A: Dowsing and Muscle Testing.)

Questions

The act of asking the question opens awareness to hearing/seeing/ feeling the answer that is already present. Stay connected to the emotion through feeling and imagery as the questions are asked. Questions are most accessible when they focus on what, who, and when; avoid why. If multiple possibilities arise, the most accurate answer will have a corresponding body sensation and feeling of flow and openness. When we find answers that have been long hidden or represent a big-picture link, we feel awakened and our whole body floods with energy.

- Right now, in this moment, am I safe? If no: Do I need to take immediate action? What action?
- Is this emotion telling me about the past, present, or future?
- What percentage is relating present-time information?
- What percentage is related to past conditioning? Clear the past by acknowledging the information.
- What percentage is relating future possibilities?
- Is the emotion I am feeling coming from another person? If yes, who is it coming from? Is the emotion my own but magnified by the energy of another person or group? If yes, who is magnifying it? Am I being manipulated by a person, group, or system? If yes, by whom?
- What action is required? What is the best action I can take? What is the time frame?
- Is this emotion attached to a limiting belief? If so, what is it?
- What does my bodymind want me to know in this moment?
- What is hidden from me?
- What have I forgotten?
- What have I lost?
- What do I need?

(A specific question for individual emotions can be found in Appendix B in Table 1: Quick Access Emotional Energy.)

Segments and Chakras

When we don't fully understand the information in our emotions, we can use body associations for added insight. Emotions arise in specific body segments, and each segment contains one of the seven physio-energetic chakras. Chakras represent different types of consciousness and hold specific growth challenges.

To use this method, locate the emotion in the body and identify the segment. Then look at the associated chakra, level of consciousness, and inherent challenge. Appendix B contains Illustration 1: Body Map of the Segments, and a table of chakra correlations can be used as a springboard to explore life issues (Table 2: Segments and Chakra Correlations).

Step 3: Directing the Energy

The ability emotions have to generate energy makes them powerful tools of consciousness. Not only do they give us direction, but they also generate force to create change. Directing the energy of an emotion involves first disconnecting from old patterns (and the thoughts that feed them) and then sending energy to enliven new choices. It also involves using emotions to charge and cleanse our system.

As explained earlier, traditional Chinese medicine says that where the mind goes, chi follows. *Mind* in this context is best understood as a feeling-thought guided by intent. We can also call it *attention*. When we pay attention to something, we connect to it energetically. Attention activates the light fibers of our chakras and sends them to explore people, places, events, and ideas. Once connected, we can choose to invest our energy, or not.

Disconnecting Energy Attachments

Past conditioning, other people's agendas, and limiting beliefs impact us because our energy is invested. We are interlaced, and before we can take forward action, we must disconnect. The difficulty is that our attachments are formed on unfinished business. We care about the person and want his or her approval or have feelings that are unresolved. We invest in limiting beliefs because they represent our view of reality. In other words, our path has moved on but we haven't.

Here is an exercise to disconnect:

Disconnecting Energy and Strengthening our Boundary

- Feel the emotion of a past attachment and follow the body sensation into the center of the feeling.

- Imagine streams of light flowing from this area and connecting to the person, past event, or limiting belief.

- Elevate your energy with a transcendent emotion and let it flow toward the subject on these streams of light. If you have trouble eliciting a transcendent emotion, send the intention to release.

- Imagine withdrawing the energy by reeling in the attachments and coiling them inside your chakra. These are your energy fibers that have been linked to others.

- Visualize the boundary of your aura as a Spiral Pillar of Light descending into the center of the Earth. Feel strong and independent.

Calling in our energy attachments means being willing to develop a new frame of reference, a new paradigm. The irony is that once we have a new frame of reference, our energy attachments automatically shift and the exercise is not necessary.

Enlivening New Directions

Once the purpose of an emotion is understood and energy disengaged from the past, we can direct our attention to fulfilling the purpose of the emotion. For example, let's say we want to make a big change in our life, but are locked in fear. We know the steps we need to take to create this change, yet every time we start to act, we are crippled by our feelings. Because fear is acting to keep us safe, we need to determine where we are unsafe. Are we moving into harm's way? Are we being impacted by past conditioning, unseen factors, other people's expectations? Are we acting from someone else's agenda? Do we need to revise what we truly want?

Understanding the hidden concern, we can direct energy into the outcome the emotion indicates. In this case, acknowledging that fear is working toward safety, we can visualize a nest of safe energy around our core and generate the feeling of being safe. The energy released from fear can be used to enliven heart-centered action.

Assisting emotions in fulfilling their function results in an immediate dissipation of emotional charge. The charge may rebuild as we return our thoughts to old patterns, and several cycles of intentional release may be necessary. (A list of the direction of flow in different emotions can be found in Appendix B, Table 1: Quick Access Emotional Energy.)

Charging the System

The effectiveness of emotions to charge our system and motivate our actions is both empowering and dangerous. It is empowering because we can use our emotions to live creative, fulfilling lives, and dangerous because it is easy to become addicted to the false high of charged emotions.

When we are connected to our core, we generate emotions that fuel the true desires of our path and purpose. When we are disconnected, we don't know what we really want or how to energize the activities of life. Consequently, highly charged emotions such as anger and fear are employed to generate energy for tackling everyday events. In time we can lose the ability to do it any other way.

For example, consider what happens when we have to accomplish a task that we dread. Maybe we need to finish a term paper, study for an exam, complete a project at work, or do our taxes. Hating the job, we procrastinate until the approaching deadline induces fear that generates enough energy to get the job done. Another tactic is to become furiously angry at our teacher, boss, or government agency, generating massive energy for attacking the job. Both strategies work, but at a cost. We burn ourselves out and deplete our physical energy. We possibly insult or hurt others as well. The technique is effective, but certainly not elegant, efficient, or enjoyable.

In this case, connecting with our dread might allow us to discover what we are afraid of. Facing the fear might help us redirect our emotional energy toward enjoyable pursuits. If life is an unending stream of dread-inducing tasks, the bigger information may be that we are calling for a life overhaul.

Transcendent emotions charge and cleanse our system. These emotions are not reserved for spiritual moments or evolved people—we all feel and use them many times through the course of a day. They are universal, and the power they generate for action is the focus of inspirational movies and books, military training, and motivational encouragement. We induce them whenever we allow ourselves to be inspired. Transcendent emotions provide the master key to choosing how to direct emotional energy. They are the bodymind's reset button, keeping us connected to our core. They are a resource we can use anytime, if we choose.

Methods to connect with transcendent emotions include:

- ❂ Meditating on an inspirational figure such as a saint, guru, or spiritual principle.
- ❂ Remembering an inspiring event.
- ❂ Remembering an incident in your life when you experienced deep connection, love, or spiritual presence.
- ❂ Reciting a prayer, incantation, or mantra.
- ❂ Opening the heart to feeling compassion, gratitude, or unconditional love.

Step 4: Heart-Centered Action

The research conducted at HeartMath institute verifies a remarkable insight: When we are focused in our heart, we naturally connect with others and participate in a reciprocal flow of energy and information. In the Body Sounding Method, the heart is the center of the chakra system and integrates spiritual and earth energy in total balance. It is the consciousness of the totality of life. In addition to linking the chakras above and below in the vertical flow of energy, the Heart chakra flows laterally as well, traveling inward to our core and outward to touch the heart centers of others. The combination of vertical and lateral flows of energy weaves us into the matrix of life. The action generated from the heart comes from our core and connects with the core of all.

There is a good visual for this in both ancient Mayan and Taoist cosmology. Imagine standing on the weaving loom of life with hands raised overhead. Energy points in the fingers and toes suspend us on the loom between Earth and Sky. Energy centers in the body connect us to the events, places, and people that weave through our life creating the tapestry of our experience. Through the energy center of the heart, all the tapestries of all entities are woven together into one whole. The heart is the nodal point connecting personal with universal consciousness.

The tapestry of life is a lovely visual that helps establish the concept, but it doesn't tell us how to achieve heart-centered awareness. Doing so is easier than one might think. There are three basic means for accessing the heart-center:

1. Use transcendent emotions such as compassion, unconditional love, admiration, and gratitude to establish connection to the heart.

2. Sense the world through the energy fibers of the Heart chakra. Imagine connections flowing out from your heart and connecting you with the world.

3. Live from your core self. Being authentic is the best way to establish connection to the Heart chakra and develop heart-centered awareness.

Most people engage the world through the consciousness of the solar plexus, the third chakra of personal empowerment and individuation. In this consciousness, the world is set up in the context of *us* versus *them*. When we shift to the Heart chakra, we align with holographic consciousness. This is not emotionally irresponsible action derived from sentimentality; it is fully grounded action inspired from being connected to the whole. It says, "If you hurt, I hurt. If you grow, I grow. While I will protect myself from harm, I will do my best not to harm you."

Heart-centered awareness shifts the basic context of events. Our actions are based on our core values and incorporate our path and purpose in life. They are not motivated by the lesser cravings for power, fame, or petty vengeance. At the same time, heart-centered action does not ignore our own personal goals and wellbeing; it expands the definition. Personal well-being and collective well-being are understood to be related.

Creating Heart-Centered Action

- Shift into the Heart chakra by focusing attention on the heart.
- Assess your motives, intentions, and hidden agendas.
- Form an intention based on the highest outcome for everyone involved.
- Create an image in your mind's eye and feel yourself there.
- Send your energy into the feeling.

Heart-centered action represents our core, and it also has greater force than action generated through other centers. It spreads like wildfire along the lines that connect people, changing direction when it meets the resistance of a closed circuit, and activating those who are responsive.

Putting It All Together

When we first begin to practice emotional subtle energy awareness, the Four-Fold Process is time consuming. Shifting into the mindful witness is elusive, especially during emotionally charged situations. We struggle to understand emotional messages and to know how to support them energetically. At first we wonder if it really works. However, with time it becomes second nature and, without thinking about it, we are practicing emotional awareness and well on the way to mastery.

How well the system works came home to me recently when I found myself at odds with a mentor of mine after making a request of him that he considered unreasonable. I greatly admire and respect Ken, and was upset when disagreement erupted in e-mail communications. Without thinking about it, as soon as the conflict emerged, I shifted into the mindful witness. I noticed my feelings of anger at having been misunderstood and also my fear at being in disagreement with a respected authority figure.

My conditioned response was to use my anger in defensiveness or to collapse in fear and withdraw. Instead, I examined my motives and grounded my response in the honesty of my intent. My entire agenda was on the table; nothing was hidden. I channeled my energy into feeling protected and safe and used heart-centered awareness to try to find a solution. In the exchanges that followed I remained true to myself and also respectful and open to Ken's point of view.

Within a few exchanges I realized that the unnamed issue bothering Ken was his belief that the integrity of his work was being imperiled. I immediately acknowledged to Ken that I respected the value he placed on his integrity. Amazingly, the energy drained from the conflict. In a short time we were through our disagreement with better understanding and much deeper respect.

After the fact, I observed that at no point did I suppress what I felt or become overwhelmed by the emotional charge. I was true to my authentic self and created heart-centered action. The real surprise was that I had not done any clearing work on my authority issues or released any past traumas. The process worked because I was able to shift out of past conditioning and limiting beliefs. More importantly, it happened automatically. My focus was on finding a workable solution that honored us both. It was a welcome change from disagreements in my past and a wonderful affirmation of the creative power of emotions.

The information in this chapter may seem untenable; however, the process works. It works because it moves us beyond the present paradigm.

Chapter 13
Meeting Emotional Challenges

The Four-Fold Process finds the message in emotions and creates constructive action. It is continually modified for different circumstances and is especially useful in excessively charged situations when it is difficult to stay present and grounded. The emotional energy in these circumstances is bound: Instead of flowing into action, it builds in intensity, disrupting our ability to respond. Situations that carry an excessive charge are typically two types: The first are emergencies, and the goal of the process is to maintain emotional presence and act for our best good; the second are situations triggered from past conditioning. In both cases, the Four-Fold Process can help keep energy flowing into constructive action.

The process accesses sacred space within. It respects our emotions and patterns while honoring the soul's need to grow. This process also aligns with the nature of energy, which is to move. Assisting the movement of emotional energy assists our ability to think and respond with the level of intensity required for the situation. The process may seem too simple to work, but don't let that keep you from trying it. It works!

Here is a quick-access summary of the Process modified for charged situations. It does not diagnose or treat psychological or medical conditions that may require treatment. Though it supports emotional health, it is not a replacement for medical care.

Modified Four-Fold Process

1. **Choose to shift.** Taking a new direction starts with making the decision. Using a physical signal, such as pressing a functionally related acupressure point, supports the shift. See Illustration 13.1, Acupressure Points on the Hand, at the end of the chapter.

2. **Fully feel the emotion, follow it inward, and name it.** Suppressing our feelings stops energy from moving. Surrender, follow the feeling, and acknowledge it.

3. **Direct the energy by intending that it flow.** Assist the movement of the energy with your mind. The energy of an emotion is fed and directed with thought. Send your energy into flow. Imagine it and say the word *flow*. You can use phrases such as, *Follow your nature and flow.* Visualize warm water, honey, or lava flowing through your body, soaking up the emotion and carrying it away.

4. **Take heart-centered action and support yourself.** The action needed during highly charged emotions is support. Ask: "What do I need to be supported?" Give it. From the Heart chakra, acknowledge, "In this moment I have everything I need."

Following are suggestions for using the process in different situations. The process modifications are a guide as to how you might approach it. The process is easily modified for personal resonance. When choosing to shift, remember to ground, center, and establish boundaries as described in Chapter 10.

Annexing Anger

Every emotion has a function—including anger. Low-level anger associated with everyday frustrations and injustices motivates action. Anger may prompt us to say no to unreasonable expectations of our time and energy: We can be motivated to confront the coworker spreading malicious gossip or stealing credit for other people's work. A day could hold many instances of boundary breeches, obstruction, or injustice, and constructive anger responds with appropriate levels of intensity and action. Constructive anger is modulated with awareness so that it doesn't spiral out of control. It maintains the opening for peaceful resolution.

Perpetual anger that lives just under the surface, erupting into rage over minor infractions, might be covering a deeper emotion and represent old trauma. In this case, anger is the easier feeling to deal with. Listening to our anger might reveal extreme hurt, anguish, humiliation, or grief among others. Anger can also be a technique to quell overwhelming anxiety and panic. Counseling helps ultimate resolution, but the simple modification of the Four-Fold Process can assist getting through upsets as they arrive.

By nature, anger is blame-oriented and wants something or someone to fight. With time, our neural circuitry becomes patterned and the body is trained to respond to any stimulation with anger. We live on the edge of eruption and our body is primed for a fight. The constant elevation of stress hormones places a drain on our adrenal glands and can undermine our immune system. It increases our risk factors for heart disease, diabetes, and irritable bowel syndrome while damaging our relationships with our partners, children, friends, and coworkers. To manage the excess energy we might become workaholics, alcoholics, or exercise addicts. Although this level of anger may protect us from deeper feelings about past injustice and hurt, it destabilizes our life, causing us to lose sight of what is important.

There are several indicators in our behavior to alert us that anger has become our conditioned response:

- We are easily frustrated by stupidity, injustice, politics, or inefficiency. Anger is often focused outward, and we may find ourselves yelling at TV presenters, newspapers, and family members about world events.

- We often feel helpless to change the obstructions and injustice that bother us. Feeling helpless may have started in childhood when we had no protection from an aggressor.

- We are critical of others. People's behavior frustrates us, and we imagine they are purposefully trying to annoy us or at best are annoyingly incompetent.

- We engage in circular thinking. Our anger is fed with repetitive thoughts as we relentlessly circulate accusations, rationalization, and blame.

- We take things personally and are easily offended. Every comment, action, or belief of someone else is seen as a direct affront, and we are deeply insulted by differences of opinion.

❧ The eruption of anger feels good in the moment, but after the energy has discharged, we often feel remorse. To feel better, we rethink all the excellent reasons why we were justified in our anger until we are angry all over again.

The hardest part of shifting anger is that in the moment of heightened emotion, we might not be sure we *want* to shift. We are tricked into thinking that the force of anger is true power. Expressing it makes us feel important, righteous, and commanding. If anger is covering fear, pain, and anxiety, anger is an alternative that provides strength. Living without anger can feel weak, and eventually we are addicted to the energy boost. Without anger the tiredness in our system surfaces. Ultimately, excess anger burns us out.

The process to intercept anger can be initiated as emotion begins to rise.

Intercepting Anger

❧ Choose to shift into mindful observer and release the power anger has over you. Press the webbing between your thumb and forefinger (LI-4; see Illustration 13.1) to stimulate the downward flow of energy, clearing your mind into a more neutral space.

❧ Shift focus away from why you are angry to how anger makes you feel. Notice the juxtaposition of power and helplessness and name that feeling anger. Notice the tension in your shoulders, neck, and jaw; notice your headache, eye strain, and stomach pain. Name it all anger. Thank your anger for defending you.

❧ Intend flow. On every exhalation, send energy out of muscle tension and into the Earth, releasing the excess charge. Send anger into your boundary and feel protected and strong.

❧ Take heart-centered action by supporting yourself. Focus on breathing through your heart and supporting your core. If desired, induce a transcendent feeling: Enlist the image of a hero to arouse admiration, a deity to conjure protection, compassion to align with your best interest, and so on. Use a phrase such as *I am more than my anger.*

Using this technique requires commitment. In the beginning, as we release our dependency on anger to fuel our power, we might experience the depletion excess anger has created in our system. Don't worry. Energy is replenished as we find different ways to power life. We are choosing to shift to new way of doing things, choosing what we will give sway to in our life, and learning that we are not at the mercy of our unhealed past. The choice we are making is powerful and freeing.

Anger that is provoked when we or someone we love are in danger is different from perpetual anger. In this case, the intensity can be lifesaving and the emotional charge strengthens our defense. Physically, the release of stress hormones creates immediate power for action. However, effective defense requires presence of mind. In life-threatening situations we must be able to think and respond. A history of using the Four-Fold Process in daily interactions entrains it so that it is second nature. Shifting into the process in extreme situations accesses the power of anger while staying grounded and in command of our actions.

Assisting Self-Defense

- Choose higher awareness. Press the webbing between your thumb and forefinger (LI-4; see Illustration 13.1) to instigate a shift into the mindful observer while also stimulating the downward flow of energy to clear your head.

- Feel the effects of anger in your body. Name anger as your ally and work with it for defense.

- Direct the energy of anger into flow: Imagine the energy flowing into your boundary, and feel protected. Direct the energy into the Earth and let the Earth power your action; direct it into your muscles for the action that you need to take.

- Heart-centered action in this case means protecting yourself. Whether you use argument, strategy, or force, move with assuredness. Avoid undue force, cruelty, or revenge.

Dealing With Difficult People

Although we want to think that difficult people are other people, chances are each of us is a difficult person at different times. We become difficult in the face of feelings we can't manage. Sometimes we are difficult because being a petty tyrant makes us feel important. Equally, we might be reacting to intimidation or the stress of past trauma. We might act poorly because we are hungry, tired, afraid, or just plain ornery!

Whether we are being difficult or someone else is, there is really only one answer: Don't play.

Stop Playing With Difficult People

- Choose to shift and not play the game. Press your thumb webbing (LI-4; see Illustration 13.1) and send excess energy into the Earth. Increase neutrality and strengthen your boundary.

- Feel the inner turmoil and name it *aggravation*.

- Withdraw your energy from the difficulty and bring it into your core. Elicit compassion for self and others.

- Bring your awareness into your heart. Take care of the logistics that need to be attended to from the heart. Repeat: *I am more than this*. If necessary and possible, return to the problem or situation later.

Diminishing Drama

Drama is not an emotion; it's the use of emotional chaos as a conscious or unconscious strategy to get what we need. It's a manipulation that comes from not believing in ourselves. The message in drama is: connect with our core. When we are disconnected, we forget we are powerful and lose our authenticity. We are unable to ask for what we need because we either don't believe we deserve it, or can't handle the rejection if we are denied. The strategy of drama brings us what we want and provides a temporary blast of self-importance and rush of superiority.

Another way we use drama is as an unconscious tool to facilitate difficult change. Sometimes we feel conflicted about something we know we must do and are unable to make a decision. We may desperately want to change jobs, leave a boyfriend, or move, but lack the confidence needed for action. Unable to own our feelings, a dramatic crisis provides the justification and energy for the positive change we seek. Although it gets the job done, it also burns our bridges.

In time, the energy boost that drama provides becomes an addiction. Repeated use trains the body to obtain energy through the highly charged emotions generated through managing chaos. Other means of generating energy, such as meeting core impulses, don't have enough charge to fully jazz our system. It's similar to the difference between the high we get from eating sugar versus eating fruit.

Sometimes we are pulled into other people's drama and are endlessly at the mercy of situations that career out of control. In this case we are codependent on the other person's addiction to drama. The following process for dismissing drama can help us separate our energy from the chaos.

Quite often we are unaware that we are choosing drama. It seems that chaos just finds us, when, in truth, we create it. Un-creating it requires an active choice. The next time people and situations are in chaos, try this exercise.

Dismissing Drama

- ☙ Choose to shift; own your feelings and act from your core. Press on the indentation on the palm side of your wrist in line with your little finger (H-5; see illustration 13.1) to increase flow to your heart center and shift you to the mindful observer.

- ☙ Feel the combination of feelings (frustration, overwhelm, revenge, and so on) that are driving you. Acknowledge the entire complex as drama. Thank drama for bringing growth. Be available to any insights that might surface to help you connect with your core.

- ☙ Breathe flow into your heart center. Allow energy to move out of the complex of drama into your core.

- ☙ Support yourself. You have a right to make choices that benefit you. Create an affirmation such as "I am enough." Look for another way to express yourself in the situation you are in.

At first, when we are shifting out of drama, we may experience a sense of emptiness as we are faced with learning how to energize life without it. Continue to use the Four-Fold Process with emotions that arise. It will help uncover the hidden reasons for participating with drama and provide a mechanism for shifting into heart-centered energy generation.

Facing Anxiety and Panic

Millions of people suffer from anxiety, waking at night with pounding heart or being stopped in our tracks with sweating palms and shaking body. We can all relate to the rush of anxiety when we realize we have made a terrible error, forgotten an important assignment, or misunderstood an essential direction. The anxiety of being in danger due to our own mistake is devastating. Equally debilitating is the anxiety of being at the mercy of events beyond our control and not knowing when the next shoe is going to drop, or having more work to do each day than we can accomplish.

The underlying feeling of anxiety is that of not knowing what is coming or whether we will be able to manage it when it does. Statistics reveal that 40 million people in the United States will experience an anxiety condition this year.[1] The same source reports that Paxil and Zoloft, two popular anti-anxiety medications, are ranked in the top-10 prescribed medications in the United States, and that 42 percent of adolescents use recreational drugs, many to control anxiety. Clearly we need new ways to interact with this complex emotion.

Energetically, anxiety builds in intensity with no means of discharge. Sensors are on high alert, causing us to feel overly sensitive, overwhelmed, and ungrounded. When our bodies become so charged that we cannot sustain it, we are driven to panic and shock. Panic starts as blind action for escape. When obstructed, panic initiates shock, the freeze reaction of the stress response. Hans Selye's well-known model for adaptation to stress reveals the initial reaction to stress is fight or flight.[2] A third response has been identified as the freeze reaction. Energetically, the freeze response protects us from blowing our circuitry with more energy than our body and/or mind can handle. It protects us from having a heart attack, nervous breakdown, or mental crisis.

Although the function of anxiety alerts us to incongruence and can reveal patterns that work against our well-being, we need to be able to intercept the intensity when the charge keeps us from enjoying life. The message of prolonged anxiety may be that the incongruence we sense comes from our high-intensity lifestyle. Are we over-extended, do we have too much job stress, or are we experiencing unhealed trauma? Making a commitment toward change and supporting it with professional help may be useful long-term strategies. In the moment, the following process for intercepting anxiety may help.

Intercepting Anxiety

- Choose to shift into the mindful observer. Support the shift by pressing the point in the middle of the inside of your wrist (HP-6; see Illustration 13.1).

- Follow the physical feelings of anxiety into the center. Acknowledge the agitation, vibration, and other sensations, and name them Anxiety. Access gratitude and be open to any insights anxiety may share.

- ☯ Direct the energy of anxiety into flow. Visualize the energy of anxiety streaming into, through, and out of your body and into the Earth. Where it has left from, only you remain. Maintaining this image will reduce anxiety in moments.

- ☯ Support yourself. Cover your heart with your hands and feel protected. Induce a transcendent emotion such as unconditional love, gratitude, or devotion. Call up an image or connect with a deity or spiritual essence that brings calming energy. State: "I am safe. There is a way through and I am enough."

Be open to the information that anxiety might share about what changes are available to you, what choices are open, and so on. Every path offers a way out, even if we can't imagine it.

My original insight into managing anxiety was inspired by the Litany Against Fear in the 1965 science fiction book *Dune* by Frank Herbert. It reads:

I must not fear.
Fear is the mind-killer.
Fear is the little-death that brings total obliteration.
I will face my fear.
I will permit it to pass over me and through me.
And when it has gone past, I will turn the inner eye to see its path.
Where the fear has gone there will be nothing...
Only I will remain.

This is an extremely powerful litany to manage anxiety.

Freedom From Manipulation

Emotions have characteristics similar to those of electromagnetics and the vibratory field of sound in physics. Individual emotions appear as measurable changes in frequency that permeate and affect the entire body, including the brain. As shown in research conducted by the Institute of

HeartMath, emotional states and information can be transmitted from one person to another through the electromagnetic energy field of the heart.[3] Although this is an exciting, empowering, and natural form of communication, as with all communications it can also be used to manipulate others.

Emotional fields are always involved when one person influences another, as when a parent intimidates a child or a charismatic leader manipulates followers. Techniques that generate emotional fields are used by cults, political leaders, motivational speakers, religious zealots, and social activists. To create change, people must be engaged through their emotions. Intellectual understanding will bring agreement, but action requires the passion of emotion. Manipulating the emotional field of followers is how politicians keep the constituents of political parties engaged in passionate argument and fighting with each other while they construct devastating change under the radar.

Energetically, manipulation brings people's frequencies into resonance with each other, often with entrainment techniques. Entrainment brings the varied frequencies of different people into step with each other through a periodic stimulus. This technique can entrain brainwave frequency and influence how we think. The step and cadence of marching, for example, is thought to bring the brainwaves of soldiers into resonance with each other. Infusing the emotional field with ideals and passion creates an easily motivated machine. Watching old film footage of Adolf Hitler's army marching in the square after a rousing speech brings home the effectiveness of this technique.

When the group mind shares a frequency, emotions can be inflamed with only a small impetus. Interestingly, leaders of this type have little power of their own. Their power is given to them as energy inputs from their followers. Once the leader has set a direction, he or she no longer has real control of where it goes. It develops its own momentum, and the leader must lead where the group mind is focused. Should he deviate from the direction he set in motion, he will be devoured.

The cadence of voice used in speeches, music, and chanting is another method for entrainment. To be clear, these techniques can be used for very good ends as well. The problem is not the technique; it's the motive. Open and honest intent is disclosed and allows for choice.

In the natural world we are entrained to the frequency of the Earth, called the Schumann Resonance. Within this frequency range, our energy field is in harmony with the larger whole of the planet, and our personal energy field is magnified. We are centered, grounded, and in control of our fate. Whenever we are out of balance, being in nature has the ability to return us to our center. The unnatural frequencies of technology destabilize our energy field, making us more susceptible to outside influence.

Here is a technique for becoming free of undue external influence.

Eliminating Manipulation

- Choose to shift to the mindful observer. Support the shift by pressing the point in the middle of the back of your wrist (TW; see Illustration 13.1) to assist the flow of energy through your bodymind.

- Feel the discomfort of being pulled out of your center and name it manipulation. Elicit compassion and be open to any messages.

- Send the flow of energy from your discomfort into your boundary. In your mind, establish the perimeter of your boundary. From your Solar Plexus chakra, imagine pushing energy outward to the perimeter. Pulse your energy away and establish "Not me." Pull your energy in and establish "Me." Let energy flow into, through, and around your boundary.

- Stand in your core. See yourself surrounded with brilliant flares of light. Be impenetrable.

Healing Through Grief

Grief is one of the most profound emotions that we can experience. Loss damages the light fibers that connect us to others as well as to our dreams, leaving us lonely, lost, and abandoned. Grief is not passive; it is a powerful force that heals our energy structures and repairs our light fibers. It prepares us for reconnection. The process is innate and does not require that we direct it. The bodymind knows how to heal. All that grief asks is that we retreat for a time from the demands of life by moving into our core and surrendering to our feelings. Healing is the natural result. However, when we resist what we feel, we can be lost in grief for a very long time.

Loss can be complicated by many layers of emotion. Losing someone we love or failing in a heart-centered endeavor activates our defenses. Grief serves to burn through those defenses to reveal the bottom line of our inner truth. Falseness cannot survive in the face of grief. The raw force of this emotion breaks through the illusions we construct to protect ourselves from our shortcomings and failings, providing clarity and self-honesty. With our defenses disarmed, we have the opportunity to reconcile our beliefs and past actions with our inner truth. Regret, guilt, unfinished conversations, and unrealized dreams are brought into the light for healing.

Support yourself in the following exercise by retreating to a quiet, comfortable place where you are safe and will be undisturbed.

Four-Fold Process for Healing Through Grief

- Once you're comfortable, take a few minutes to center, ground, and shift into mindful observer. Choose to surrender. One at a time, press all three of the acupressure points in Illustration 13.1 (H-5, HP-6, and Lu-6), alternating back and forth.

- Allow your defenses to fall and your feelings to rise. Let regret, guilt, and painful memories be present. Let the loneliness, fear, and uncertainty speak. Try not to hide. Instead, allow the pain of grief to burn through each feeling. Listen for the truth embedded within your memories and feelings. Allow the bigger picture to be revealed.

- Allow the energy of grief to flow into your core, fortifying your inner strength.

- Breathe light into your pain and allow grief to direct your healing.

Releasing Hatred

Hatred is generated when the foundation and core of our life are threatened. Someone tries to destroy the empire we've built, turn our spouse against us, or viciously violate someone we love. Threats to our core are personal and all-consuming. The hatred they inspire snaps our attention into focus and marshals resources we didn't know we had. Hatred is an all-consuming emotion with enormous capacity to destroy. One incidence of true hatred is enough to last a lifetime.

When we survive an attack to our core and overcome the threat, we achieve previously unimagined abilities, insight, and strength. It is common, after time has passed, to be thankful for the gifts the challenge brought. When we do not overcome the threat, hatred fosters the desire for vengeance. These two emotions together—hatred and vengeance—will either destroy us or set us free.

Hatred provides the force to survive extreme deprivation and abominable abuse. Without taking away from the survival benefits, when we are in thrall to hatred, its message is: *Look within*. It is a call to address our inner shadow. The shadow is a concept developed by Carl Jung, the Swiss psychiatrist who studied under Freud. Jung's work bridges modern psychology and spirituality, and his innate grasp of the manner in which spirit achieves psychological form is the foundation of many of the concepts we have today regarding the workings of the subconscious mind and how to interact with it through active imagination.

In the shadow concept, we submerge parts of our self that we are not proud of in our subconscious, forming a shadow self. Not liking this part of us, we project it to the outside world where we can focus our anger and disgust at trying to change it. We can spend our life hating something external that is merely a reflection of our internal shadow. The key to shadow work is to accept all parts of who we are. In the words of Carl Jung, "We cannot change anything unless we accept it. Condemnation does not liberate, it oppresses."[4]

In this way of thinking, all hatred that is not formed from an extreme threat to survival is really self-hatred. Hatred is a nuclear bomb on a seek-and-destroy mission; when the external target proves to be a projection from self, we must dismantle it or be destroyed. By accepting our shadow we can integrate the unhealed parts of us that we project out and return home. Change and growth come through acceptance. When hatred raises its head, it is a message from our core to initiate compassion.

Energetically, hatred mobilizes our energy in externally focused aggression. It creates a fortress around our core that keeps all energy, including that of love and forgiveness, from penetrating. It is usually generated from our solar plexus, yet takes over our entire system. Intercepting it is accomplished only through a true desire for change and willingness to examine self. If we do, hatred can illuminate the darkness within and reveal that there is no separation. What we hate in another is a reflection of self, and we truly are all one.

When hatred toward someone else is taking you over, try this process.

Intercepting Hatred

- Shift into the mindful observer. Support the shift by pressing the point in the webbing of the thumb (LI-4; see Illustration 13.1) to stimulate downward-flowing energy.
- Follow the feeling of hatred into the center of your heart and name it self-rejection.

- ❷ Visualize the energy that surrounds your heart and core softening and becoming liquid. Send it into flow by imagining it streaming through your body and into the Earth.

- ❷ Support self-love. Imagine your heart as a beautiful room—warm, cozy, and inviting. See the presence of your spirit guides inviting you home. Accept the invitation. Welcome the person you hate to join you in sanctuary and know that we are one.

Resolving Conflict

Conflict occurs with the closing of the resonant field between people. Communication is difficult because the emotional energy field is not conductive. Consequently, we are stuck in a mindset of *us versus them* and connect through the consciousness of the Solar Plexus chakra. The benefit of this consciousness are self-empowerment and reliance. Some of the challenges are finding ways to work with others, allowing space for another's truth, and acknowledging other people's contribution. Resolving conflict requires finding one emotional agreement that can allow flow between the parties. This can be as simple as agreeing to disagree, finding a common point within the conflict, or simply affording each other human respect.

The problem is that conflict brings up many past patterns. Every past conflict leaves its mark and influences our present response. If defensiveness is our pattern, we will become argumentative and fight for our perspective. If fear is our pattern, we will collapse and give away our dreams. If manipulation is our pattern, we will seek to find the other person's emotional buttons and push them. If drama is our pattern, we will create chaos. Often the last thing on our minds in a conflict is to find a solution; all we really want is to win. Moving into heart-centered awareness changes the dynamic to one in which a solution can be found.

Conflict is about engagement. We think we are at opposite ends of the pole from our opponent; however, the pole is connecting us. When we are in conflict, our energy entwines with the other person in an intense embrace. Resolution requires disengaging our energy from the conflict and finding one place of agreement that can create flow in the situation. The best way to do this is through a transcendent emotion or the development of empathy.

Resolving Conflict

- ❸ Choose to shift into the mindful observer and support the switch by pressing a point in the middle of the back side of your wrist (TW-4; see Illustration 13.1). Move into heart-centered awareness and engage empathy.

- ❸ Follow the feelings of conflict into your body. Name them point of view. Acknowledge their merits and their failings.

- ❸ Direct energy into flow. In order to flow into a solution, disengage your energy from the conflict. Pull your attachments back in to your center. Send energy along the lines of tension into the one single area of agreement you can find. Discharge excess energy by flowing tension out of the muscles and into the Earth. Flow into your Heart chakra to support your core needs. Stand in your center.

- ❸ Take heart-centered action by being emotionally congruent. When you are emotionally congruent you are grounded, centered, and strong. Put your agenda on the table and back it up with your energy. Look for a place of agreement that can bring about a win-win solution and be open to hearing another perspective. Everything is point of view. Imagine sharing the same one.

When you use this approach you have no control over whether the person you are in disagreement with will step up or not. However, assuming the other person will not and using your mistrust to stay in opposition makes you the one who shirks resolution. Take the higher ground and be willing to walk away from the table if need be.

Undoing Stress

Stress is not a single emotion, but a complex of emotional and physical reactions that arise in response to challenge. In itself stress is not harmful; it helps us meet life demands as well as emergency situations through the production of cortisol and adrenaline. However, in prolonged situations these hormones undermine our health. Sustained stress causes problems such as weight gain or loss, insomnia, high blood pressure, high cholesterol, elevated glucose (diabetes), suppressed immune function, increased inflammation, and acceleration of aging. And of course, stress can create negative health habits such as drinking, smoking, and overeating, too.

This list of health issues alone is sure to elevate stress levels! The truth is that everyone lives with some type of prolonged stress, such as job insecurity, an unhappy marriage, financial uncertainty, or even abusive situations that we are afraid to leave. It's easy to see the toll stress can take on our physical health. Emotionally, stress creates distortion so that we are unable to see and perceive situations clearly. Consequently, our judgment is off and so is our ability to communicate. Decisions and relationships suffer.

On the bright side, stress is a reaction, not a condition, and we can change our reactions. We may not be able to change all of the conditions in our life that are stressful, but we can change how we respond. Studies reported in Chapter 14 suggest that those who are well nurtured handle stress better than those who are not. In addition, many of the conditions that cause stress are self-created. We pile on one expectation after the other, filling our life to the brim with things that we have to do. Is this because we are hiding from something, or are we looking for something?

Stress may be asking us to look at our priorities and reorganize our life. The World Happiness Report for 2012 identified Scandinavian countries as having the happiest citizens in the world.[6] The report found that money is not the top indicator of happiness; quality of relationship is. If we are trading the quality of our relationships in order to make more money so we can be happy, we may want to rethink our strategy.

Undoing Stress Exercise

- ❧ Choose to shift into the mindful observer. Support the shift by pressing the point in the webbing of the thumb (LI-4; see Illustration 13.1) to stimulate downward-flowing energy and reduce the frazzle of stress.

- ❧ Feel and follow the tension of stress into the body. Move your body to follow the twists and turns of stressed tension. Twirl, roll, curl, and stretch into the position that relieves your stress. Stay in this position and notice what you feel. What do you need nurtured? Can you give it to yourself? What's missing in your life?

- ❧ Direct the energy by letting the tension flow from your muscles out through your feet and into the Earth. Send energy flowing into your heart to strengthen your core.

- ❧ Create heart-centered action and give yourself whatever feels nurturing for you. Support your core and your dreams, and allow yourself to relax. You are enough.

Victim Mentality

The victim mentality is not an emotion; it is a way of thinking that impacts the way life unfolds. It consists of blaming others for every mishap that occurs. This is not the same as being the victim of violent crime, domestic abuse, or persecution. If you are the victim of abuse, it is not your fault. Find a safe place and get help.

In a victim mentality, we are unable to see the connection between our own actions and the events in our life. For example, we think we lost our job because our boss doesn't like us, overlooking the fact that the dislike originates from our inability to be on time or finish our workload. Here's an example: Ted asks Karen what she would like for her birthday. Karen responds, "Oh, don't worry, I really don't want anything more than a nice evening at home with you." When Ted brings home a bouquet of flowers, Karen is disappointed, thinking, "He doesn't really care about me. If he did he would have known how much I would love a gold bracelet." Not only has Karen made herself a victim by not saying what she really wanted, but she has made Ted her victimizer. No matter how hard Ted tries, because he can't read her mind, he will always in some way cause her pain.

The interesting thing about having a victim mentality is that we really seem to enjoy the pain we bring on ourselves. Sometimes it makes us feel heroic: *Look at all I suffer; only a very strong person is subjected to this much.* Other times it makes us feel special: *God has chosen me to suffer the pain of the world for others.* The fact that neither of these perspectives is true doesn't matter. When we are victims we don't want to take responsibility for our choices, behaviors, or challenges. Maybe we are afraid we aren't strong enough or that we will be judged, or maybe we want to take the easy road and entice someone to rescue us.

A surprising number of people are willing to ride in on a white horse and rescue the victim. They are willing to agree that the person is blameless in exchange for the emotional lift of being the rescuer. Ted may have started out as a rescuer, but eventually Karen's self-sabotage made him to blame for her unhappiness. Their marriage can be saved, however, if they listen to the message of victimhood as a call to claim their personal power.

As with all the changes initiated in this chapter, shifting from being a victim requires shifting out of our established point of view. We must choose to meet every challenge with personal responsibility. Not surprisingly, when we shift out of victim mode, we often slide to the other end of spectrum, heaping blame and self-loathing on our heads. It takes effort to swing back and forth, consistently avoiding the center. However, we all have a mindful observer who knows exactly what we are doing. Shifting the victim mentality requires listening to the observer part of self.

When you meet with obstacles and want to shift from the victim mentality, try an approach like this.

Shifting out of Victim

☯ Choose to shift to the mindful observer. Press a point in the pad of your thumb (Lu-6; see Illustration 13.1) to support the shift.

☯ Follow the feelings of victimhood inside. Feel the resentment, longing, anger, and shame, and name them all victimhood. Acknowledge the inner victim and listen to any message it has. Ask yourself: What am I afraid to hear or see?

☯ Direct your energy into your core. Acknowledge the powerful being you are. Let your energy radiate out from your core.

☯ Take heart-centered action. Express gratitude for all the good things in life. Forget about finding someone to blame, and look for solutions.

Illustration 13.1: Acupressure Points on the Hand

Illustrations by Colin Andrews

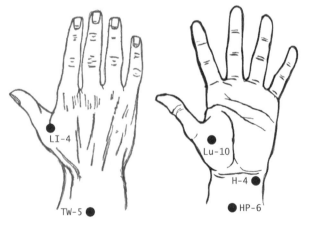

Meridian abbreviations:

LI = Large Intestine

TW = Triple Heater

H = Heart

HP = Heart Protector

Lu = Lung

Chapter 14

Emotional Dynamics of Health

Using the Four-Fold Process to shift the energy of overwhelming emotions is a step toward better health. It's no surprise that emotions and physical health are linked. The body responds to every thought and feeling we have. If we take offense at something said to us, or are startled by a noise in the basement, the body doesn't ask whether anger and fear are warranted; it immediately goes to the sympathetic nervous system and produces stress hormones to initiate fast and effective fight or flight. As stressful situations end, fear and/or anger subside and the body switches back to the parasympathetic nervous system that favors rest, digest, and repair mechanisms. In this state, the cascade of chemicals includes endorphins and dopamine—feel-good molecules.

We can think of sympathetic and parasympathetic as the defense and nurture responses of the body; the yang and yin, respectively, of our body-mind. We are meant to move between the two in dynamic balance, changing in and out of different states as needed.

When basic survival needs are met, the natural human state is happiness. Undercurrents of less-comfortable emotions nudge us out of complacency and into action. This is healthy and even enjoyable; however, prolonged stays in emotions that stimulate the sympathetic nervous system can produce harmful health effects.

Although indirect links between emotions and health are abundant (as seen concerning stress in Chapter 13), the question arises: Can emotions really impact our health in direct and measurable ways? Direct links between emotions and physical health have not always been accepted. This changed with the publication of the Adverse Childhood Experience (ACE) study, the largest investigation to date into the relationship between childhood trauma and adult health problems. The research was conducted from 1995 to 1997 at Kaiser Permanente in collaboration with the Centers for Disease Control and Prevention, and involved 17,000 participants.

The findings of the ACE study suggest that childhood trauma is one of the most important risk factors for adult health problems.[1] The authors concluded that the study "...documents the conversion of traumatic emotional experiences in childhood into organic disease later in life."[2] Some of the conversion of emotional trauma into poor health can be related to behavior. For example, children who have learned to not value themselves are more likely to adopt unhealthy lifestyles as they grow up: eating poorly, smoking, drinking, and becoming involved in high-risk behaviors.

The results also went beyond behavior to include organic predispositions. The ACE study looks at how health is impacted by *past* emotions, but it's no secret that maintaining a positive mental outlook and happy emotions improves our health in the present. For one thing, stress is decreased, which automatically lowers health risks and increases immune function. Psychoneuroimmunology is the study of how mind and emotions affect the endocrine, nervous, and immune systems. Substantial evidence points to the roles that mind and emotions play in health. The power of positive prayer and thinking is also well documented.

It is tempting when first looking at the impact of emotions on health to feel afraid of feeling afraid. In other words, we judge that every "negative" emotion is going to cause an illness. The result is that many people try to suppress emotions that they consider harmful or transform them into something else, which is just another form of suppression. We need not be afraid of what we feel. We must remember that each emotion has function, and emotional awareness helps us receive the message that allows the emotion to subside. Using the Four-Fold Process to work through and release both current and submerged emotions provides a path to better health. In short, our past does not have to determine our present.

Some of the following sections explore current science, experiments, and studies. However, science is not necessary to experience the concepts. The exercises that are included are all that is needed to experience the healing benefit of emotion.

Physio-Emotional Health

One of the reasons overcoming past trauma is challenging, whether from adverse childhood experiences or traumatic experiences at any age, is because the memory is stored in our tissue at a cellular level. The stored memory impacts muscle tension, which can create chronic muscle pain (as explained in Chapter 5). Our body language, pain patterns, and armored segments all provide clues into how we have stored the trauma from our past.

The body's cellular responses are similar to those of single-celled organisms. Like an amoeba confronted with pain, the cell contracts and withdraws; when confronted with pleasure, the boundary softens. We see this in action when we place our hand into hot water. If the water is scalding, our muscles contract and pull our hand out of the water. The contraction begins as a cellular retraction combined with a motor reflex initiated from the spinal cord. By the time the brain knows about the event, the hand is already being withdrawn. Equally, if the water is pleasingly warm, the cell boundary softens, circulation increases, and relaxation occurs.

The body's desire to avoid pain also includes the pain of emotion. Painful emotions create body discomfort, and muscles in the segment where the emotion occurs contract around it in an action called muscle splinting (see Chapter 5). When muscle splinting occurs around a physical injury, the tightened muscles reduce the risk of further damage. When splinting occurs around emotional pain, muscles are also trying to limit the amount of harm. There is only so much emotional pain a person can handle, and splinting is one way to manage it.

In time, splinting hardens into patterns of unconscious muscle holding known as body armor. (Appendix B includes a map of body segments and a table of corresponding emotions.) The problem is that whereas muscle contraction of a segment might reduce the feeling of emotional pain, it also diminishes the feeling of all the other emotions associated with that area. The armor that blocks pain and grief blocks joy and love as well. Armor that protects against anxiety in the pit of the stomach also numbs the satisfaction of achievement.

The suppression of painful emotion not only blocks healthy emotions, but it also reduces mobility in the area. This can cause skeletal pain and spinal restrictions that compress the nerve roots traveling to the organs in the dermatome segment of the muscle armor. The loss of nerve innervation may in some cases create organ dysfunction.

When the body is armored against grief, sadness, and other painful emotions, our emotional life is flat-lined. The normal ups and downs that occur as emotions are interacting with our environment are dulled. Along with a sense of humor and fun, we lose perception and insight. The isolation created by muscle armor reduces blood and nerve flow to the tissue, and also reduces the flow of energy to and from other people and our environment. Isolation is the major cause of illness.

Although suppressing emotions may help us manage in the short term, it is clear that at some point we must release them. On the positive side, understanding the process of emotional holding also provides the key to letting it go.

Energy Cysts

The concept of an energy cyst was developed by Dr. John Upledger, an osteopath who created the CranioSacral Therapy balancing system derived from the original work of Dr. William Sutherland published in 1930. The term describes the energetic result of emotional trauma in the body.

An energy cyst occurs when the energy of an emotion becomes trapped in the fascia of muscles and organs due to a physical injury. It can also be called an emotional hotspot as the cyst contains the emotion that the person felt at the time of the accident as well as the energy of the impact. The site of the energy cyst can be where the injury actually occurred or where the force of the impact stopped its travel into the body. A bad fall onto the tailbone, for example, can create an energy cyst at the site of impact, or the force can travel up the spine and create a cyst where the motion was stopped by the snapping of the neck, or both.

When an energy cyst forms, healing of the injury proceeds until it contacts the emotional hotspot. At that point, the emotion of the accident must be addressed. Otherwise, healing cannot continue, which results in chronic pain. For example, a person who is thrown headfirst into the windshield during a car accident may develop an energy cyst in the neck or head. In the weeks after the accident, the pain of the physical injury continues to recede until it reaches a point where it no longer gets any better. Nothing physically shows up as wrong in x-rays or CAT scans, and the problem is considered to be in the soft tissue (muscle and fascia). Physical therapy and massage may help, but they will eliminate the pain only if the emotional energy that traveled into the body is acknowledged, processed, and released.

An energy cyst can contain a variety of emotions. It may hold the energy of fear present at the time of the accident as well as the deeper primordial fear of death. It may contain anger at the driver that would be too debilitating to acknowledge, or it might encompass the helplessness of being out of control. Whatever is lodged there, it will interfere with the healing process until it is released.

Healing Past Trauma

Unprocessed emotions must be cleared to experience optimal health. Yet, many people have no idea of how to do it. Healing emotional or physical trauma is no different from learning how to contact and release emotional patterns (as discussed in Chapter 13). The process is initiated through the desire to shift, then feeling and following the emotion into the body, contacting and acknowledging its message, and allowing it to flow. Although we can do this ourselves, by using techniques such as the Four-Fold Process, the Emotional Freedom Technique, and others, a more powerful change occurs when contacted through bodywork focused on emotional processing.

Bodywork that incorporates emotional processing, such as Jin Shin Do® Bodymind Acupressure®, SomatoEmotional Release, Reiki, or any number of others, has the advantage of adding a witness and guide to the process which more firmly grounds it in reality and also maintains safety. A list of contacts to find such a practitioner is found in Appendix C.

When an emotion that is lodged in the body shifts, the energy contained in the tissue is released. Any of these manifestations might occur as the body discharges excess emotional energy: shaking, yawning, crying, laughing, sighing, profuse sweating, and trembling. Rather than being concerned or upset, allow the process to complete and move out of the system. These signs indicate a major change has occurred.

Releasing past trauma does not have to include reliving the trauma, although it might; it can be as simple as making a choice. Here is an example.

Shirley was a client who came in with pain from a past skiing accident. At the time of the injury, she was a relatively new skier and wanted to go with her husband on an extended ski trip. After taking a dozen lessons and mastering the easy slope, she decided to prove she was ready for the trip by tackling an advanced slope.

As Shirley rode the ski lift to the top of the trail, she looked down at the mountain and knew she wasn't ready. Her heart pounded and she shook with trepidation. Determined not to let fear get the best of her, she suppressed her feelings and forced herself to head down the mountain. Not too far from the top, she had a severe accident that resulted in a concussion. A year later, she still suffered neck and shoulder pain, along with recurrent migraines. Although she was able to function and was still intent on learning to ski, every time she put on skis, her vision blacked and she was paralyzed with fear.

People who heard Shirley's story confirmed her conclusion: Fear had sabotaged her attempt to ski the big slope. If she had not been afraid, everyone agreed, she would not have had the accident. Shirley underwent hypnotherapy and psychotherapy hoping to reduce her fear and alleviate her symptoms, to no avail. She used visualization and relived the event while seeing herself calm and collected and skiing perfectly. She used affirmations, telling herself she was safe. Nothing worked.

During a bodywork session, Shirley allowed herself to fully feel the terror she had experienced before and during the accident, and followed the feeling to where it originated in her body. Using body processing techniques, she dialogued with the feeling. Shirley started the session angry at her fear for sabotaging her; however, the process allowed her to understand that her fear had wanted only to warn her so that she might avoid getting hurt.

"What was I supposed to do?" she asked. "Let fear control me?" Even as she asked the question she knew the answer: She was supposed to let the fear guide her. She had not been ready for the slope, and although she wouldn't admit it, she knew it. Suppressing the fear severed her connection to her information system and undermined her choice. If she had listened to how she felt, taken a few more lessons, and practiced on the intermediate slope, she might have been ready for her husband's ski trip. Acknowledging the message in her fear allowed release. At this point Shirley felt a deeper, more pressing question: What had she needed to prove to her husband? What had she really been afraid of?

Once the energy that was stored in her tissue was released, Shirley felt a significant inner change. Believing that her emotions had sabotaged her, she had lost self-trust. After understanding how her emotions had been working to protect her, she felt profound gratitude and moved into greater self-trust.

She returned to taking skiing lessons with no further episodes of blacking out. In letting go of the past, she did not need to relive the accident; she only needed to acknowledge the message and discharge the energy.

Here is an example of how to use the Four-Fold Process for healing past trauma.

Healing Past Trauma

- **Choose to shift.** Move into the mindful observer and make the decision to forgive the past, accept the unacceptable, and move on.

- **Feel and follow.** Feel your physical pain and relax into it. Instead of resisting and suppressing, surrender. Think of your pain as an entity outside of yourself, such as an animal, spirit, or being. Talk to it. Tell it everything you feel. Detail your disappointment, fear, anger, and resentment. It doesn't matter how many times you have said these things before; say them again from the perspective of non-judgment. Tell your pain what you want: Do you want it to go away, disappear, heal, or what? When you have said everything there is to say, stop and listen. Pay attention to feelings, images, sensations, and sudden knowings.

- **Direct the energy.** Energy may simply discharge in a rush of tingles, inner vibration, or trembling. Let it go. Direct the energy into flow. Disengage any attachments you have to the past.

- **Create heart-centered action.** Allow yourself to feel a transcendent emotion such as appreciation, gratitude, or joy. Use the energy of these emotions to support and nurture yourself. Feel the unobstructed flow of positive energy through your body. Let every cell receive it. What else would you like to create with this energy? Imagine it!

DNA and Emotions

DNA is the genetic blueprint or instruction manual for the development and function of an organism. A gene is an identifiable unit of DNA that produces a specific trait, and the genome is the complete set of genes in an organism. The Human Genome Project was designed to map the human genome. When the project began in 1990, scientists hoped to chart the genetic causes of disease.

Initially scientists anticipated finding a minimum of 100,000 different human genes. As the project went on, however, they discovered the number of genes that make a human is about 25,000—the same number as less-complex life forms such as fish. A NOVA program, "Ghost in Your Genes," that aired October 16, 2007, on PBS, states, "Even more startling, it turned out the same key genes that make a fruitfly, a worm, or a mouse also make a human. Chimpanzees share 98.9 percent of our genome."[3]

The complexity of life turns out to have as much—if not more—to do with *how* genes are expressed as what genes are present. How behavior, nutrition, and environmental factors influence the expression of our genetic code is a field of study called *epigenetics*, and it may hold insights into why childhood trauma impacts adult health.

Scientists learned that nature has devised ways for silencing genes that we don't want expressed by covering them with a molecule called a methyl group. Methyl coverings are called tags. Methyl tags are imprinted on our genes as part of a learning process and in many cases are inherited.[4] The ability to turn genes on and off involves creating and removing tags, which requires an adequate supply of methyl groups, proper enzymes, and correct information. Nutrition, toxic exposure, emotions, and stress are key factors in assuring an adequate supply of methyl groups and are therefore factors in our genetic expression.

Genetic research with rats helps us understand the ACE study findings. As explained on NOVA, the gene that lowers stress hormones in the blood of rats is turned on in those rats who are licked and nurtured by their mothers, and turned off in those neglected by their mothers. In other words, less-nurtured rats were programmed from childhood to have elevated levels of stress, such that events that carry little stress for well-nurtured rats carry significant stress for neglected rats. Although we can easily see the relationship between poor parenting and limited stress skills in our human experience, this study reveals the genetic link.

Says neuroscientist Michael Meaney of McGill University in the NOVA interview, "If you grow up in a family that involves abuse, neglect, harsh and inconsistent discipline, then you are statistically more likely to develop depression, anxiety, and drug abuse. And I don't think that surprises anyone. But what is interesting is that you are also more likely to develop diabetes, heart disease, and obesity. And the stress hormones actively promote the development of these individual diseases."[5]

These studies open the door to the realization that emotions may be as important as nutrition and toxins in turning genetic material on and off. In addition, the study provides a mechanism for understanding how emotions impact our health, and may have profound effects on treatment and prevention of disease. In my opinion, however, they stop short of asking the bigger question: Can we overcome early programming with positive steps in adulthood? My answer is a resounding yes.

Epigenetics demonstrates that the use of methyl tags for gene silencing is a form of learning. In the rat experiment, for example, the early experience of maternal abandonment turned off the stress-lowering gene. Can positive experiences turn it back on? Can we learn to express our genetic material differently by how we manage our emotions later in life? Experience indicates that what we do with emotions generated from adverse childhood experiences is as important as the experiences themselves. As children we don't have a choice in how we experience ACEs. As adults, we do have a choice in how we re-experience them.

Insights From Our Elders

Reducing childhood trauma is the first and foremost desired outcome of this research. Healthy living in spite of our past trauma must be the next. Surprisingly, people who have addressed and overcome childhood trauma consider what they learned to be the gift they have to give the world. Like James Kirk in *Star Trek V: The Final Frontier*, they see their pain as an integral part of their strength, success, and happiness. Is it possible that the emotions that produce poor health are not negative by the fact of existing but are negative by the choice of what we do with them?

Insights come from our elders. Although science has often thought long life to be primarily a function of our genes, study after study of our oldest citizens reveals that positive attitude and resiliency to stress are key attributes. In the Longevity Genes project at the Albert Einstein College of Medicine's Institute for Aging Research, a study of 243 Ashkenazi Jewish adults between 100 and 107 years of age showed that emotions are important factors. Says Dr. Nil Barzilai, a study coauthor, in an ABC interview, "The results indicated they [centenarians] had two things—a positive attitude for life, meaning they are optimistic, easygoing, extraverted, laughed more; and expressed emotions rather than bottling them up."[6]

What is most significant is that these people did not avoid pain and suffering as children or adults. Quite the opposite: Some child survivors of Nazi concentration camps, certainly the most horrific ACE we can imagine, are now octogenarians. What they seem to have done differently is not suppress, hold on to, or repress their stress, grief, and pain, but felt it, processed it, created action, and moved on.

In light of this research, the empowered position is that our health and longevity are not solely in the hands of our past or our genes. Good nutrition, exercise, clean air and water, and a toxin-free environment form the foundation for good health, but our mind and emotions are equally important. The choices we make today in how we live with our emotions and how we align them with our mind is our most commanding ally. Using techniques such as the Four-Fold Process is our path to better health. When we bring our mind into alignment with our emotions, we are activating the most powerful tool we have: intention.

Energetic Considerations

We have said that emotions have electromagnetic field characteristics and that individual emotions appear as measurable changes in frequency that permeate and affect the entire body, including the brain. Neuroscientist Dr. Candace Pert suggest that our emotional field coordinates internal processes. In an interview posted at *www.6seconds.org*, Dr. Pert explains the mechanisms at work.

Essentially, every cell has receptor sites for the peptides that carry emotions. The specialized cells of nerve ganglia have thousands (see Chapter 4). As a cell's receptor site is activated, Pert says, an electrical charge is passed inside the cell, initiating a biochemical response. At the same time, the charge changes the cell's electrical frequency, which influences the vibration of the energy field. Says Pert, "We're vibrating like a tuning fork— we send out vibration to other people. We broadcast and receive. Thus the emotions orchestrate the interactions among all our organs and systems to control that."[7]

Pert isn't the only scientist thinking outside of the box. The HeartMath Institute studies the field effect of emotions in relation to DNA based on the theory of heart intelligence proposed by Doc Childre, stress expert, author, and creator of the HeartMath system. Childre proposes that DNA act as antennae tuned to the organizing electromagnetic field produced by the heart. Heartfelt positive emotions are said to increase the flow of information and therefore positively impact the epigenetics of DNA. In a study authored by Rollin McCraty, when heartfelt emotions were coupled with intent to interact with DNA, changes in the configuration of DNA were reported.[8]

When considered along with the research into the electromagnetic waves of DNA by Nobel Laureate Luc Montagnier, the HeartMath results don't seem as impossible as they otherwise might. In the same way that it is difficult to understand how the dark matter of the universe creates the scaffolding of matter, it is difficult to link the concept of subtle energy as an organizing field of life with current scientific research. Attempts are in their infancy and will surely grow and develop. As with all science, some aspects will be proved correct, and some will be put aside or will move in a new direction.

We don't need to wait for science to prove what we already feel and interact with. We know that we feel and look more vital, and experience better health when we are in our natural state of happiness. When we curtail this state by holding on to emotions that are past their use-by date, we know it is unhealthy by how we feel. Although understanding the mechanisms is interesting, our ability to interact with our emotions comes from our experience.

Research is important in its ability to change the condition it reveals. In this case, we can promote healing by letting go of past pain and moving on. Although physical illness or disease requires physical attention, we have the power to shift even the most difficult physical illness into a better direction. The body is designed to heal; our intent can be the tipping point. Never stop medical treatment; offer your body additional support with the following process.

Intentional Health Exercise

- **Choose to shift into the mindful observer.** Move beyond judging your health status, emotions, or state of mind; accept what is.

- **Feel and follow.** Take your awareness into the area where your illness resides. Imagine your illness as a being separate from yourself—perhaps an animal or spirit. Notice how much of your energy is entwined with the illness. Tell the illness everything you feel about sharing your body. Don't hold back; share everything. Consider what will change in your life if your illness is gone. Tell the illness exactly what you want to do once it leaves. Stop and listen for any response.

- **Direct the energy.** Disengage your energy from your illness. Send energy from your core into your cells and allow flow into all of your cells.

❷ **Create heart-centered action.** Build the energy in your core through your breath. Imagine your core as a diamond and allow the diamond energy to brightly shine. Hold the intent of returning to the ideal expression of your ideal blueprint. Imagine shining the diamond light of your core into, through, and around the DNA in every cell in your body. Radiate health. Support your belief with action.

If we can apply the epigenetic studies to our emotional process, then what we learn can be inherited by our children. In fact, it becomes part of the legacy we pass on to the next generation.

Chapter 15
Emotional Opportunity

Employing emotions to create better health is only one of the many ways we can use our emotional intelligence. The constant flow of energy that creates the current of our emotional life offers an untapped resource for living an empowered life. Through our emotions we have access to greater information and unlimited energy. We can use this wisdom, guidance, and energy to enhance all aspects of our life. This chapter presents a few ideas for directing our emotional energy into life-enhancing action.

Decision-Making

Emotions guide every decision we make, even the most logical. As brain research shows, emotions hold the memory of past lessons, and intelligence integrates facts and logic with emotional wisdom.[1] Our mind may rationalize our choices, justify our actions, and convince us of something we know is not right, but our emotions are the voice of our inner truth. Because emotions sense shifts of subtle energy, they provide indications of when to move and in what direction. Accessing this information adds a new dimension to decision-making; the key to success lies with intent and imagination.

Are you one of those people who always chooses the line at the grocery store that takes the longest? Next time try this simple technique: Disregard the length of the line and imagine yourself standing in one line after another while holding the intent of leaving the store as soon as possible. Try to detect a subtle difference in the flow and openness of your energy (as discussed in Chapter 12) as well as any change of emotion when imagining yourself in the different lines. The intent you hold in this exercise is important: Changing the intent could change the best line. For example, the intent to be in the line that will bring the highest good might produce a different result to intending to get out of the store quickly. There could be someone in one line whom you might want to meet.

When we are making a decision and the facts are lining up in a clear direction that feels good, the choice is obvious and easy. Regardless of whether the decision is as important as what investment to make or as unimportant as the line in a grocery store, how we feel guides our decision.

Sometimes one choice clearly seems to be the best, yet a nagging feeling holds us back. We know something is not right because we feel it. The thought that something is wrong without the feeling to go with it has little force. On the other hand, the feeling that something is wrong is often enough to stop us from action even when we can't find a single reason to substantiate it. That is because information beyond our conscious awareness wants to be heard. Emotions can help us tune in to those other factors.

The decision-making exercise begins after we've gone through the steps of reason. First, clearly define the need and the options. Whether we are deciding to stand up for ourselves in the workplace or purchase an item such as a car, or are choosing a career path, we can't make a decision unless both the need being addressed and the options before us are clearly defined. In most cases, multiple selections can easily be narrowed to two, or at most three, possibilities.

If there is no obvious choice between the remaining options, examine underlying assumptions. Many times decisions are difficult because they are framed as either/or situations in which the best choice is not on the table. For example, we are often told we have to choose between environmental health and economic growth. The idea that there is a third option such that environmental health supports economic growth is not considered. Are the choices we're looking at false choices? Are all the options on the table?

Once we've clearly outlined the benefits and challenges in the possibilities we've identified, we can take a look at core impulses. What core impulse is being met in the situation? How well does each choice meet the impulse? If the situation has been looked at in every light and all information collected, yet a clear choice that both our body and mind agree with hasn't emerged, use the Map to Decision-Making Exercise.

The Map to Decision-Making Exercise

- **Choose to shift** into the mindful observer and separate from an investment in either outcome.

- **Feel and follow** by imagining living each answer. Live the choice; see, feel, and be in the choice. Feel the emotion of it. Use active imagination to see yourself one day from now, one year from now, and five years from now. You don't need to know what happened during that time period; just hold the intent of being there and notice how you feel. What emotions are present? What sensations are in your body? Is your energy enlivened or dampened? Is it heavy or light? Upwardly or downwardly mobilized? Do you feel opened or closed?

- **Direct the energy** by looking for the decision that opens the flow. Follow the flow of energy into the scenario and magnify it.

- **Take heart-centered action.** Visualize the outcome and send all of your energy into its success.

Once a decision has been made and acted on, don't second-guess. One of the ways we sabotage ourselves is to make a choice and then withdraw our energy from it so that we don't succeed. Make the choice and support it.

Confusion

When confusion reigns in decision-making, it is a sign that we are not listening to all the aspects of our inner self or are not honoring the totality of our core. Maybe we are listening to one core impulse at the expense of another—weighing our need for creativity over our need for security, for example. Maybe we are listening to the inner critic and imagining what others will say, or are listening to the inner victim and imagining how everything will go wrong. Or perhaps we are not listening to our heart.

The best approach is to sit with the core impulses described in Chapter 9 and observe how the decision under consideration affects each impulse.

Which is most important at this time? What damage might be done if one or two impulses are neglected? We need to give a voice to the part of us that represents each impulse and listen to each one. Chances are we will discover an unacknowledged core need. Sometimes this additional voice will prompt a different choice or require an addendum to our direction. Often it only needs to be acknowledged and held in observance so that we aren't blind-sided later when this need isn't met.

Resistance

When we feel resistance to the choices before us, it is a sign that inner and outer flows are not in alignment. Something is off and we don't have all the pieces to move forward. Resistance is our bodymind maintaining integrity. Maybe something is hidden and resistance is slowing us down because we don't have all the information needed for the best decision. Maybe it is keeping us aligned with proper timing. Perhaps it is telling us that, under the surface of events, someone has a hidden agenda that is driving our choice. Or maybe it is revealing our own state of denial.

Whatever resistance is trying to say, slow down and listen. Honor the part that is reading the current and not liking the direction the river is going. Swim against the tide a little, be uncomfortable, and use the Four-Fold Process to find out what is hidden in resistance.

Developing Presence and Personal Power

Presence is an emanation from our core that reflects the depth of who we are along with our thoughts, unhealed traumas, past conditioning, beliefs, attitudes, and emotions. Through resonance, presence acts as our ambassador, attracting people, events, and conditions while negotiating the circumstances of our life. Sometimes the tone rings clear and sometimes it carries harmonics that reflect how we are responding to challenges. Consequently, our presence changes at different times, in different circumstances, and through varying degrees of stress.

The element that best establishes the power of our presence is emotional congruence. This is the state achieved when who we are internally matches our external expression. It's what is meant by being authentic, or true to our self. What people see is what they get. Our energy emanation is clear and solid. On the other hand, when we are emotionally incongruent, what we say and do does not match who we are. Our presence is infused with projections of our inner confusion, pain, hidden agendas, and so forth, making us energetically incoherent. We have lost touch with our core.

There are many reasons for losing touch with the core, but the bottom line is pain. We have been trained to believe that pain diminishes us and therefore we conceal it from others and try to convince ourselves that it is gone. Our own emotional incongruence lets us know that it's not. At different times and in different challenges, we are all susceptible to losing touch. When we are, it is not a call to judgment; it's a call to awakening.

When we are emotionally consistent, we have abundant personal power. There is no confusion distorting our core self in the goals we enact. Consequently our energy follows our mind in a straight line without divergences of inner whims and fantasies. Personal power produces actions based on clear intent and core values. A focused mind and heart have the power and presence to do anything.

Presence is built on our ability to ground, center, and maintain our boundary, as discussed in Chapter 10. Practicing those skills daily changes our relationship to our emotions. The exercise in Chapter 9, Honoring the Core, invests our presence with our heart. It is reproduced here and modified into the steps of the Four-Fold Process.

Honoring the Core and Building Presence Exercise

- **Choose to shift.** Take three deep, cleansing breaths, inhaling diamond-like clarity and exhaling everything you do not need. Imagine your breath penetrating all parts of your body. Breathe all the way into every extremity, including the ends of your hair and out into your aura.

- **Feel and follow.** Focus your attention on the center of your Heart chakra, in the center of your body, in the center of your chest. See it as a small spark of diamond-light, radiating in all directions. Feel its quality, tension, and texture. Does it have a color?

- **Direct energy.**
  - With your breath, imagine light from your spiritual source descending into your Crown chakra and connecting with the diamond in your heart.
  - Inhale light into your heart, expanding its size and brilliance. Exhale and allow the radiance of your heart to grow.

- ❷ Inhale energy up from the Earth, ascending through your body into your diamond heart. Exhale and allow the radiance of your heart to grow.
- ❷ With each inhalation, let your heart-diamond grow in size and brilliance. On the exhale, allow the radiance to shine.
- ❷ With each breath, feel the boundary of your aura expand and your presence grow.
- ❷ Feel yourself grounded and centered with your heart full.

❷ **Take heart-centered action.** Elevate with gratitude.

Expanding Creativity

Creativity is one of the most important aspects of being human. Simply put, to create is to experience the divine in our nature and also to glimpse the nature of the divine. Through creativity we express the impulse of our spirituality. Creativity is unique, generative, and fundamentally fulfilling. No person's creative expression is ever the same as another's. A thousand people can paint Motif #1, the harbor at Rockport, Massachusetts, and no one will paint it with exactly the same color, light, composition, or emotion. Creative interpretation is personal and reflects our own relationship with the cosmos.

Despite the importance of creativity to well-being, it is not something that can be artificially initiated. Energetically, the creative impulse shoots through our system and loosens our anchors. It melts our conceptual boundaries, dissolving the lines of connection that organize people, events, and ideas. The creative leap that brilliantly reorganizes the ordinary into something extraordinary rarely emerges in a step-by-step format. More often it arrives in a flash—a burst of insight that brings the same components together in all new configurations. Once we see the new array, it takes hold of our imagination and demands that we discover the steps, talent, or rationale to reveal it.

The creative inspiration is expansive. It induces excitement, passion, enthusiasm, and commitment. It commandeers our attention and energy. As much as it engages us, it also consumes us and borders on obsession. Demanding expression, creative inspiration wants to be seen, shared, and used in new ways. It does not let go of us until we follow its demands.

The worst experience for someone in the thrall of a creative vision is to experience a creative block. This is an interruption in energy flow that can arise in the face of self-doubt, deadlines, stress, and lack of sleep as well as poor health or the absence of needed information. The frustration that ensues, however, is its own salvation. Frustration snowballs into desperation whose function is to push us out of the box. Desperation jumpstarts creative insight. If we sit in the feeling of our frustration and desperation without trying to avoid the discomfort, we will emerge with the needed expression in hand.

Although we cannot force creative ideas or induce inspiration, we can support the spiral flow of creative energy that travels through the chakra system to land in the heart. It is initiated by a cascade of energy that enters through the top of the head and descends through the core of the body to the Base chakra. When we are struck with a creative insight, energy spirals through this course in nanoseconds. Bringing energy into the path and assisting its flow helps reveal where the creativity is blocked and offers support.

The Creativity Spiral Exercise

- **Choose to shift.** Close your eyes and take three deep breaths while engaging the mindful observer in heart-centered awareness.

- **Follow and listen.** Hold the creative question, project, or desire in your mind and heart. Feel, see, and sense it.

  - **Direct the energy.** Initiate the Creative Spiral (see Illustration 15.1). Imagine inspiration as bubbling energy that is pouring into the top of your head.

  - See/feel the energy cascading in a waterfall through the center line of your body, generating excitement as it fills your Base chakra with light.

  - Ground this energy in your Base chakra and allow it to gather substance and energy.

  - Visualize the energy arcing out of the left side of the Base chakra and spiraling upward into the Third Eye chakra.

  - See the energy flowing into the left side of the Third Eye, filling the chakra and enlivening it as it initiates creative vision. Affirm that you are able to see in new ways.

  - From the Third Eye, the energy continues its spiral by leaving through the right side of the chakra and arcing downward into the right side of the second chakra.

- Imagine the second chakra filling with watery light and inspiring creative passion. Support your passion with appreciation.
- See/feel the energy leaving the second chakra out the left side and arcing upward to the Throat chakra, entering the left side of the throat, where creative expression is initiated. Allow the excitement to grow as you affirm your commitment to creative action.
- Visualize the energy flowing out the right side of the Throat chakra and arcing downward to enter the right side of the solar plexus.
- In the solar plexus, allow your creativity to be empowered. Support your commitment, allowing the creative seed to further excite your system.
- See/feel empowered creative inspiration leaving the left side of the Solar Plexus chakra and arcing upward into the heart.

- **Take heart-centered action.** Visualize your heart growing in light and passion, and imagine your creative expression flowing from your heart out into the world. Affirm your creative essence.

This visualization is excellent at supporting the elements that are blocked, weak, or isolated from our creative spirit.

Growing Intuition

At 5 a.m. on a summer day in the early 1980s I was in the driver's seat of a rented car parked on the side of a deserted thoroughfare. I was working with Greenpeace in Canada on a campaign to protest the movement of uranium from a mine in Saskatchewan across the countryside by train to a port in Montreal. Its ultimate destination was a refinery in Russia. On this particular morning, we had failed in a night-long vigil to intercept the train in a staged protest.

I sat in the car next to a phone booth where another Greenpeacer, Kai Millyard, was talking to a campaign coordinator. Suddenly I was overwhelmed with agitation and annoyance. I ignored my emotions, imagining that I was reacting to our failure, which was on my head as one of the co-ordinators. I stayed in the car. The agitation returned even stronger and the

Illustration 15.1: Creativity Spiral

Illustration by Wayne Mason

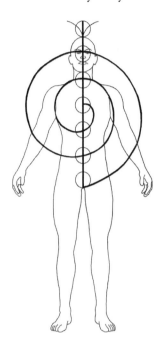

annoyance turned to anger. Unable to sit with the energy, I stormed from the car and walked over to the phone booth.

As I approached, Kai looked over my shoulder and his mouth dropped in bewilderment as he tried to express what he was seeing. A van had crested the hill behind us and was driving at high speed toward the car. I turned in time to see the van hit the back of the car, buckling it and blowing out the doors as it careened across the street. The van flipped over. Fortunately everyone inside was okay. I had a vision of my fate if I had stayed in the car and was overwhelmed with gratitude. Many years later I recognized it was percipience expressed through my emotions that sent me from the car and saved me from tragedy.

This incident is a good example of how intuition and psychic abilities are functions of subtle energy awareness. In this event, my energy field acted as an antenna. It picked up the bow wave of the impending accident and transmitted the information into my body via my chakras. The energy information was conveyed by the chakra through the emotion of anger (protection) supported with the physical sensation of agitation. As demonstrated in Dean Radin's experiments (Chapter 9), the magnitude of the emotion in the approaching event increased the strength of my reaction. The extent of injury and devastation that would have occurred had I stayed in the car was the force that propelled me out of harm's way.

A similar agitation, minus the anger, presaged my first meeting with my husband, lifting me from my conference chair and directing me into the hallway where we met. This time it was the immensity of positive emotion that provoked action. This type of event is not unusual. Most people reading this will have had similar experiences. We continually receive emotional impulses resulting from energy intuition: we just don't always notice it. At this particular juncture in history, many people are awakening to their inner abilities.

We can monitor our intuitive development by correlating inner impressions with outer omens. The force of emotions that signal intense or important events often arrives with synchronicity to underscore them. Synchronicity is the concurrence of unrelated events in a meaningful manner. It represents a flow of energy that initiates external actions at the same time that it stimulates our emotions. When we are in harmony with this flow of energy, we may notice opportunities opening before us: People, information, and resources arrive just when we need them. We feel full, awake, and alive.

More people than ever are opening to their intuition and feeling part of the larger flow. The increase isn't because psychic abilities are suddenly emerging, or synchronicities are increasing. Rather, we are starting to pay attention to what has always been present. As we do, we discover that intuition doesn't need to arrive with the clout of a strong emotion as in the cases just described; it can be elegant and arrive on the whisper of a feeling. To hear it, however, we must listen to the current of emotion riding under the surface of events and interactions. We can do this by connecting to life through our chakras.

Connecting and sensing through the chakras is best described as extending our awareness as a projection from our energy centers. The energy fibers that explore and sense the world are directed through attention. Where we put our attention is where our energy flows; it is automatic. Whenever we focus on something and try to understand it, we are probing with our energy senses. Visualizing the exploration of our energy sensors allows us to connect what we feel to the information we receive, thus opening the channel for conscious awareness.

Developing intuition works best when we switch two of the steps of the Four-Fold Process and direct energy before we feel and follow. Emotional intuition is safest when we are grounded and centered, and have strong boundaries. Ground, center, and establish boundaries before beginning (see Chapter 10). It is especially interesting to use this technique during standard activities of daily living.

Emotional Intuition Exercise

- ❧ **Choose to shift.** When the phone rings, choose to shift into to the mindful witness.

- ❧ **Direct the energy.** Before answering, connect to the person calling through the heart center. Imagine your energy sensors flowing to meet and greet the caller.

- ❧ **Feel and follow.** Follow your energy and be open to sensing who is calling and what he or she is calling about. Feel the emotional mood the caller carries. Let an image form in your mind.

- ❧ **Take heart-centered action.** Send a stream of welcoming energy to meet the caller as you answer the phone.

Try the same thing when you're phoning someone. Before placing the call, see the person clearly in your mind's eye and connect with him or her through your chakra energy. Because emotions are the language of energy, send a strong emotion of caring and connection for a moment or two before placing your call. You might be surprised how often the person answers with surprise to say that he or she was just thinking of you.

While in conversation with people you meet, try focusing on your chakras and notice your impressions, emotional read, and physical sensations as you talk. Try connecting to past inhabitants in old houses, parks, and historical places and see what impressions you pick up. One thing is sure: Life is never boring with so much to explore, and, more importantly, we begin to gain insight into how we are energetically interacting with the world around us. The point of developing intuitive ability is to expand awareness.

Cautions

There are important cautions to keep in mind when developing energy intuition. First, there is danger in assuming that the information we perceive is absolute truth. Whereas trusting our impressions is important, it is equally important to respect the truth of another. Assuming we know what is best for someone else, know his or her path and purpose, or know someone else's motives is egotistical. The truth is always bigger than one person and we should seek information for support, not to create advantage or self-importance.

Intuitive information is subject to our own bias and influenced by our beliefs. Ignoring facts and dispelling logic to take large risks based only on intuitive information is foolhardy. Intuition sets the direction; reason and hard work create the path. This is how the mind and heart work together.

Finally, opening our intuition carries a responsibility. When we open the door to intuitive information, we may experience psychic overload from picking up impressions and feelings without having intended. It can be difficult to feel the difference between our own feelings and something we've picked up from another. Use the discernment exercise in Chapter 12 to help.

Maintaining healthy boundaries is essential in developing intuitive work of any kind, not only to protect us from overload or psychic invasion of another, but also to ensure we don't violate someone's privacy. It is important to do energy-clearing work and the boundary exercises in Chapter 10 along with holding clear intent and emotional congruence.

Radiant Relationships

We are in energy exchange with everything and everyone around us. The exchange is kept inside prescribed boundaries based on how intimate we are. Romantic relationships are the perfect medium for practicing emotional awareness skills, because the resonance of love brings the heart-fields of lovers into sync and the force of feelings is a perfect carrier wave for thoughts and emotion. It is natural for energy to be transferred between lovers.

There are several key elements to building a radiant relationship. Love, respect, and trust are foremost, but the single most important trait of a radiant relationship is empathy. Empathy is not an emotion; it is the ability to feel what another person is feeling. In a love relationship, empathy allows two different and unique people to act with a single intent. Without empathy, each person in a relationship is ultimately motivated and directed from personal viewpoints and desires. With empathy, people are still acting from personal vantage points, but because they can feel from the other person's perspective, their vantage point is expanded. Now the definition of receiving what you want includes your partner receiving what he or she wants as well. There is no personal happiness that leaves our partner's happiness out of the equation.

Empathy reduces our internal resistance to love. Any time we resist love, finding empathy reestablishes it. Even when we cannot condone a behavior or stay with a partner who is out of integrity, empathy allows us to remain heart-centered. When exchanging energy with a partner, empathy governs the quality of energy being exchanged. Critical and judgmental thoughts are destructive and diminish our relationships. Unconditional love, acceptance, and support elevate the quality of relationships. Empathy allows us to switch from one to the other.

In my book *The Path of Energy* (Career Press, 2011), a chapter is devoted to energetically building relationships. Essentially, anytime we put our attention on other people, we're interacting with them energetically whether they are physically present or at a distance. As with all energy interactions, we sense them through our emotions. The strongest relationships form connections between lovers through all seven chakras. This happens naturally in the presence of unconditional love, creating an unusual depth of intimacy and a degree of personal safety that few people experience.

The Conscious Connect exercise following is not a practice we can do without the other person's permission. When the power of our will is used to create bonds that are not wanted, attention becomes hooks and projections in another person's energy field. In short, we would be perpetrating a type of psychic attack, albeit unintentionally. Always connect energetically with permission and awareness.

Conscious Connection Exercise

- **Choose to shift.** Move into the mindful observer and choose to make heart-centered connection with your friend or partner with whom you have agreed ahead of time to link. You can do this with each other simultaneously.

- **Follow and listen.** Imagine your attention as a spotlight illuminating the person.

  - Using active imagination, internally acknowledge the person and ask for permission to connect. Assure respectfulness and observe that you cannot see anything the person doesn't want to disclose.

- ❂ Notice your impressions, sensations, and feelings.
- ❂ Direct your energy.
  - ❂ Send your senses to explore the space within the spotlighted area.
  - ❂ Imagine streams of energy leaving your chakras and respectfully knocking at the boundary of your partner's aura.
  - ❂ Pay attention to physical sensations, changes in audio/visual perceptions, and shifts in mood. Correlate them with gut feelings, inner visions, synchronicities (candles flaring, blasts of wind, and so on), metaphors, and so forth.
- ❂ **Take heart-centered action.** Ask if your friend or partner is open to a transmission of love, and if yes, send and receive love. Allow the radiance between you to grow.

The Wonder of Happiness

In the book *The Emotional Revolution*, author Norman Rosenthal describes the four traits of happy people. He reports that happy people like themselves, feel in control of their lives, and are optimistic and extroverted.[2] I would add that happy people accept life; they enjoy the positive and let go of the not-so-much. On first reading this list, many of us might feel on the outside of several—if not all—of these traits. That doesn't mean we can't use them. Remembering that our body reacts to our thoughts and emotions, we can begin to think and act as if we are happy until our body believes it and we are.

Building Happiness Exercise

- ❂ **Choose to shift.** Unzip the unhappy shell you show the world and step out of it. Be your authentic self.
- ❂ **Feel and follow.** Remember a time you felt really happy and fully engage the memory. See the people, smell the air, and feel the atmosphere. Allow the feeling of happiness to pervade your senses and every one of your cells.
- ❂ **Direct the energy.** Envision all of the following traits and direct your energy into the images.
  - ❂ Practice liking yourself. Remember things you have done that you are proud of and relish that feeling. Imagine stretching

beyond your capabilities and succeeding. Send your energy into the feeling of pride.

☯ Imagine being in control of your life. You may not have control over many things, yet you always have control over how you respond and how you receive. Consider all the nuances that you do have control over and accept the areas where you do not. Imagine giving the areas you truly have no control over to a higher power. Take control by using energy exercises to creatively shift elements in your life. Send your energy into self-determination.

☯ Imagine greeting your life with optimism. Dispute pessimistic thinking by remembering a moment of awe or admiration. Direct your energy into transcendent emotions. Things really can work out! Choose it!

☯ Imagine engaging with other people and having fun. Think of people who might want to hear from you, or people who are shut in, and call them. Give of yourself in order to get out of yourself. Send your energy into positive exchange.

☯ **Create heart-centered action.** Support your belief with action. call people; become a mentor; exert authority over your moods, words, and choices. Believe in yourself, and if you can't do that, believe in a higher power, and if you can't do that, believe in the beauty of nature. Trick yourself into feeling happy until you do!

Chapter 16
Intentional Living

As far as we can discern, the sole purpose of human existence is to kindle a light in the darkness of mere being.

—Carl Jung, *Memories, Dreams, Reflections*, 1962

We live within a sea of energy from which the circumstances and conditions of our life unfold. Changing our circumstances requires changing the frequency, or vibration, of our energy field. We can't create something different from the same mindset with which we have created the old; we must align to something new in order to make a shift. Although most people grasp the concept, many wonder how. How do we change our frequency? How do we align to a new one?

There are many methods that work to answer these questions. Some shift frequency by using the vibration of sound, the feng shui of sacred geometry, or prayer; some recommend aligning to religious doctrine, gurus, saints, and angels. Regardless of the method, shifts in frequency always correspond to changes in emotional states. Emotions are the key to shifting

233

frequency because emotions correspond to changes in consciousness and the frequency of emotion is mutable.

Our frequency changes every time we move in and out of an emotional state. We use this knowledge to perform daily functions. Whether we are responding to stimuli or initiating an action, emotions mobilize energy according to their function. In response to stimuli, emotions arise with a message and we use their energy to fulfill it. When we desire to create a particular action, we conjure the specific emotion that will fulfill the function we need and deliver the energy to enact it. In this way emotions are our allies: We use them continuously, never even realizing that we are.

On the other hand, emotions also, they have the ability to drive our behavior. Each of us has experienced being driven by emotions, especially when we are feeling out of balance. The most stressful period of my life occurred when I decided to go back to graduate school and become a naturopathic physician. During the four years of the program, every aspect of my life—personal, financial, and professional—had to withstand enormous strain. The stress was considerable and my behavior reflected it. Every undeveloped inner aspect surfaced and acted out; I was not pleasant to be with. Fortunately, when we fall prey to our own worst moments, we can use them as opportunities to find a deeper place of truth within and grow to encompass it more fully.

We can use transcendent emotions to shift into the frequency required for creating a better life. Aligning with gratitude, joy, admiration, unconditional love, awe, and compassion raises our vibration, alters our perceptions, and elevates our consciousness. Then attitudes change and suddenly our view of life is different. How we behave and what we create is aligned to a new frequency. We enjoy life not necessarily because our conditions have changed (though they probably will), but because *we* have changed. Life becomes infinitely more interesting and significantly less irksome.

Aligning with transcendent emotions does not mean avoiding the rest of our emotional range; this would limit our energy vocabulary and perception. It means that we know we are not at the mercy of our emotions. Emotions arrive with energy and a message. What happens from that moment forward is a choice: We choose what do with the information, how to direct the energy it releases, and what we will align with. We choose how our emotions will be our emissaries.

The change we are talking about is encompassed by the idea of living with intention. The exercises in this book are suggestions of one way to accomplish this. If it appeals to you but seems too complicated, just remember the formula: Choose, feel, flow, and act from the heart. It doesn't matter how many times you forget; it's how many times you remember that is important.

Manifesting

Manifesting the life we want is really not that big a secret; we already use the tools in creating the life we have. Shifting to manifesting what we want is a matter of awareness.

Essentially, we have the life we are capable of sustaining with the energy we have created to fund it.

Positive change requires that we expand. In the early stages of a venture, we can usually generate the energy for expansion. The excitement of our vision generates energy. We are jazzed and create goals, draw up action plans and time lines, and back up our vision with positive action. However, unless we can sustain the inner shift that is generating energy, in time it will dissipate and the doors our emotional emissaries were opening no longer open as easily. Flow and synchronicity ebb away. At this point most people say that their dream "is not meant to be" or "the universe doesn't support it." More likely, either our emotions are not supplying enough energy to sustain the change we initiated or our dream isn't inspiring our emotions.

Most of us generate the energy for our life through a specific set of emotions, and often use anger and fear more than we realize. Although anger and fear are great emotions for their purpose, they are not meant to be the fuel for creative change. Their function is survival. If we are using anger and fear to generate change, what we create will reflect those functions and we will be living in survival mode.

One reason we choose emotions that don't fit the function at hand is because we are stuck in a set of limiting beliefs. We may be stuck in the hamster wheel of habitual thinking, moving around the same points over and over, generating the same level of energy. Habitual thinking is seductive; we know where each visualized event will take us and what energy lift it will provide. As much as we may want to change, if we don't know another way to generate energy, we probably won't. Utilizing the energy of transcendent emotions is the way out.

Limiting Beliefs

To sustain a shift, we must be able to see ourselves living in the world we are creating. If we want change and aren't able to manifest it, look to the many ways expansion challenges our self-image, relationships, beliefs, and so on. There is sure to be something within that doesn't want to grow and thus siphons our energy away from success, sabotaging the golden opportunity we would create.

For example, a woman created an exciting educational children's game that she wanted to market. The idea was stupendous and she received massive support, even obtaining funding. As success snowballed, she was expected to participate in marketing decisions, create infomercials, do radio and television interviews, and give presentations at fundraisers and workshops. Her original vision stopped at creating the prototype and convincing educators of its usefulness. She had not envisioned how large she would need to become in order to fulfill the potential of her idea and so was caught short of energy.

Immediately, problems started developing. Family crises occurred to keep her from meetings and speaking engagements. She felt torn between her creative vision and her family life, and started to think that she was wrong for "wanting it all." When obstacles began to appear, she decided the lack of flow must mean she wasn't meant to create the project.

Very quickly she started to believe that she needed to make a choice: sell her vision or ruin her family. This was a false set of assumptions and inside she knew it. Her emotional response to feeling forced into a decision led her to self-examination. Most of us never make it to this first shift; we are caught in the intensity of turmoil. Because she wanted to expand, she did the emotional work to discover the belief that limited her.

She discovered that her initial limiting belief was that she didn't deserve to have what she wanted and, if she became too visible, she would lose the quality of her family life. Consequently, her emissaries created obstacles. There was some truth in her belief, and, rather than discard it, she, her husband, and their children did creative visioning together. The result was a family committed to a shared, creative goal that included making some sacrifices for the dream and creating boundaries to protect the family.

Timing

In addition to having enough energy to sustain our vision, we must also have enough energy to ride the ups and downs of the paths related to timing and positioning. Both play key roles in the advancement of our goals, and this is where emotional awareness really pays dividends. Paying attention to our emotions can help us stay connected to what is missing in our plan, feel when to move, and know what opportunities will serve us. Paying attention to our emotions helps us navigate the terrain of other people's agendas, alerting us to inconsistencies and pitfalls. In the right frame of mind, this journey is an exciting game.

Directing energy into our life dreams consists of using our mind to open a pathway. Where we send our mind is where energy flows. Energy is like water. It flows toward least resistance. The most powerful use of energy creates a potential, then removes the inner resistances to flowing towards it. If we have created a vision and directed our energy yet nothing is happening, we need to look at our inner resistances. Are they telling us the timing is not right, that we don't have all the pieces to the puzzle? Are they telling us that what we are creating doesn't match our authentic self, that we are not honoring the best that we can be? Examining our resistance can create the coherence needed to create the life of our dreams.

Path and Purpose

Finding our path and purpose is another key element in manifesting. Does what we want match our authentic expression of our path? Many of us vacillate about knowing what our path and purpose is, sometimes feeling stopped in going forward because we aren't sure of our purpose.

Psychologist Dave DePalma writes that the common human purpose in life is to know peace, feel love, and express joy.[1] He explains this is a universal purpose everyone shares. Each person's personal purpose is to express this universal purpose in our own unique expression that best fulfills our inner spirit. It's worth taking a moment to consider how we know peace, feel love, and express joy in our life.

Creating Our Dream Exercise

- ☛ **Choose to shift into mindful observer.** Connect with gratitude and take three deep breaths as you shift into alignment with this frequency. Inhale peace, feel love; exhale joy, feel love.

- ☛ **Feel and follow.** Imagine your dream. Create all aspects of it in your mind's eye. Envision it in all its brilliance. Soak it in. Notice how large you must be to live this dream. What needs to grow?

What will challenge you and drop you to the floor? What will sustain you?

- ❧ **Direct the energy.** Let your vision jazz your energy. The more you invest in your dream, the more it should feed your joy. If there is no joy when you look at your dream, there is no energy to direct. When you have a good buzz of joy, direct your attention to your vision and energize your dream. Create a circuit between yourself and your vision. Feel yourself expand as your dream is enlivened with the energy you send.
- ❧ **Create heart-centered action.** Support your belief with action.

...before a dream is realized, the Soul of the World tests everything that was learned along the way. It does this not because it is evil, but so that we can, in addition to realizing our dreams, master the lessons we've learned as we've moved toward that dream. It's the point at which most people give up. It's the point at which, as we say in the language of the desert, one "dies of thirst just when the palm trees have appeared on the horizon."

—Paulo Coelho

When we first begin to work with our emotions, we tend to tune in to the information that reflects our place in the world; we try to discern people's intentions, feel for the right direction, look for clues to our path and purpose. At some point, however, we lose the self-importance that places our desires at the center of our exploration. Like Copernicus moving from an Earth-centered celestial vision to a Sun-centered vision, we move from our own vantage point to that of higher consciousness.

At this point we desire to use emotional and energy awareness to create a better world. Joining with others sharing a similar intent creates exponential change, as experiments in meditating for peace and healing show. To learn more, check out Lynn McTaggart's Intention Experiments at *www.theintentionexperiment.com/the-peace-intention-experiment* and the Global Coherence Initiative at *www.glcoherence.org*.

Non-Ordinary Reality

Paying attention to shifting emotions brings us into awareness of eddies and currents of a different dimension of reality. Some refer to this as *non-ordinary reality*; others call it spiritual or dimensional reality. For me, it is the realm of subtle energy. Additional life forms live within this realm with whom we share the universe. They have different names in different traditions: spirits, angels, fairies, ETs, and so on. Whatever they are called, we live side-by-side, separated only by the veil of perception.

Carlos Castaneda writes that the only true goal of life is the enhancement of awareness. Working with subtle energy reveals an essential truth: Reality as we know it is only one vantage point. There are other outlooks; vistas into innumerable dimensions interacting with ours at all times. In the same way that we are unaware of the interactions of microbes without microscopes, or the interface of subatomic particles without quantum accelerators, without developed energy senses we are unaware of the multiple domains that exist around us. Through the expansion of awareness we peek into the smallest corner of these domains.

As with microbes and subatomic particles, we may not be able to see subtle energy, yet we can perceive its activity. By paying attention to how we feel, we can track the movement of energy through delicate changes in the body and subtle shifts in our emotions. The bodymind, our vehicle for consciousness, is designed to navigate these domains.

Developing proficiency at perceiving subtle energy shifts our vantage point. In the ancient Vedic system, the seven physio-emotional centers called chakras are the portals that provide access to other realities. According to Carlos Castaneda, his Yaqui mentor Don Juan describes 600 assemblage points within our aura that connect with different dimensional landscapes.

Immediately the questions arise: Is it safe to interact with these other domains? Do negative entities exist that will harm us?

Universal Forces: Positive or Negative?

In Taoist philosophy, the whole of reality is divided into two forces called *yin* and *yang*. These two forces are equal and opposite actions in a world of changing cycles. Similarly, cosmology of the ancient Maya was organized according to cycles that correlate to planetary movements within the solar system as well as the movement of the solar system through our galaxy. Like the phases of the moon, it is a characteristic of a cycle such that half is spent building up, then the other half falling away. This sequence is seen in all things: the coming and going of civilizations, the growth and decay of ecosystems, and the anabolic and catabolic processes of the body.

When a cycle changes, thoughts, ideas, and constructs shift into a new paradigm. We are engaged in such a shift right now. Structures that are based on the old fall apart and are destroyed as new structures and systems that are in agreement with the new alignments are built. This transition can be difficult, and old patterns stir as new light emerges. Often people label different parts of the cycle or the forces behind them with positive or negative energy.

We tend to like growth phases and become attached to what is created, falsely labeling the diminishing phase as negative. To know this label is false we need only look at the cancer that is created when a cell's growth is unimpeded. Because diminishing phases ask us to eliminate what is unessential, we find it uncomfortable. Further, we decide that forces are good or bad depending on whether they help what we are trying to achieve or seem to work against it.

Another option is to see the forces as neutral: How we align to them makes them helpful or harmful. If we can align activities with the phase of the cycle that will exalt it, we might change how we view it. For example, when we are trying to get rid of an old habit, it is useful to align it with a cycle that is ending or a force that dismantles. When we want to create something new, we might attach it to a growth phase or generative force.

This idea of neutrality extends to the entities that lie within these domains as well. We label an entity as evil if it challenges us and good if it supports us. Is it possible that entities such as goblins and "evil" spirits are like Tolkien's Gollum character and have function that we don't understand? Perhaps these entities temper our spirit like gold in fire, burning off impurities. Perhaps they reveal our self-doubt so that we can learn confidence. Maybe they even show us that they are only a reflection of the shadow-self that we hide from. We decide whether or not we align with such beings by the quality of our emanations—the quality of our heart and spirit.

Possibly, similar to our emotions, all forces have function for different purposes at different times. It is the action we create that can be rightly labeled good or evil. This is a difficult concept to grasp. We want to blame an outside force for the pain, cruelty, and injustice in the world. However, the force is neutral. It is our intent, our level of awareness, that creates these outcomes. Expanding consciousness is how we can learn to foster the intent that fulfills our universal purpose: know peace, experience love, express joy.

Discernment

The idea of evil and good forces is pervasive in all of our doctrines. We are told we must align with the positive forces of the universe, leaving us to wonder whether the positive is yin or yang. And if we decide that one is good, does that mean we have to fight against the other? Consider the actions created in the name of God as people's emotional fields are manipulated so that they attach bombs to their bodies, and join crusades, jihads, inquisitions, witch hunts, and holocausts. Is this really the best we can imagine?

At some point in our inner growth we come face-to-face with the largest question that we as humans face: How can the beauty and love that we feel in the presence of God/Divine/Oneness exist be juxtaposed to the pain we bear in the face of horrendous loss? We wonder how there can be design and purpose to living when our pain has the power to shatter everything in existence. From this pain we develop the concept of good and evil, for surely only evil could bring us so thoroughly to our knees.

This is perhaps the biggest dichotomy: that the totality of the universe contains both pain and delight—that we are both human and Divine. When people undergo an expansion experience their life is transformed. As with the pain of loss, in near-death experiences, out-of-body ascension, and Kundalini rising, reality is shifted and we expand. Our body literally grows in energy and we are able, somehow, to embrace the totality. We experience the bliss state, a moment of transcendent love.

We return permanently altered; we never see the world in the old way again. There may be times when we are impatient, are angry, or make poor decisions; we may have visions we are unable to fulfill; however, we have an understanding that can never be erased. The beauty of our experience converts us and we live for something greater, no matter how imperfectly we achieve it. We may never have another such experience, and yet we never doubt the reality or meaning of the one we lived.

A caution arises that illusion can also cause a temporary sense of expansion. We can align with people who manipulate us, filling us with energy so that we perform an action in their agenda. Equally, an undeveloped aspect within self might attach to a force that expands it and we are deluded into thinking we are more spiritually advanced than we are. False gurus, drugs, or even mental illness such as schizophrenia can produce such effects; however, there are distinctions that help in our discernment.

Real upliftment:

- Is followed by peaceful and productive action and improved effectiveness in life.
- Does not require continued inputs of energy to keep it alive. It will rise and fall as all experiences do, but it will never be lost.
- Leaves us more attuned to the beauty of the world and divinity of life, even though nothing in our circumstance has changed.
- Increases tolerance and love of others.

Experiences derived from illusion:

- Are often followed by an inability to be effective in our life, or by violent action.
- Dissipate unless repeated inputs of energy from the drug or guru are imbibed.
- Are often followed by depression and despair—a message from our bodymind to examine the situation more closely. People often find the world an ugly place.
- Increase the desire to enact judgment on others.

The frequency that we call the Divine is the frequency of the totality that governs the cycles of existence. Through expansion of consciousness, we seek to engage the totality more fully and with all parts of our self. We seek to enter and travel in these realms; our safety lies with our emotions and intent. Love represents the consciousness that embraces the Divine; it provides the glue of reality. If we wish safe passage through the levels of consciousness we are engaging, the ally to align with is love.

You are already naked. There is no reason not to follow your heart.
—Steve Jobs

Enjoy the journey.

APPENDICES

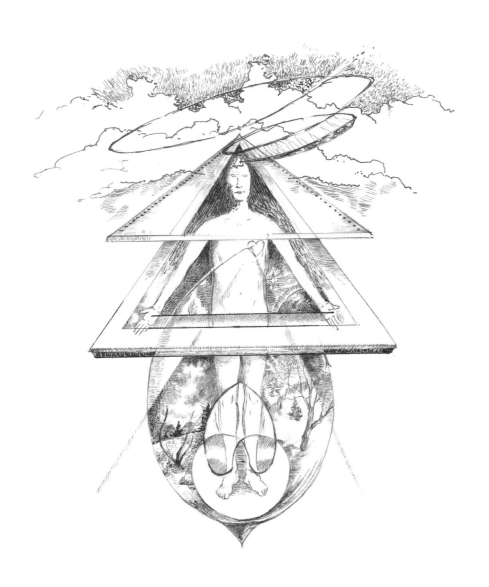

Illustration by Mark Johnson

Appendix A
Dowsing and Muscle Testing

Dowsing and muscle testing are techniques that allow us to ask yes or no questions of the bodymind. Answers are reflected through a strengthening or weakening of the body's electrical signal as reflected in increasing or decreasing muscle strength, signifying yes and no answers respectively. We use these techniques in emotional awareness exercises when we are unsure of the body's messages.

How to Dowse With a Pendulum

For the best information on Dowsing contact the American Dowsing Society at *www.dowsers.org*.

Pendulums are made of strings or chains around 8 to 10 inches long with a weighted object on one end. Most people use a crystal or another sacred object, but almost anything you can tie on will work. *You* are the dowser; the tool is not.

Step One: Clear your mind and focus your intent: Breathe, ground, and center.

Step Two: Learn how your pendulum speaks to you. This step only has to be done once; the next time you dowse you can use the same patterns.

- Hold the end of the chain so that the weighted end is hanging down. Swing it in a circle and ask the pendulum to show you a yes response. After a few minutes the pendulum will change from swinging in a circle to swinging in a straight line, either back and forth, or up and down—this is your yes response when you are asking questions.

- Return the pendulum to swinging in a circle, steady your hand, and ask the pendulum to show you a no response. Once again, after a few minutes it will begin to swing in a straight line, this time in a different direction from the last time.

- Now ask it to show you a maybe answer. *Maybe* can be another straight line in another direction, can be a dead stop, or can be continuation of a circle.

Step Three: Once you know your three response patterns, begin to ask yes and no questions. The questions need to be accurate, specific, and clear.

Self-Muscle Testing

Muscle testing has the advantage of not using a tool other than your own body.

Step One: Clear your mind and focus your intent: Breathe, ground, and center.

Step Two: Using your non-dominant hand, touch the tip of your little finger to the tip of your thumb, making an "O" shape.

Step Three: Insert the index finger of the other hand through the "O" and hook it around your finger-thumb connect. Apply force to the area where the pinky and thumb meet. Resist the force with your finger and thumb and try not to let your index finger break the connection.

Step Four: Ask for a yes response and try to pull the "O" open. It should be pretty strong. Ask for a no response and repeat; it should be easy to break the connection. Practice asking yes and no questions and using the same amount of force to experience what strong and weak feels like.

Step Five: As in dowsing, use this technique to explore issues by asking yes and no questions that are clear, accurate, and specific.

Appendix B
Emotional Charts

Table 1: Quick-Access Emotional Energy Chart

Emotion	Function/Question	Send your energy to:	Feel yourself:
Anger	Protection What are my motives?	Strengthen the boundary	Strong
Anxiety	Congruence What is missing?	Enliven your sensors and core	Complete
Apathy	Connection Where is my value?	Contain your boundary	Valued
Boredom	Engagement What have I lost?	Discover your core	Creative/ passionate

Contentment	Flow Where is my alignment?	Connection with others	Aligned with others
Denial	Core protection What am I protecting?	Surround the core	Capable
Depression	Assessment What have I forgotten?	Connect with the core	Enough
Desperation	Creative discovery What don't I see?	Release energy anchors	Courageous
Disappointment	Dispel illusion What am I afraid to see?	Inward to explore the core	Trusting
Discouragement	Non-judgment Where do I need help?	Surrender energy attachments	Supported
Envy	Self-esteem What part of me is hiding?	Strengthen the core	Visible
Excitement	Motivation Can I believe?	Mobilize the system	Successful
Fear	Warning Where am I unsafe?	Mobilize flight or fight	Safe
Grief	Repair energy connections Can I maintain connection?	Energy attachments	Connected
Guilt	Pride Where have I abandoned myself?	Strengthen connections and boundaries	Reconciled
Happiness	Self-reward What do I deserve?	Charge the system	Flowing
Hatred	Protect the core Can I survive?	Surround and strengthen the core	Illuminated

Inspiration	<u>Support the core</u> What needs expression?	Radiate from the core	Creative
Jealousy	<u>Self-regard</u> Where am I not seeing myself?	Cleanse the boundary	Respected
Joy	<u>Self-expression</u> What brings me joy?	Radiate from the core	Authentic
Love	<u>Unity</u> Where do I resist love?	Radiate from the core	One with all
Obsession	<u>Self-value</u> What is lost?	Strengthen the boundary	Full
Passion	<u>Growth</u> What is outgrown?	Charge the system	Powerful
Sadness	<u>Find core connection</u> Where have I left myself?	Connect with the core	Whole
Shame	<u>Restore integrity</u> What is in the way of forgiveness?	Connection with others	Loved
Wonder	<u>Awaken potential</u> Where are my limits?	Open the core	Expanded

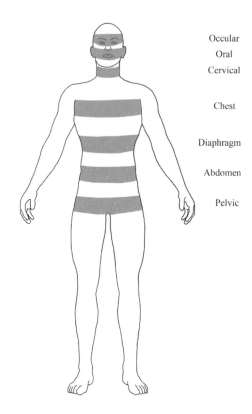

Occular
Oral
Cervical

Chest

Diaphragm

Abdomen

Pelvic

Illustration 1: Body Map of the Segments

Illustration by Wayne Mason

Table 2: Segments and Chakra Correlations

This chart shows some basic correlations between segments and chakras.

SEGMENT	Emotion	CHAKRA	Issues
	Elevation Arrogance Connection Universal love Universal compassion	**Crown Chakra** Universal Consciousness Opening to spiritual impulse and inner knowing	Dogmatism Authoritarianism Superiority Higher perspective Wisdom Expanded awareness Enlightenment Awakening

Ocular (Eyes, ears, and sinuses)	Desire Longing Neediness Peace Conviction	**Third Eye Chakra** Creation Consciousness Opening to Truth and insight	Percipience Problem-solving Righteousness Visualization skills Using intent Concentration Bigger picture concepts
Oral	Determination Expression Trust Expresses feeling originating in other parts of the body	**Throat** Clarity consciousness Opening to intuition	Creative expression Interaction Avoidance Communication
Cervical	Resistance Adventure Controlling		Mediates between heart and head Tempers emotions for expression
Thorax: includes **Shoulder.** **Arm.** **Chest.**	Responsibility Fear of performance Protection Love Joy Happiness Appreciation Grief Sadness	**Heart Chakra** Holographic consciousness Opening to empathy Unifies, focuses, and translates feelings	Compassion Unconditional love Forgiveness Betrayal Loss Self-protection

Diaphragm (includes organs immediately under diaphragm)	Anger Anxiety Pleasure Surrender Pride Control Courage Guilt Power	**Solar Plexus** Personal consciousness Opening to gut feelings Opens to personal perspective and empowerment	Self-importance Ability to defend self Ability to allow pleasure Need to be right Need to control Issues around confrontation Self-trust
Abdomen	Shame Pride Desire Lust Fear of feeling Fear of connection Passion	**Sacral Chakra** Creative consciousness Opening to inspiration Connects heartfelt feelings to genitals Allows creative passion	Humor Interpersonal connection Ability to create Family relationships Sexual desire Material excess
Pelvis and legs	Mortal fear Faith Grounding Inner strength Stability	**Base chakra** Survival consciousness Opening to instinct	Letting go Stability Sense of direction Personal safety Material well-being

Appendix C
Resources

Innumerable books and Websites provide excellent resources into these explorations. Following are my personal favorites. Asterisked books are special picks.

Books

Andrews, Synthia

- *The Path of Energy*. New Page Books, 2011.
- *The Complete Idiot's Guide to the Akashic Record*, with Colin Andrews. Alpha Books, 2010.
- *Acupressure and Reflexology for Dummies*, with Bobbi Dempsey. Wiley, 2007.

Andrews, Colin

- *Signs of Contact*, with Stephen J. Spignesi. New Page Books, 2003.

Becker, Dr. Robert, and Gary Selden
- ❧ *The Body Electric.* Quill Press, 1985.

Bodanis, David
- ❧ **E=mc2: A Biography of The World's Most Famous Equation.* The Berkley Publishing Group, 2000.

Brinkley, Dannion
- ❧ *Secrets of the Light: Lessons from Heaven,* with Kathryn Brinkley. HarperOne, 2009.
- ❧ *Saved by the Light: The True Story of a Man Who Died Twice and the Profound Revelations He Received,* with Paul Perry. HarperOne, reprinted 2008.

Castaneda, Carlos
- ❧ **The Teachings of Don Juan: A Yaqui Way of Knowledge, 3rd edition.* University of California Press, 2008.
- ❧ All the rest of his books!

Dychtwald, Ken
- ❧ **Bodymind.* Tarcher/Putnam, 1977.

Gallegos, Eligio Stephen
- ❧ **Personal Totem Pole: Animal Imagery the Chakras and Psychotherapy, 3rd edition.* Moon Bear Press, 2012.

Goleman, Daniel
- ❧ *Emotional Intelligence: Why It Can Matter More Than IQ.* Bantam Dell, 1994.

Keyes, Ken
- ❧ **Handbook to Higher Consciousness.* Eden Grove Editions, 1997.

Marcinak, Barbara

- *Path of Empowerment: New Pleiadian Wisdom for a World in Change.* New World Library, 2004.
- *Family of Light: Pleiadian Tales and Lessons in Living.* Bear and Company, 1998.
- *Earth: Pleiadian Keys to the Living Library.* Bear and Company, 1994.
- *Bringers of the Dawn: Teachings from the Pleiadians*, with Tera Thomas. Bear and Company, 1992.

McTaggart, Lynn.

- *The Field: A Quest for the Secret Force of the Universe.* Harper Perennial, 2002.

Mitchell, Dr. Edgar

- *The Way of the Explorer, Revised Edition.* New Page Books, February 15, 2008.

Myss, Caroline

- *Anatomy of the Spirit: The Seven Stages of Power and Healing.* Three Rivers Press, 1997.
- *Sacred Contracts: Awakening Your Divine Potential.* Three Rivers Press, 2002.

Oschman, Dr. James L.

- *Energy Medicine: The Scientific Basis.* Churchill Livingston Publishing, 2000.

Pert, Dr. Candace

- **Molecules of Emotion: The Science Behind Mind-Body Medicine.* Simon & Schuster, 1999.

Pond, David

- **Chakras for Beginners: A Guide to Balancing Your Chakra Energies.* Llewellyn Publications, 1999.

Radin, Dean

- *Entangled Minds: Extrasensory Experiences in a Quantum Reality.* Paraview Pocket Books, 2006.
- *The Conscious Universe.* Harper Edge, 1997.

Rosenthal, MD, Norman E

- *The Emotional Revolution.* Citadel Press, 2002.

Schultz, Mona Lisa

- *Awakening Intution: Using Your Mind-body Network for Insight and Healing,* Harmony Books, 1998.

Shumsky Susan G., and Dannion Brinkley

- *Exploring Auras: Cleansing and Strengthening your Energy Field.* New Page Books, 2005.

Small Wright, Machaelle

- **M.A.P.: The Co-Creative White Brotherhood Medical Assistance Program, 3rd edition.* Perelandra, Ltd., 2006.
- **Behaving as if the God in all Life Matters.* 3rd revised edition, Perelandra, Ltd., 1997.

Teeguarden, Iona Marsaa

- **Joy of Feeling.* Japan Publications, May 1987. 7th printing, May 2006, by the Jin Shin Do® Foundation for Bodymind Acupressure.

Tipping, C. Colin

- *Radical Forgiveness: Making Room for the Miracle.* Quest Publishing & Distribution, 2002.

Tolle Eckhart

- *A New Earth: Awakening to Your Life's Purpose.* Plume Books, 2005.

Willimas, Paul

- ❂ **Remember Your Essence.* Entwhistle Books, 1999.
- ❂ **Das Energie.* Entwhistle Books, 1982.

Young-Sowers, Meredith

- ❂ **Spirit Heals: Awakening a Woman's Inner Knowing for Self-Healing.* New World Library, 2007.
- ❂ *Wisdom Bowls: Overcoming Fear and Coming Home to Your Authentic Self*, with Caroline Myss. New World Library, 2006.

Websites
Bodywork for Emotional Processing

- ❂ CranioSacral-Somatoemotional Release: *www.craniosacraltherapy.org*
- ❂ **Jin Shin Do® Bodymind Acupressure®: *www.jinshindo.org*
- ❂ Matrix Energetics: *www.matrixenergetics.com*
- ❂ **Myofascial Release: *www.myofascialrelease.com/fascia_massage/public/sem_courses.asp*
- ❂ Rubenfeld Synergy Method: *www.rubenfeldsynergy.com*
- ❂ Trager Approach: *www.tragerus.org*

Additional Emotional Processing

- ❂ **EMDR: Eye Movement Desensitization and Reprocessing: *www.emdr.com*
- ❂ Emotional Freedom Technique: *www.emofree.com*

Interesting Organizations and Websites

- ❂ American Society of Dowsers: *www.dowsers.org*
- ❂ Academy for Future Science: *www.affs.org*
- ❂ Consciousness Research Laboratory: *www.deanradin.com*
- ❂ Association of Research and Enlightenment: *www.edgarcayce.org*
- ❂ Crop Circle Research: *www.colinandrews.net*

☯ HeartMath: *www.heartmath.com*

☯ The Global Coherence Initiative: *www.glcoherence.org*

☯ Intentional Peace Experiment: *www.theintentionexperiment.com/the-peace-intention-experiment*

☯ Institute of Noetic Sciences: *www.noetic.org*

☯ Institute of Consciousness Research: *www.icrcanada.org*

☯ Path of Energy and Emotion Website: *www.thepathofenergy.com*

☯ Perelandra: *www.perelandra.com*

☯ Stillpoint: *www.stillpoint.org*

Appendix D
Glossary

active imagination: a tool for listening to and dialoguing with the subconscious by using the imagination in a state of deeply relaxed, alert awareness

Adverse Childhood Experience (ACE) study: an investigation into the relationship between childhood trauma and adult health problems

Albert Einstein: the revolutionary scientist who developed the Theory of Relativity and designed the formula $E=MC^2$

altered state of awareness/mind/consciousness: any state of awareness markedly different from our normal state of waking consciousness, generally characterized by beta brain waves

ambiance: the atmosphere, mood, or feel of an environment, especially as it relates to the energetic and emotional vibe

amygdala: the area of the temporal lobe of the brain that processes memory and emotion

anabolic processes: metabolic processes that construct molecules from smaller units; the pathways that build

Andrew Armour: a neurocardiologist conducting research in conjunction with the HeartMath Institute who places the heart in the center of the emotion-energy matrix as an informational processing center

anthropomorphic: the attribution of human characteristics (or characteristics assumed to belong only to humans) to other animals, non-living things, phenomena, material states, objects, or abstract concepts, such as organizations, governments, spirits, or deities

anthroposophy: "a path of knowledge aiming to guide the spiritual element in the human being to the spiritual in the universe," according to Rudolph Steiner; also thought of as wisdom of the human being, and awareness of one's humanity

assemblage points: energy foci within the aura that are portals to different dimensional landscapes, as described by Carlos Casteneda

attention: the primary instrument of mindfulness; when combined with intent, the most powerful tool we have to interact with energy

aura: the energy field that permeates, supports, and emanates from the body.

authentic self: the part of a person that speaks from the power of his/her own inner truth and is connected to the divine essence in life

awareness: the ability to perceive, to feel, or to be conscious of events, objects, or sensory patterns

Barbara Brennan: originally a NASA scientist and intuitive who developed Western concepts of human energy structures and psychology

being in the body *or* **being present:** connecting external events with feelings of subtle energy in our body and the emotions they evoke; also, being fully present in the moment, paying attention with a quiet mind

bliss response: described as divine union by Candace Pert

body armor: muscle splinting that protects us from feeling undue emotional pain that in time hardens into patterns of unconscious muscle holding

body segments: horizontal sections of the body in which muscular tensions in the front, back, and sides are functionally related

body sounding: a model for working with subtle energy that includes mind, body, spirit, and emotions, developed by Synthia Andrews

bodymind: a term for the combined unit of the body and mind seen as different interactive aspects of one whole

boundary: the outer border of the energetic space around each person, generally about 3 feet away from the body and aligned with the outer layer of the aura, although it can expand and contract as needed

brainwaves: electromagnetic emissions from the brain that are generated by the oscillation of neurons as they communicate with each other; the five primary wavelengths are delta, theta, alpha, beta, and gamma

cadence of voice: rhythms of speech; used here in the context of rhythms used in speeches, music, and chanting as a method for entrainment.

Candace Pert: the neuroscientist and pharmacologist whose identification of the opiate receptor earned the lab where she worked a Nobel Prize. She developed the current concept of the role of peptides in emotional conveyance between the body and mind, and has published more than 250 scientific articles.

catabolic processes: metabolic processes in the body that break down larger molecules into smaller units to be used as raw material for creating other products

centering: the ability to bring our attention to the core of our being where our authentic self resides. When we are centered we are connected to our inner truth and able to perceive more clearly.

chakras: centers of energy emanating from the center line of the body with radiations front and back that look like rotating vortices. They are considered focal points in the body for the reception and transmission of subtle energy.

clarity consciousness: the consciousness of truth and intention of the Throat chakra

coccyx: commonly referred to as the tailbone, the final segment of the vertebral column in tailless primates

coherence: the state of being united: bringing different aspects into alignment and making a stronger, unified force

consciousness: the quality or state of being aware of an external object or something within oneself

constructive anger: anger modulated with awareness so that it can be used to maintain personal boundaries without causing undue harm; maintains the opening for peaceful resolution of conflict

core self: the authentic self or essence

Cosmic Egg: Joseph Chilton Pearce's name for the aura

Cranio-Sacral Therapy: a body balancing system created by osteopath John Upledger that focuses on the movement of cerebral spinal fluid and the spiritual and energetic components of health

creation consciousness: the awareness of divine constructs that organize life and life events

Cymatics: the study of how sound vibration organizes matter; coined by Swiss naturalist Dr. Hans Jenny

Daniel Goleman: an internationally known psychologist who introduced the concept of emotional intelligence

dark energy: in physical cosmology and astronomy, a hypothetical form of energy that permeates all of space and tends to accelerate the expansion of the universe

dark matter: a type of matter hypothesized to account for a large part of the total mass in the universe; cannot be seen directly with telescopes; thought to be the scaffolding of matter

dark matter scaffolding: the matrix out of which physical matter is constructed

David Bohm: a nuclear physicist; one of the fathers of quantum physics

déjà vu: The act of recognizing something despite encountering it for the first time

Dean Radin: the head researcher at the Institute of Noetic Sciences; researcher and author into the field of parapsychology; provides unique insights into the energy field effects of our awareness and the link between energy and emotion

discernment: the ability to read information and make choices based on what is most beneficial, according to personal perspective

the Divine: the frequency that governs the cycles of existence

DNA: the genetic blueprint or instruction manual for the development and function of an organism.

Doc Childre: a stress expert, author, and creator of the HeartMath system

dowsing: the use of devices such as a pendulum or dowsing rods such that the energy of the correct answer to a dowser's question is transferred from the bodymind through movement of the device

drama: not an emotion; the use of emotional chaos as a conscious or unconscious strategy to get what we need

E=MC² (energy = mass x the speed of light squared): energy and matter are the same substance; the difference between them is simply the speed at which they vibrate

EEG (electroencephalograph) and EKG (electrocardiograph): two devices that record the electric fields of the brain and heart respectively

the Eight Strange Flow Meridians: according to traditional Chinese medicine system, the underlying root of all the body's energy systems. Not attributed to a physical body system, they are the source and blueprint that makes manifest all the systems and structure of the body.

electromagnetic spectrum: the range of all possible frequencies of electromagnetic radiation emitted or absorbed by a particular object

emotion: a direct response to internal and/or external stimulation; an innate quality of consciousness that includes feeling

emotional intelligence: the concept that emotions provide important information to our decision-making and includes the ability to identify, assess, and control the emotions of oneself, of others, and of groups

Emotional Kaleidoscope: dynamic model of the synchronistic flow of emotions through the TCM cycle of transformation created by Iona Marsaa Teaguarden, creator of the Jin Shin Do® Bodymind Acupressure® method of bodywork

empath: a person who receives intuitive information through the emotional field of another

empathy: the capacity to recognize feelings that are being experienced by another sentient being

endocrine glands: organs in the endocrine system that secrete different types of hormones directly into the bloodstream to regulate the bodymind

endorphins: neuropeptide molecules that relieve pain and induce a feeling of well-being, similar in action to morphine

energy attachments: flows of energy that connect us to others; can become overly invested in past conditioning, other people's agendas, and limiting beliefs

energy awareness: a state of perception that pays attention to the flows of subtle energy inside and outside of the body

energy cyst: a focus of emotion and energy that has become trapped in the fascia of muscles and organs during physical trauma; the bigger the emotional charge, the larger the energy cyst; coined by John Upledger, DO

energy fibers: energy extensions of the chakras that sense the world around us and anchor our frame of reference

energy matrix: an energy field that forms templates that organize matter into discernible form

entanglement: in quantum physics, the idea that once two particles have met they continue to reflect the same state and influence each other even when separated

entrainment: brings varied frequencies into rhythm through the application of a periodic stimulus

fascia: a band or sheath of connective tissue that supports or binds together internal organs or parts of the body

feelings: the sensation of emotions

filaments of light: another name for energy fibers

five core impulses: the basic needs that we strive to fulfill in living a meaningful and empowered life; similar but not identical to Maslow's Hierarchy of Needs

five-element TCM: in traditional Chinese medicine, there are five basic elements that are divisions of yin and yang: Wood, Fire, Earth, Metal, and Water. Each element governs a pair of meridians in the body (Fire governs two pairs).

flow: the movement of subtle energy through the body and the material world

fMRI: functional magnetic resonance imaging

the Four-Fold Process: shift awareness, receive information, direct the energy, create heart-centered action; provides a framework to explore the non-ordinary reality within our emotions

four known forces of physics: gravitational, electromagnetic, strong, and weak

freeze reaction: a closing-down of awareness that protects the body from overwhelming emotional trauma that occurs during the extreme stress of shock

frequency: either the number of traveling waves in a specified period of time or the rate at which a particle vibrates

functionally related acupressure point: acupuncture points on different meridians that support each other's function; can be influenced with the application of needles, finger pressure, magnets, or electric current

future/past transmission: picking up psychic information from past or future events

ganglia: nerve cells in concentrated complexes

gene: an identifiable unit of DNA that produces a specific trait

genome: the complete set of genes in an organism

Gnosis: immediate inner knowing

grounding: being connected to the Earth

Hans Jenny: the Swiss doctor and naturalist who developed Cymatics and principles describing how vibration and waves impact the organization of matter

Hans Selye: the author of well-known model of Stress Adaptation revealing fight-or-flight reactions as the initial response to stress

Hara line: a line of energy running through the center of the body; coined by author/researcher Barbara Brennan

heart-centered awareness: actions are based on core values that incorporate path and purpose in life; not motivated by the lesser craving for power, fame, or petty vengeance

HeartMath Institute: founded in 1991 by Doc Childre "to develop effective and scalable methods and technologies to help people self-regulate emotions and behaviors": *www.heartmath.com.* The institute conducts cutting-edge research into the neuroenergetics of emotions and created EM-wave technology.

heightened states of being: a state of being more aware, knowledgeable, or conscious

hippocampus-amygdala: area in brain that deals with the development of perception, memory, emotion, and mood, among other things

hologram: a three-dimensional representation of an object in which every part contains all the information possessed by the whole

holographic consciousness: connecting with the construct and interconnectivity of the totality while still seeing the individuality and independence of the components

human energy matrix: a field of energy that forms the template of our physical body and is the medium through which we are connected to other points of life in the larger universal matrix

hypnagogia: a state of consciousness between wakefulness and sleep

illusion: something that deceives by producing a false or misleading impression of reality

inner shadow: a concept developed by Carl Jung, a Swiss psychiatrist who studied under Freud; consists of disliked parts of self that are submerged into the subconscious, forming a shadow-self that we project into the outer world as an external force

intuition: perception of truth, fact, etc., independent of any reasoning process

Iona Marsaa Teeguarden, LMFT: psychotherapist who developed the Jin Shin Do® Bodymind Acupressure® method of bodywork

Jin Shin Do® Bodymind Acupressure®: a system of bodywork that combines the theories of classic Chinese acupuncture, a traditional Japanese acupressure technique, Taoist philosophy, and Qigong (breathing and exercise techniques) with Western psychological tools like Reichian segmental theory and principles of Ericksonian psychotherapy. It is a brilliant synthesis of body-centered emotional processing and meridian methodology.

Jonathan Haidt: a professor at the New York Stern School of business who taught psychology for 16 years at the University of Virginia; research focuses on the psychological basis of morality; developed the concept of self-transcendent emotions

Kundalini: spiritual energy that lies dormant in the base of the spine and carries the seed of spiritual awakening

light fibers: another name for energy fibers

Longevity Genes Project: a study into the factors of longevity; revealed that positive attitude and resiliency to stress are key attributes to long life

low-level anger: anger associated with everyday frustrations and injustices

Luc Montagnier: Nobel Laureate who was one of the Nobel prize winners in 2008 for discovering the link between HIV and AIDS, and whose current research demonstrates electromagnetic waves of DNA

Masaru Emoto: the author who conducted experiments that purport to shows that different thoughts and emotions create different crystallization patterns in frozen water

matrix: a surrounding substance and structure within which something else originates, develops, or is contained

meridians: pathways in the body along which vital energy flows

methyl coverings: methyl tags imprinted on our genes that aid in the suppression of specific genes such that they do not express in the physiology

methyl group: a molecule consisting of a carbon atom attached to three hydrogen atoms used in processes throughout the body

methyl tags: methyl groups used as DNA coverings

mindful witness: the part of self that observes our actions from a place of non-judgment and acceptance

mindfulness: the art of *being* in a world obsessed with doing

morphic field: the energy-field effect of consciousness; coined by biologist/author Rupert Sheldrake as part of a theory for the transference of information among members of a species

muscle armoring: muscle tension that results from chronic muscle splinting

muscle splinting: adjacent muscles in an area tighten around an injury or painful emotion, limiting movement and protecting from further damage

muscle testing: using the body's response to assess answers to properly worded questions

Nadis: the channels through which, in traditional Indian medicine and spiritual science, the energies of the subtle body flow; they connect at special points of intensity called chakras

nerve plexus: the network of intersecting nerves

neuroendocrine system: made up of the nervous system and the endocrine system, which work together to keep the body functioning regularly

neuropeptides: small, protein-based molecules used by neurons to communicate with each other; once thought to be specific to the nervous system, but the work of neuroscientist Candace Pert demonstrates that all cells can make and receive neuropeptides

nodal point in matrix: individual ampoules of consciousness

non-locality: in classical physics, the direct influence of one object on another, distant object

Norman Rosenthal: psychiatrist who researches the role of emotions in health and well-being

nucleotides: molecules that, when joined, make up the individual structural units of the nucleic acids RNA and DNA

oneness-consciousness: the awareness of all life as an interactive whole

orgone: psychiatrist Wilhelm Reich's term for life-force

paradigm: describes distinct concepts or thought patterns in any scientific discipline or social system

parasympathetic nervous system: the branch of the autonomic nervous system that governs functions related to rest, digest, and repair mechanisms

particle: a small localized object to which can be ascribed several physical properties such as volume or mass

past emotional patterns: patterns developed from past situations that left a lasting impression or were unresolved; they govern our conditioned responses and often occur below the level of awareness

peptides: different types of amino acid chains; called neuropeptides when related to the nervous system; Dr. Candace Pert believes they transmit emotional information

perception: the organization, identification, and interpretation of sensory information

percipience: the power of perceiving, especially perceiving keenly and readily

perpetual anger: anger that lives just under the surface, erupting into rage over minor infractions; might be covering a deeper emotion such as grief or fear, and may represent old trauma

personal presence: the essence of who we are and the state of being we are in; the overall frequency we emit

Phineas Gage Syndrome: a brain injury to the pre-frontal cortex that occurs later in life, after the brain is fully developed, and leaves the person unable to fully engage life and experience a full range of emotions

psychoneuroimmunology: the study of how mind and emotions affect the endocrine, nervous, and immune systems

physio-emotional: the connection between the body and emotion; used when discussing how emotional memory is stored in the body's tissues at a cellular level

physio-energetic chakras: energy centers in the body that represent different types of consciousness and hold specific growth challenges

portals: doorways; openings

post-traumatic stress disorder: a type of anxiety disorder that can occur after seeing or experiencing a traumatic event

precognition: also called future sight and second sight; a type of extrasensory perception that would involve the acquisition or effect of future information that cannot be deduced from presently available and normally acquired sense-based information

presentiment: a vague thought or feeling that something bad or good is about to happen

psychic perceptions: another term for extra-sensory perception

receptor: a site on a cell membrane that binds substances such as hormones and neurotransmitters

repressed emotion: the containment of the action associated with a strong feeling

resonance: in physics, the oscillation of waves that increase in amplitude when two waves come into phase with each other; in spiritual terms, the harmonization of different energies that amplify each other and create another unique energy that vibrates in synchronization

Richard Davidson: a neuroscientist who headed study at the University of Wisconsin that looked at what effects gamma brainwaves may produce and what part of the brain is active during gamma wave emission. He used functional magnetic resonance imaging (fMRI) to view eight monks' brain activity while they meditated in Gamma wave states that were verified by EEGs.

Rollin McCraty: a research scientist working with the HeartMath Institute on concepts of physiologic coherence and who has published many scientific research papers

Rupert Sheldrake: biologist and author who describes the sharing of collective information as an energy-field effect of consciousness called the morphic field; access to the information stored there is obtained through resonance

seat of consciousness: according to some, the pre-frontal cortex area of brain where self-awareness resides

self-transcendent emotions: Jonathan Haidt's term for emotions that lift us out of self-interest, orienting us toward something more important than our usual concerns

sentience: the ability to feel, perceive, or be conscious, or to have subjective experiences

seven segments: according to Wilhelm Reich, horizontal sections of the body in which muscular tensions in the front, back, and sides are functionally related

Shen: a word in Chinese that roughly translates as the root of the spirit; the heart meridian is considered the home of the Shen

signature frequency: the unique frequency emitted by a person, object, gas, substance, and so on

solar plexus: the part of the abdomen directly below the chest between the two sides of the rib cage

somatic events: events pertaining to the body

spiritual essence: individual energy (spirit/soul) in its purest form

SQUID (Superconducting Quantum Interface Device): used for magnetic field imaging of the heart, brain, and other organs

standing: the right to be in charge of one's own life; the ability to be self-determined

string theory: active research in particle physics that attempts to reconcile quantum mechanics and general relativity; a contender for a theory of everything (TOE)

subluxed vertebrae: a dysfunctional biomechanical spinal segment that is fixated

subtle energy: the medium through which consciousness acts; the carrier wave for consciousness, etheric energy; life force—that which makes the difference between inert material and life

Superstring Theory: everything in the universe, from galaxies to subatomic particles, is made up of microscopic strands of vibrating energy

suppressed emotion: avoidance of feelings that we don't want to experience

sympathetic nervous system: the system that produces stress hormones to initiate fast and effective fight or flight

synchronicity: the experience of two or more events that are apparently causally unrelated or unlikely to occur together by chance, yet are experienced as occurring together in a meaningful manner

the Tao: the larger spiritual reality; the entirety of all that is

TCM: abbreviation for Traditional Chinese Medicine

theosophists: proponents of an esoteric philosophy seeking direct knowledge of presumed mysteries of being and nature, particularly concerning the nature of divinity

transcendent emotions: emotions that elevate from the mundane world. They uplift and inspire, making us want to show our own greatness and look for the best in the world. They include compassion, unconditional love, admiration, gratitude, awe, joy, and devotion.

transference: a phenomenon characterized by unconscious redirection of feelings from one person to another

trauma: an emotional response to a terrible event such as an accident, rape, or natural disaster

the Twelve Organ Meridians: pathways of energy in the body in TCM; each one is associated with a particular body part

universal consciousness: the all-encompassing hologram of existence

vibration: the deepest, most indivisible level of matter that forms templates for physical matter in the energy matrix

vibrational matrix: the idea that the material world is an expression of vibration based on resonance, proportion, and harmonics

victim mentality: not an emotion, a way of thinking that impacts the way life unfolds; consists of blaming others for every mishap that occurs

visualization: the practice of constructing images in the mind's eye; used as a tool for creating action

waves: a swell, surge, or progressive movement

wei-wu-wei: doing without doing (Chinese)

Wilhelm Reich: the Australian psychiatrist and psychoanalyst who developed ideas of the movement of life force through the body in relation to psychology and body tension, created the concepts of body armor and segmental patterns of tension, among others, and is considered the father of body-centered psychotherapy and emotional processing in bodywork

yin-yang: the two original forces separated from the Tao, or all that is. Yin and yang are not opposing forces (dualities), but complementary and interconnected forces that interact to form a greater whole with dynamic balance.

Notes

Introduction

1. Casteneda, Carlos. *The Teachings of Don Juan: A Yaqui Way of Knowledge*, 1968.
2. The Complete Site on Mahatma Gandhi, *www.mkgandhi.org*.

Chapter 1

1. Goleman, Daniel. *Emotional Intelligence: Why it Can Matter More Than IQ. 10th Anniversary Edition*. New York: Bantam, 2006.

Chapter 2

1. Hall, Stephen S. "Iceman Autopsy." *National Geographic* (Nov. 2011), page 131.

2. Dorfer, L., M. Moser, F. Bahr, K. Spindler, E. Egarter-Vigl, S. Giullén, G. Dohr, and T. Kenner. "A Medical Report From the Stone Age?" *The Lancet* 354 (1999): 1023–1025.

3. White, John, and Stanley Krippner. *Future Science.* Norwell, Mass.: Anchor Press, 1977.

4. Greene, Brian. *The Elegant Universe: Superstrings, Hidden Dimensions, and the Quest for the Ultimate Theory.* New York: Vintage Books, 2003, pp. 15–16.

5. Pettersson, Peter. "Cymatics: The Science of the Future?" World-Mysteries.com. *www.world-mysteries.com/sci_cymatics.htm.*

6. Jenny, Dr. Hans. *Cymatics: Bringing Matter to Life with Sound.* MACROmedia video, 1986.

7. Bohm, David. *Wholeness and the Implicate Order. Re-issue edition.* New York: Routledge, 1996.

8. "Dark Energy, Dark Matter." Nasa Science: Astrophysics. *http:// science.nasa.gov/astrophysics/focus-areas/what-is-dark-energy.*

9. Trimble, Virginia. "Existence and Nature of Dark Matter in the Universe." *Annual Review of Astronomy and Astrophysics* 25 (A88-13240 03-90). Palo Alto, Calif.: Annual Reviews, Inc., 1987, pp. 425–472.

10. "Dark Energy," op.cit.

11. Massey, Richard, et al. "Dark Matter Maps Reveal Cosmic Scaffolding." *Nature* 445 (2007): 286–290. *www.nature.com/ nature/journal/v445/n7125/full/nature05497.html.*

12. Sanders, Robert. "'Dark Matter' Forms Dense Clumps in Ghost Universe." UC Berkeley News Press Release, November 5, 2003. *http://berkeley.edu/news/media/releases/2003/11/05_darkmatter .shtml.*

13. Emoto, Masaru. *Messages from Water, Vol. 1.* Hado Publishing, 1999.

14. Jenkins, J.S. "The Mozart Effect." *Journal of the Royal Society of Medicine* 94.4 (April 2001): 170–172. *www.ncbi.nlm.nih.gov/ pmc/articles/PMC1281386.*

Chapter 3

1. Horký, K., and J. Widimský Jr. "Role of the Heart as an Endocrine Organ." *Cor Vasa* 33.6 (1991): 441–450. Department of Medicine, 1st Medical School, Charles University, Prague, Czechoslovakia.

2. HeartMath.com.

3. Lowndes, Florin. *Enlivening the Chakra of the Heart: The Fundamental Spiritual Exercises of Rudolf Steiner.* Sophia Books, 2005.

4. Brennan, Barbra. *Light Emerging: The Journey of Personal Healing.* New York: Bantam Books, 1993.

5. Ibid.

6. Teeguarden, Iona Marsaa. *The Joy of Feeling.* Japan Publications, 1987. 7th printing May 2006 by the Jin Shin Do® Foundation for Bodymind Acupressure® (*www.jinshindo.org,* P.O. Box 416, Idyllwild, CA 92549).

Chapter 4

1. Schwartz, Gary E.R., and Linda G.S. Russek. "Registration of Actual and Intended Eye Gaze: Correlation with Spiritual Beliefs and Experiences." *Journal of Scientific Exploration* 13, No. 2 (1999): 213–229.

2. Persinger, M.A., and K. Makarec. "The Feeling of a Presence and Verbal Meaningfulness in Context of Temporal Lobe Function: Factor Analytic Verification of the Muses?" *Brain Cognition* 20.2 (Nov. 1992): 217–226.

3. Bartlolmei, F., et al. "Rhinal-Hippocampal Interactions During Deja-Vu." *Clinical Neurophysiology* 123.3 (March 2012): 489–495.

4. Armour, J. Andrews. *Neurocardiology: Anatomical and Functional Principles.* Institute of HeartMath, 2003, pp. 9 and 15.

5. McCraty, PhD, Rollin. *The Energetic Heart: Biolectromagnetic Interactions Within and Between People.* Institute of HeartMath, 2003, p. 3.

6. Ibid, p. 1.

7. Ibid., p. 3.

8. Ibid., p. 1.

9. Ibid., p. 7.

10. Hecht, Laurence. "Luc Montagnier's Revolution in Biology: New Evidence for a Non-Particle View of Life." *21st Century Science & Technology* (Winter 2010–2011). *www.21stcenturysciencetech. com/Articles_2011/Winter-2010/Montagnier.pdf.*

11. Pert, PhD, Candace. *Molecules of Emotion: Why You Feel the Way You Feel.* Scribner, 1997, p. 179.

12. "Candace Pert, PhD: Biography." *www.candacepert.com.*

13. Pert, *Molecules,* p. 245.

14. Schwartz, "Registration," pp. 213–229.

Chapter 5

1. Upledger, John E. *SomatoEmotional Release and Beyond.* UI Publishing, 1990, p. 15.

2. Dychtwald, Ken. *Bodymind.* Tarcher/Putnam, 1977, p. 101.

3. Ibid., p. 102.

4. Ibid., p.103.

5. Teeguarden, Iona Marsaa. *A Complete Guide to Acupressure, Revised.* Japan Publications, September 1996; Revised edition 2002; 3rd printing July 2009 by the Jin Shin Do® Foundation for Bodymind Acupressure® www.jinshindo.org. PO Box 416, Idyllwild, Calif. 92549.

Chapter 6

1. Mott, Maryann. "Did Animals Sense Tsunami Was Coming??" *National Geographic News,* Jan. 4, 2005. *http://news. nationalgeographic.com/news/2005/01/0104_050104_tsunami_ animals.html.*

2. Pert, PhD, Candace. *Molecules of Emotion: Why You Feel the Way You Feel.* Scribner, 1997.

Chapter 7

1. Radin, PhD, Dean. *The Conscious Universe.* New York: Harper Collins, 1997, p. 271.

2. Talbot, Michael. *The Holographic Universe.* New York: HarperCollins, 1991, p. 17.

3. Sheldrake, Rupert. *A New Science of Life: The Hypothesis of Morphic Resonance.* Park Street Press, 1981, pgs.115–118.

4. Pert, Candace. Interview at *www.6seconds.org.*

5. Armour, MD, J. Andrew. *Neurocardiology: Anatomical and Functional Principles.* Institute of HeartMath, 2003, p. 10.

6. McCraty, PhD Rollin. *The Energetic Heart: Biomagnetic Interactions Within and Between People.* Institute of HeartMath, 2003, pgs. 1, 9.

7. McCraty, Rollin, et al. *The Coherent Heart: Heart–Brain Interactions, Psychophysiological Coherence, and the Emergence of System-Wide Order.* Institute of HeartMath, 2006, p. 3.

8. Haidt, Jonathan, and James Morris. "Finding the Self in Self-Transcendent Emotions." *Proceedings of the National Academy of Sciences* 106.19 (2009): 7687–7688.

9. "Admiration." *Chambers English Dictionary.* W & R Chambers Ltd. and Cambridge University Press, 1988.

10. Haidt & Morris, "Finding the Self," p. 7688.

11. Haidt, J. "The Positive Emotion of Elevation." *Prevention & Treatment* 3.3 (March 7, 2000).

12. Ibid.

Chapter 8

1. Lipton, Bruce. *The Biology of Belief: Unleashing the Power of Consciousness, Matter, and Miracles.* Mountain of Love/Elite Books, 2005, p.133.

2. Kenyon, Tom. *Brain States.* United States Publishing, 1994, p. 38.

3. Ibid., p. 39.

4. Ibid, p. 39.

5. Ibid, p. 40.

6. Rutgers University. "Effect of Gamma Waves on Cognitive and Language Skills in Children." *ScienceDaily.com*, October 21, 2008. *www.sciencedaily.com/releases/2008/10/081021120945.htm*.

7. Kaufman, Marc. "Meditation Gives Brain a Charge, Study Finds." *Washington Post*, January 3, 2005. *www.washingtonpost.com/wp-dyn/articles/A43006-2005Jan2.html*.

8. Ibid.

9. Holzel, Britta K., et al. "Stress Reduction Correlates With Structural Changes in the Amygdale." *Social Cognitive and Affective Neuroscience Advance Access* (September 23, 2009). *www.nmr.mgh.harvard.edu/~lazar/Articles/Holzel-SCAN-2010.pdf*.

10. Hoopes, Aaron. *Zen Yoga: A Path to Enlightenment Through Breathing, Movement, and Meditation*. Kodansha International, 2007.

11. Ranganathan, Vinoth K., Vlodek Siemionowa, Jing Z. Liu, Vinod Sahgal, and Guang H. Yue. "From Mental Power to Muscle Power: Gaining Strength by Using the Mind." *Neuropsychologia* 42 (2004): 944–956.

Chapter 9

1. Radin, Dean. *Entangled Minds: Extrasensory Experiences in a Quantum Reality*. Pocket Books, 2006, pps. 164–169.

2. "Mind." Merriam-Webster.com. *www.merriam-webster.com/medical/mind*.

3. Rosenthal, MD, Norman E. *The Emotional Revolution*. Citadel Press, 2002.

4. Pert, Candace. *Your Body Is Your Subconscious Mind*. Sounds True, Inc., 2004.

5. Tolle, Eckhart. *A New Earth*. New York: Penguin, 2005, p. 53. (Kindle edition.)

6. Ker Than. "New Theory: How Intelligence Works." *Live Science E-Journal*, September 11, 2007. *www.livescience.com/1863-theory-intelligence-works.html*.

7. Rosenthal, pgs. 15–18.

8. Rosenthal, p. 19.

9. Talbot, Michael. "The Universe as a Hologram: Does Objective Reality Exist?" Holography.ru. *www.holography.ru/files/univhoe2.htm.*

10. Burns, PhD, Martha. "Left Vs. Right: What Your Brain Hemispheres Are Really Up To." *Scientific Learning E-Journal*, July 12, 2011. *www.scilearn.com/blog/left-brain-right-brain-hemispheres.php.*

11. "The Brain's Left and Right Side seem to Work Better Together in Mathematically Gifted Middle-School Youth." American Psychological Association Press Release, April 11, 2004. *www.apa.org/news/press/releases/2004/04/interhemispheric.aspx.*

12. "Mind." Merriam-Webster.com.

Chapter 11

1. Pert, Candace. *www.6seconds.org.*

Chapter 13

1. "Anxiety Statistics." AnxietyCentre.com. *www.anxietycentre.com/anxiety-statistics-information.shtml.*

2. "Stress Management: Start Here!" MindTools.com. *www.mindtools.com/pages/article/newTCS_00.htm.*

3. McCraty, PhD, Rollin. *The Energetic Heart: Bioelectromagnetic Interactions Within and Between People.* HeartMath Research Center, 2003, p. 7.

4. "Quotations by Author: Carl Jung." The Quotations Page. *www.quotationspage.com/quotes/Carl_Jung.*

5. "World Happiness Report 2012: Scandinavian Countries Are Happiest on Earth." *The Huffington Post*, April 6, 2012. *www.huffingtonpost.com/2012/04/06/world-happiness-report-2012_n_1408787.html.*

Chapter 14

1. "Adverse Childhood Experiences (ACE) Study." Centers for Disease Control and Prevention. *www.cdc.gov/ace/.*

2. Pick, Marcelle. "Emotions, Health and Stress: How Emotional Experience Determines Your Health." Women to Women. *www.womentowomen.com/emotionsandhealth/emotionalexperience.aspx.*

3. "Ghost in Your Genes." PBS NOVA Transcripts, airdate October 16, 2007. *www.pbs.org/wgbh/nova/transcripts/3413_genes.html.*

4. "Epigenetics and Inheritance." Learn.Genetics: Genetic Science Learning Center, at The University of Utah. *http://learn.genetics.utah.edu/content/epigenetics/inheritance/.*

5. "Ghost in Your Genes." PBS Transcripts, NOVA.

6. Carollo, Kim. "Centenarians' Positive Attitude Linked to Long Life." *ABC News*, June 5, 2012. *http://abcnews.go.com/Health/centenarians-positive-attitude-linked-long-healthy-life/story?id=16494151.*

7. Pert, Candace, *www.6seconds.org.*

8. McCraty, Rollin, Mike Atkinson, and Dana Tomasino. *Modulation of DNA Conformation by Heart-focused Intention.* CITY: HeartMath Institute, *www.heartmath.org.*

Chapter 15

1. Rosenthal, MD Norman. *The Emotional Revolution: How the New Science of Feelings Can Transform Your Life.* Citadel Press Books, 2002.

2. Ibid., pgs. 382–385.

Chapter 16

1. *www.heartvoice.com.*

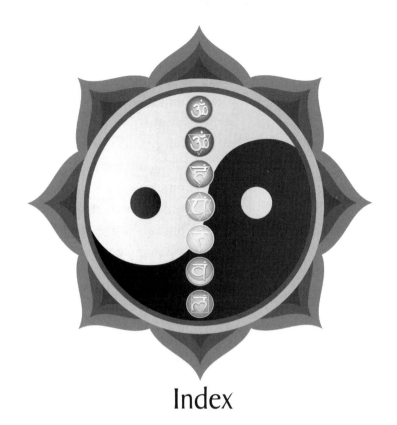

Index

About the Author

Dr. Synthia Andrews is a licensed naturopathic physician with 30 years of experience as a massage therapist and energy intuitive. Her work focuses on the emotional and spiritual dynamics in health and healing. Facilitating people's energy awareness is her life's work, and she is passionate about exploring the connections among the human body, the subtle energy matrix, and the emotions. The Emotional Compendium in this book (Chapter 11) is the result of her own personal growth and her experience working with clients. She is author of *The Path of Energy* (Career Press, 2011) and is the primary coauthor of three other books on healing, subtle energy, and consciousness. She teaches energy awareness workshops, lectures around the world, and maintains a private subtle energy–oriented naturopathic practice in Guilford, Connecticut.